ISLAM BEYOND TERRORISTS AND TERRORISM

*Biographies of the
Most Influential Muslims in History*

Iftekhar

University Press of America,® Inc.
Lanham · New York · Oxford

Library of Congress Cataloging-in-Publication Data

Mahmood, Iftekhar.
Islam beyond terrorists and terrorism : biographies of the most
influential Muslims in history / Iftekhar Mahmood.
p.   cm
Includes bibliographical references and index.
1. Muslims—Biography. 2. Islam—Appreciation.
3. Terrorism—Religious aspects—Islam. I. Title.

BP70 .M34 2002
297'.092'2—dc21   [B]   2002023834 CIP

ISBN 0-7618-2275-5 (paperback : alk. ppr.)

Dedicated to the memory of the victims of the September 11, 2001
terrorists attack on the World Trade Center
And the Pentagon

CONTENTS

Preface

It was a relatively mild winter in February 1993, in Kansas City, Missouri where I was a graduate student working on my doctorate degree in Pharmaceutical Sciences. As was my regular practice, I came back home from my laboratory for my evening tea, news and dinner. As I turned on my television, I realized that something was terribly wrong in New York City. Soon I found out that there was a bomb blast in the World Trade Center and many people were killed. It was a gruesome scene around World Trade Center. The faces of injured people with pain and misery, the frightened people running away from the World Trade Center, the faces of the people waving from the windows of this high rise building to be rescued and the struggle of the police and fire fighters are all still fresh in my memory as if this was an incident of just yesterday. Naturally within hours, the focus was turned on those who had masterminded and carried out such an atrocious attack. A few days later the news came that the "Islamic militants" were behind the bombing. The word 'Islamic militants' drew my attention. Is Islam a militant religion? Were those who carried out this malicious attack on innocent people really Muslims? Do these people understand Islam? Is there any religion which teaches violence? I was puzzled, angry and sad by the incident. I am not a religious scholar but even I understand that Islam is not a militant religion. I could not find any justification behind the act of these "Fundamentalist Muslims" (if we can call them Muslims). Their cowardly act was probably the first serious blow to Islam and its credibility in the twentieth century. Islam as a religion was defaced and defiled by the act of these people. The pain and sorrow these terrorists inflicted to those who were in the World Trade Center was unimaginable.

The incident forced me to think and analyze Islam and Muslims. I know for fact that the contribution of the Muslims in the field of science, philosophy, literature, mathematics, arts and even in music is immense. Their work in a wide variety of fields proved to be beneficial to mankind irrespective of their religion, race and culture. From the birth of Islam to the Fall of Baghdad, Granada, Delhi and Istanbul, Islam remained a predominant religion in the world for more than one thousand years with enormous contribution to human race.

The people who bombed the World Trade Center were Muslims by faith but Islam certainly is nothing to do with their heinous crime. It was also annoying to see that these people used the name of a peaceful religion to commit a crime against fellow human beings. It was obvious to me that these people do not understand Islam and are also ignorant about the teachings of Islam. Then everything became calm and life returned to normal. By the end of 1993, I obtained my doctorate degree and moved to Maryland. The incident of February 1993, however, never left my memory.

The plotters of the World Trade Center were caught and sentenced and then everything appeared to be quiet and probably forgotten. Then in 1995, there was a bomb blast in a federal building in Oklahoma City which killed hundreds of people. The initial speculation was that this was also a work of the Muslim terrorists. Mercifully, this time it was not but I thought how much Islam and the Muslims have to bear the burden of being labeled as "terrorists". Then in 1998, the American embassies in Kenya and Tanzania were bombed that cost more than 200 lives of innocent Kenyans and Tanzanians who worked in these embassies. Once again the 'Muslim terrorists' were suspected and indeed the investigations later confirmed that the fundamentalist Muslims were behind the bombings. Like the rest of the world, I wondered what was wrong with the Muslims and their course of action. Islam does not allow the killing of innocent people under any circumstances. In both the cases (bombing of the World Trade Center and the American Embassies), I could not find any justification by the terrorists to target innocent people, especially in the name of Islam and the Muslims. Once again Islam and a vast majority of the Muslims were under scrutiny and on trial for something for which they had nothing to do with.

The twentieth century was coming to an end and everywhere people were getting ready to celebrate the new millennium. In this context, in the fall of 1999, the reputed television channel 'Arts and Entertainment' presented a program about the lives and achievements of 100 most influential people of the last millennium. The program opened with Suleyman the Magnificent, the great Ottoman sultan in the sixteenth century. At the end of the program I found out that he was the only Muslim and was ranked last among the 100 most influential people of the last millennium. It was very surprising to me. With the exception of a few, the whole program consisted of only European and American names. Influence of some of these people was considered enormous by the narrator but I disagreed. I know for fact that there were many people whose influence on human civilization was far reaching than the influence of some of the people presented in the program. The names of numerous influential Muslims who contributed significantly to the human civilization were simply missing from this list. Was it a prejudice against the Muslims? Or was it simply ignorance? It was my anticipation that the people who selected these influential people of the last 1000 years may not be aware about other cultures and religions. While going through the magazines, commentaries, and the news media, I surprisingly found that very little is known about Islam, the Muslims and the contributions of the Muslims to the world. I concluded that it was ignorance not prejudice and the selectors simply did not know about Islam, the Muslims and their contributions to mankind. At that point (fall 1999), I decided to write a book to highlight the contributions of the Muslims to the human civilization. I also wanted to prove a point that Islam like other religions is a peaceful religion and its basic moral teachings are no different than other religions. Like all other cultures and civilizations, the Muslims had their both glorious and dark moments. Like all other cultures and civilizations, the Muslims have contributed significantly to all human beings and a vast majority of the Muslims are neither fanatics nor terrorists.

Though conceived in December 1999, I did not commence writing the book before 2001. The progress of my writing was painfully slow. Then the horrible incident of September 11, 2001 occurred. It was such a tragic, painful and sad incident that it is impossible to describe the magnitude of this incident in words. Thousands of innocent people died due to the sick mentality of few people. Once again, those who masterminded and committed this inhuman crime were Muslims by name and faith and Islam was once again on trial. This time media, politicians and the American people were all very confused about Islam as a religion and the Muslims as its followers. It became obvious to me that the Muslims round the globe have to work very hard if they want to restore the credibility of the Muslims and Islam in the eyes of the civilized world. At the moment it appears to be an uphill task especially when a vast majority of people in the western hemisphere are unfamiliar with the true Islam and the contribution of the Muslims to the world.

At a time when Europe was going through the dark ages, the Muslims introduced the intellectual and scientific knowledge to the human civilization. They preserved the Greek, Persian and Indian heritage and introduced new dimensions to the knowledge of Aristotle and Plato. Between the eighth and the thirteenth century, the Islamic civilization was at its peak and the Muslims contributed significantly in the area of medicine, science, mathematics, astronomy, philosophy, history and political science. They revised and corrected the old theories and developed new methods and techniques in a wide variety of fields. It is widely believed that the European Renaissance was motivated and influenced by the works of the Muslim scholars and intellectuals.

Considering that even the Muslims of today are not aware about their great intellectual heritage of the past, the objective of this book is to provide a reader with a brief introduction of the life and achievements of influential Muslims and their place in history. The book is an effort to educate both Muslims and non-Muslims. I anticipate that those people in the western hemisphere who want to know about the contributions of other religions and cultures (especially these days there is a lot of focus on Islam) but cannot find these information in a condensed form in a single book will find this book interesting. It is very important to understand other cultures, races and religions since the mutual respect for all human beings can be established by knowing each other's contribution to human civilization. This mutual respect may help to bring an end to hostility to each other.

I hope that the Muslims round the globe will also find this book interesting since it describes their heritage and contributions to the world. I particularly hope that this book will be inspirational to the young Muslim children. The future generation of the Muslims will depend on those who are children today but it is not very inspiring to me when I see the young Muslim children learning and memorizing the Quran in madrasas without having even faintest idea about Islam and its teachings. It is also very painful to see the children being misguided about Islam and other religions and cultures by the religious groups. I hope these short biographies will help the Muslim children to realize that the glorious days of Islam were due to the progressive and constructive thinking, ability to learn from and respect other cultures and religions and above all living in peace and harmony with other religions and cultures. Orthodoxy and fanaticism brings isolation and destruction to the nations and no religion and culture is immune to destruction if it does not learn to live in peace and harmony with others.

In these biographies, I decided not to include Prophet Muhammad and the first four caliphs (Hazrats Abu Bakr, Omar, Osman and Ali). So much have been written and known about them that any description about their lives and achievements in this book will be of little significance. Therefore, I decided to focus mainly on the intellectuals, scientists, philosophers, military commanders, rulers, historians, statesmen, religious scholars and reformists. The life sketch of an individual is though short but it provides a clear picture to the reader about the life and achievements of that individual. This list by no means is complete but it is also beyond the scope of this book to describe the lives and achievements of every significant Muslim in history. Therefore, I have selected only those who have enormous contribution either to Islam or to the human civilization. I have avoided rating the people as number one, two or three rather they appear chronologically. For example, a person born in 700 AD is listed earlier than the person born in 720 AD.

I hope this book will help both the Muslims and non-Muslims to understand the contributions of the Muslims to the world. It is also important for the Muslims to realize that the existence and glory of a nation, race, culture or religion lies in its ability to contribute to the human civilization not in sabotage and destruction. Their past is the proof.

Iftekhar Mahmood
December, 2001

Introduction

Islam as a growing religion in the western hemisphere is drawing a lot of attention and there is a renewed interest in knowing Muslims and Islam. Unfortunately, Islam as a religion has been completely misunderstood by the western world. This misunderstanding may be due to the fact that in the modern western hemisphere very little efforts are made to understand other cultures and religions. Furthermore, the fundamentalist Islamic groups have depicted a very different picture of Islam in the minds of non-Muslims. This picture of Islam is completely misleading and put both Islam and the Muslims in an unfavorable position. Though the conflict between Islam and Christianity dates back to the era of Crusades but in modern time both the Muslims and the Christians have been living in relative peace and harmony. In fact the Crusades proved to be beneficial to the Western Europe as the intellectual curiosity began taking shape in the Christian societies. By the early fourteenth century, both the Muslims and the Christians were proving Ibn Khaldun's philosophy of history a correct phenomenon. The great Islamic civilization in the Middle East and Spain was in decline due to the lack of innovations, political decay and the rise of Islamic fundamentalism. On the other hand, the Europeans had come out of their own isolation and were following the same paths and inquisition which had created the great Islamic empire.

The Ottomans (1281-1922) and the Mughals (1526-1857) created two great Muslim empires in Europe and in India, respectively, but they failed to create the magnificent seat of learning which once Baghdad and the Muslim Spain were famous for. Islam's glorious days were over by the thirteenth century. By the nineteenth century, the mighty Ottomans in Europe and the Mughals in India were in sharp decline. From the sixteenth century onward the European intellectualism, inventions and discoveries were at their peak. The economical need forced the Europeans to go out of their continent and explore the possibilities of improving their economy. This started the European imperialism and the desire to colonize other nations. The two world wars in Europe weakened the western imperial powers and the movements for independence resulted in the emergence of many independent countries in Asia, Africa and Latin America. Many independent Muslim nations also emerged, especially in North Africa, Middle East and Far East. Countries like Pakistan and Bangladesh appeared on the global map. Despite their independence, the Muslim countries faced enormous challenges. Financially some Muslim countries became very rich due to oil production whereas many remained poor without much needed resources. The greatest challenge these Muslim countries face today is lack of political stability, modern education and failure to establish a modern and intellectual society. Another major hindrance in the progress of the Muslim nations is lack of democratic institutions and inability to discard the old and outdated social and religious practices.

A sound democratic structure is very vital for the progress of a nation but the Muslim countries seem to be unfamiliar with the word 'democracy'. Even in the twenty first century, the Muslim nations are ruled by the civilian or military dictators as well as by despotic monarchs. The so-called leadership in these countries does not allow their citizens any kind of human rights. Some of these countries are dependent on the very nations from which they liberated themselves. The judiciary system is flawed and corrupt. The power-hungry rulers of these countries lack political vision and understanding of modern day political structure. The most corrupt regimes are in the Middle East where the socio-political structure remains outdated.

At a glance it appears that the whole Muslim world lacks modern thinking and seems to be unable to adjust and adopt the necessity of a modern day life. This, however, should not be interpreted that every Muslim is backward or uneducated. Tremendous individual efforts have been made by millions of Muslims from every region of the world to obtain higher education and they are quite capable to compete in the modern day society. These are individual efforts without support of their government and sometimes even without the support of their own families.

There is no doubt that the educated elites of the Muslim societies have distanced themselves from the orthodoxy. They follow Islam as their faith but they no longer are influenced by the mullahs or so called Ulemas (religious scholars) rather their interpretation of the Islamic laws is much broader, sensible and constructive. Despite the presence of such educated elite groups, the overall picture, however, is very gloomy as the Muslim world lacks modern education, and free and rational thinking. The Muslim nations appear to be more emotional than rational and pragmatic. As if the monarchs and dictators are not enough to hamper the Muslim progress in the modern world, the greatest danger both the Muslims and Islam face today is the emergence of the fanatics or the fundamentalists. These Muslim fundamentalists are no different than those Christian fundamentalists who bomb abortion clinics or Hindu fundamentalists who want to destroy every monument in India which has Muslim imprint. This does not necessarily mean that all fundamentalists are violent. Unfortunately, in Islam a small fraction of fundamentalists has emerged who wants to resolve every issue by violence.

In Islam, the struggle between the fundamentalist and the moderate Muslims is nothing new. The animosity between the religious groups and the rationalists existed since the early eighth century. This kind of tug of war between the religious zealots and the rationalists, however, is prevalent in every religion and every culture. The golden era of Islam prevailed for centuries due to the rational and progressive thinking. This was the time when the Muslims preserved the Greek and Indian knowledge, made discoveries in science and technology. Intellectual thinking and debates about the political, social and religious matters were at the zenith. The rationalists or the liberal groups within Islam believed in God and his prophet and obeyed the laws of Islam despite the accusation of the orthodoxy that the practices of these rationalists are unIslamic.

Many factors contributed to the building of great Islamic civilization. Islam's teaching of equality among human beings irrespective of their background was highly attractive to the downtrodden people of many non-Islamic societies. The tolerance against other religions, race, culture, and language helped spread Islam. As a result, millions embraced Islam due to its tolerant and mild nature and its basic teachings. By living under the auspices of Islamic empire the people of different cultures and religions brought their knowledge and experiences which proved to be beneficial to the Muslims and Islam. Within one hundred years after its birth in the Arabian Desert, Islam was a dominant religion and culture in the world. The glorious achievements of the Muslims were due to their open mindness, free and intellectual thinking, respect for other cultures and religions and a great desire for innovations and progress. Islam absorbed the experiences and knowledge from other great civilizations and expanded it to the benefit of all mankind. On the other hand, the Islamic religious groups realized that they were losing their power and appeal to the general masses. These groups in the pretext that the Islamic societies were getting corrupt tried to turn the clock towards a non progressive and nonintellectual society. By its own definition this was a non-Islamic society as Islam is not against innovations and does not limit its followers to only religious education. One should, however, make a clear distinction between the two classes of orthodoxy; one who sincerely wanted to keep the society free of corruption and immorality without jeopardizing the scientific and intellectual progress within Islam. This group mainly consisted of theologians, philosophers, intellectuals and scholars on religious matters. The other group mainly consisted of madrasa (religious school) educated mullahs who were rigid and lacked proper understanding of basic Islamic teachings and were against all sorts of innovations within the Islamic societies. The graduates of these madrasas were neither theologians nor religious scholars rather they were 'street smart mullahs' whose ignorance ultimately led to the decay of the great Islamic civilization and the fall of the Muslim empire.

Memorization of the Quran by heart without understanding its basic teachings does not prepare a madrasa educated mullah to give statements about Islam or issue fatwas (religious decree). This should be left to the scholars and the theologians of Islam who have better understanding of the religion and are in a better position than a mullah to provide the Muslims with proper guidance.

To the fundamentalists, Islam was always in danger either due to moderate Muslims or from foreign elements though they never provided any evidence that Islam was really in danger. Over the last fourteen hundred years, among the Muslim communities again and again the so called defenders of the faith have emerged. Two very well known orthodox reformists in Islam were Ibn Taymiyya (1263-1328) and Muhammad Wahhab (1703-92). Both of these failed to gain support at the grass root level among the Muslim communities. Muhammad Wahhab's success was mainly of political nature. The House of Saud accepted his views of Islamic purification mainly for its political gains. Though Muhammad Wahhab's followers are also found outside Saudi Arabia, they remain largely invisible or non-influential. Besides Ibn Taymiyya and Muhammad Wahhab, there were many other fundamentalist reformers who frequently emerged but failed and their movement disappeared quickly. These fundamentalists were not always unsuccessful rather some of these even succeeded in building their own empire. Almoravids (1056-1147) and Almohads (1130-1269), the two Berber Empires in North Africa were examples which originated due to the fundamentalist views of their founders. These empires, however, did not survive long due to their rigidity and lack of progressive thinking. The rise and fall of Almoravids and Almohads was perfect example of Ibn Khaldun's philosophy of history. These two empires due to their discipline, ambition, and objectivity initially rose to great heights but their rigidity and uncompromising principles isolated them from others. Such close and unaccommodating societies never prosper and ultimately destroy themselves.

The street smart Mullahs have an amazing habit of converting a simple issue into an Islamic conflict if it serves their purpose. A common statement of Mullahs is that 'Islam is in danger'. Yes, Islam is in danger and it is due to the ignorance of the Mullahs and the misguidance they provide to the general Muslim masses. If Islam was ever in danger it was due to these madrasa educated mullahs who have no understanding of Islam. Unfortunately these mullahs have been contaminating the minds of those Muslims who are not well aware of the reality and in such a way these mullahs create hatred against the people of other religions and cultures. These mullahs are also brain washing young Muslim children. The madrasas have become happy hunting grounds for these mullahs where they are busy in teaching hatred and their brand of Islam to the innocent minds of the future Muslim generations. These close minded shallow mullahs interpret Islam based on their limited knowledge and ignorance. For example, these mullahs advocate that women should remain behind the veils and should be deprived from education. Islam in its original teachings has given women enormous rights and rates them equal to men (first class citizen) and yet these ignorant Mullahs are misinterpreting Islam declaring women a second class citizen. Neither Islam allows it nor can the Muslims in this age and time afford keeping half of their population behind the closed doors.

The Muslim women have played important roles on many fronts. The patience and piousness of Raabah Basri, the philanthropic works of queen Zubaidah (wife of caliph Harun Rashid), the administrative skills of Razia Sultan (daughter of Altamsh), the wisdom of Noor Jahan (wife of emperor Jahangir), and the heroic efforts of Jamila Bo Pasha of Algeria against the French imperialism are well known in the civilized world. In recent past Pakistan and Turkey had women prime ministers. Current head of states of Bangladesh and Indonesia are women. These examples clearly indicate that women are as capable as men. There are millions of Muslim women who have enormous talents but orthodox mullahs wants to put them behind the veils and deprive the Muslim communities from benefiting from these talented women.

The word "Jihad" or holy war has also been misinterpreted by these mullahs. The Muslim theologians have interpreted the word "Jihad" with extreme caution and proper understanding. Abd al-Qadir Jilani, founder of the Qadiriyah order, waged jihad against self. His concept of jihad was to purify one's soul and submission to God. Unfortunately, to a mullah jihad is always associated with war and violence against others.

It should also be recognized that the Islamic orthodoxy was always challenged by the liberal thinkers of Islam. In modern times, social and political reformists like Muhammad Abduh, Jamal ad-Din Afghani and Sir Syed Ahmad Khan tirelessly worked to change the mentality, isolation and the decay of the Muslim societies. Muhammad Abduh as the Mufti of Egypt played a vital role by bringing reforms in the Egyptian society, thus freeing the Egyptians from irrational customs and practices imposed by the ignorant mullahs. He also modernized Al-Azhar University by introducing new curriculum and new methods of teaching. Sir Syed's contribution to the Muslims of the Subcontinent is unforgettable. Not only he wrote books and pamphlets to caution the Muslims of India about their obsolete social practices and thinking but he also tried to educate them by first establishing a school where modern education was provided to the Muslim children. The school became a college and ultimately a world renowned university (Aligarh University). The conservative Muslims of the Subcontinent created all sorts of hurdle for Sir Syed and to neutralize his educational plan they established a madrasa at Deuband. Time proved that the graduates of Aligarh University were far more productive for the advancement of the Muslim culture and intellectualism in the Subcontinent than the graduates of Deuband.

The orthodoxy always claims that the fall of the Muslim societies is because the Muslims do not practice Islam in its true spirit. Therefore, there is a need to create Islamic states where the Muslims will follow the strict Islamic laws and will live within the boundaries of Sharia. Let's examine the progress and achievements of two countries where strict Islamic laws have been imposed and the people of these two countries have been forced to practice Islam in its true spirit (according to the understanding of the enforcers).

I start with Iran. More than twenty years after Islamic Revolution of Iran, today Iranians are demanding more freedom and liberty in every aspect of their life. Even moderate clergies now realize that the harshness of the Islamic revolution suffocated the Iranian society and halted all sorts of progress in Iran. The freedom of speech and individual human rights were all ceased by the Islamic revolution. The revolution, in the name of Islam put half of its population (women) behind the closed doors and made them a second class citizen, quite opposite to Islam's teaching about the treatment of women. Twenty years after orthodoxy established an Islamic state (in the mind of orthodox Iranian clergy) in Iran, the Iranian society is isolated from rest of the world and going back in time. Today a majority of Iranians realize that if they want to compete in the modern world once again, they have to rebuild their society by abolishing orthodoxy and bringing modern themes and practices. The current tug of war between the Iranian educated elites and the orthodox mullahs is a clear example that orthodoxy has failed in Iran.

Another country where orthodox Islam is practiced is Saudi Arabia. It has been almost seventy years now since King Saud established Saudi Arabia and Wahhabi brand of Islam was imposed in the country. Despite the fact that there is no room for monarchy in Islam, Saudi Arabia remains a country run by a royal family. Basically the country is a police state with no human rights and no freedom of speech even for the Saudi citizens. The judiciary system is based on the Islamic laws yet the laws are different for the ruling class, the religious groups, and the common citizens. Islam preaches a strong democratic government and equal laws for everybody but Saudi Arabia's political and social structure belies the basic principles of Islam. Unfortunately, many Muslims consider Saudi Arabia a true Islamic country but reality is that Saudi Arabia is anything but a true Islamic country. Due to its rigid Islamic practices (in many ways the practices are really not Islamic rather both the ruling class and the mullahs use Islam as a tool for their own objectives), the country has failed to produce scholars, scientists, politicians and intellectuals and is heavily dependent on the foreign talents. Saudi Arabia is a very rich country due to oil revenue, yet it lacks progress in every aspect of life. In Saudi Arabia, women are second class citizens and for the reasons best known to the mullahs and the monarchy, women can not drive cars or take part in politics.

The above two examples clearly demonstrate that orthodoxy has failed to establish both political and social stability in these two countries. There is hardly any progress in any direction in these two countries. The decaying political and social plight of Iran and Saudi Arabia under the influence of orthodoxy should discourage other Muslim nations to follow the footsteps of these two countries. A majority Muslim but secular country like Turkey is more likely to be successful in the modern world than the countries like Iran and Saudi Arabia.

It is generally propagated by the street smart Mullahs that the USA and other western countries are against Islam. These Mullahs, however, have failed to provide any kind of proof of their allegation. After the Crusades there was never any open military conflict between the Christianity and the Islam. The conflicts in Spain between the Muslims and the Christians and in Europe between the Ottomans and the Christian states were of pure political nature rather than a conflict between Islam and Christianity. The war between Iraq and the coalition led by the USA in1990 was also not a conflict between Islam and Christianity rather it was a war of political need and political interest. Therefore, there should be a clear distinction if a conflict between a Muslim and a non-Muslim country is a war against Islam or it is a political conflict. I wonder how the Muslim clergy will describe the ten year war between Iran and Iraq? Some clergy may interpret it as an intrigue against Islam by foreign powers. The reality is that two dictators in order to keep their grip on power misguided their own people.

Let us not forget America's role in resolving the Balkan issue in the nineties. In Bosnia and Kosovo when the Muslims were being butchered by the Serbs, the USA and the Western powers, by military operations, forced the Serbs to stop the killing of the Muslims. How many Muslim countries came forward or dared to challenge the Serbs militarily to stop the mass murder of the Muslims in Bosnia and Kosovo? There is no denial that some financial aid to the Muslims of Bosnia and Kosovo did come from many Muslim countries but overall, the Muslim role both politically and militarily in Bosnia and Kosovo was negligible. After peace was established in Balkans, many Muslim religious groups appeared there and tried to preach their brand of Islam. One can also conclude that the Muslim countries both politically and militarily are so weak that they are unable to stop the bloodshed of Muslims in any part of the world or take any measure to safeguard the interest of Muslim countries.

One should not also forget the religious liberty and freedom the Muslims enjoy in the USA and many western countries. The freedom of religion and speech these Muslims enjoy in these countries is far more than the freedom they have in their own respective Muslim countries. In the USA and in the Western Europe, the Muslims are free to establish their religious schools and free to practice their religions as they choose. In the USA and in many Western countries, the Muslims are also free to practice their religious beliefs without any fear of persecution. Muslims have built their own societies, mosques and religious schools and live in harmony and peace with other religious groups. On the other hand, there are many Muslim countries where the persecution of one religious group by the other is quite common. The internal feud between different Islamic sects is also common. What is troubling that most of the time these feuds become violent and hundreds and thousands of innocent people are killed. The reality is that both the Muslims and Islam are safe and appear to be prospering in the USA and in Western Europe than in majority of the Muslim countries. Unfortunately, a small number of fanatic Muslims has infiltrated into the moderate Muslim societies of the USA and Western Europe and the fanatic views and acts of these people are creating a bad image of Islam and the Muslims.

The events after the incident of September 11, 2001, also reflect the thinking of American society, media and its politicians. After some Muslim fanatics crashed their planes into the World Trade Center and Pentagon, a backlash against the Muslims in America was inevitable. Some unpleasant incidents did happen when the Muslims were targeted, mosques and Muslim properties were damaged but given the magnitude of September 11 incident in which thousands of innocent people died (a vast majority being Americans), the American Muslims did not really face the wrath of the American public. The credit goes to the American government, the politicians, the media, and most of all to the American people. In this whole incident the American democracy stood taller than ever before, protecting its minority. The president and the politicians made all possible efforts to ensure that the American Muslims remain safe and protected. The constant assurance of the president and the politicians to the American public that Islam is a peaceful religion and a vast majority of American Muslims have nothing to do with the horrible events of September 11 was a remarkable feat in an attempt to protect the rights of a nation's minority. The president, many senators, and the congressmen went to the mosques, met the Muslim leaders and condemned the violence against the Muslims. They separated the Muslims and Islam from the terrorists and tried to instill respect for Islam and the Muslims in the minds of the American people. The media again and again showed documentaries on Islam, presented discussions among leaders of different religions in an effort to demonstrate the true face of Islam which helped a great deal to calm down the situation. Then there were Americans as a nation who for a moment though, overcame by emotions but then showed their compassion, tolerance and understanding towards the American Muslims and Islam. They fully understood that the inhuman acts of a few can not be used to malign a religion or all of its followers. This is a true face of American democracy and its people and if there is any nation on this planet who needs to learn from this whole incident is the Muslims.

To the sharp contrast of the American attitude, the acts of many Muslims in many countries were just appalling. Many newspapers (mainly run by the orthodox Muslim religious groups) in the Islamic world misguided the Muslims by fabricating the stories of atrocities on the American Muslims. This is a sheer example of poor and dishonest journalism and also shows how the orthodoxy in Islam does not hesitate to lie and distort facts to achieve its objectives. In Pakistan, the killing of sixteen Christian worshippers in a church by the hands of fanatic Muslims was a savage act and should be condemned by every Muslim. Once again these fanatics who claim to be the staunch followers of Islam forgot the teachings of Islam. Under the influence of ignorant mullahs many Muslims in the Islamic world fail to realize the damage these fanatics are causing to the image of Islam and to the Muslims. In the attack on the World Trade Center, hundreds of Muslims from many parts of the world were killed.

The support of many Muslims to the terrorists and their leaders against the 'war on terrorism' undermines the ability of the Muslim world to grasp the grim reality of the current situation. The Muslims round the globe should understand very clearly that this is not a war against Islam or the Muslims rather against a bunch of uncivilized thugs who are willing to put the whole human civilization on fire just to achieve their evil objectives. Their whole act is unIslamic and runs contrary to their claim and if they are allowed to continue, it will be Islam and the Muslims who will burn first. The Muslims have already isolated themselves from the normal streamline thinking of the rest of the world and their support to the fanatics is not going to help their cause and may even undermine their own existence.

In the twenty first century, the most urgent need for the Islamic world is to search for honest and sincere leadership. The democratic institutions must be established at every level of the Muslim society. There should be no room in the politics of Islam for orthodox religious figures, monarchs, and the dictators. The religion and state must be separated (secular states) and the constitution and the government of a modern Islamic country should parallel the western democracy where the rights of every person irrespective of the religion, culture, language, and race are respected and protected. In the first quarter of the twentieth century, Mustafa Kemal Ataturk established a secular state in Turkey (though failed to establish democratic institutions), therefore, there is no reason why in the twenty first century the Muslims can not establish democratic institutions and secular states? They should focus on abolishing the conservative and irrational views, building their societies around progressive and rational thinking and practicing their religion in its true spirit. This is the time that the Muslim world should come out of its own imposed isolation and be rational rather than emotional. The street smart mullahs are continuously busy in convincing the Muslims that the non-Muslims are their enemies and are determined to destroy Islam and the Muslim culture. This is of course a fabrication and the Muslim world should not pay any heed to such utter nonsense. Let us face the grim fact that at the moment the Muslims are living in their own created dark age and unless they start searching for the light, history and the historians will not be kind to them.

A Brief History of Islam

By the early seventh century in the desert of Arabia, emerged a new faith 'Islam'. The word Islam means submission or surrender to the Will of God (Allah). For the next six hundred years, Islam remained politically and culturally a dominant religion in and outside Arabia. Today, more than one billion people known as 'Muslims' are the followers of Islam. Though, passed its prime and golden age, Islam is still one of the leading religions of the world.

Prophet Muhammad, the founder of Islam belonged to a prominent tribe of Western Arabia known as Quraysh. He was born in 570 AD in Mecca after the death of his father. He spent the first eight years of his life under the care of his grandfather. After the death of his grandfather, the future prophet was under the care of his uncle. As a caretaker of the business of a rich businesswoman Khadija, he made several trading journeys to Syria. Khadija was so impressed by his honesty that she proposed marriage which he accepted and got married to her at the age of twenty five. At the age of forty, Muhammad (peace be upon him) had the vision of Angel Gabriel who told him that Muhammad (peace be upon him) was the messenger of God or Prophet. After this first revelation, he received many other revelations or messages directly from God. All these revelations were compiled in the form of a book, the Quran (the sacred scriptures of Islam).

At that time, the tribes of Mecca were of polytheistic faith and the new Prophet preached monotheism (existence of one God) which directly collided with the faith of the common people of Mecca. There were, however, many people in Mecca who accepted his teachings and joined him in prayers. To the majority of Meccans, this was an attack on their faith and hostility against the Prophet and his followers began. By 622, Prophet Muhammad decided to migrate to Medina, then a small town about two hundred fifty miles northeast of Mecca. This migration is known as 'Hijrah' and the Muslim calendar begins from the time of Hijrah (July 16, 622 AD).

In Medina, the Prophet got support from different Arab tribes and there he set up his administrative policies. With the passage of time, more and more people embraced Islam. The Meccans, however, were not ready to accept the emergence of a new faith in Arabia and there were numerous battles between the Muslims and the Meccans. The Muslims had a decisive victory at the Battle of Badr (624) but at the Battle of Uhud (625) lost the initial advantage due to the lapse of the archers guarding the Muslim flank. If Battle of Uhud was not a victory for the Muslims it was also not a defeat. In 627, the Meccans laid siege of Medina with ten thousand men but resolute trench defense of Medina by the Muslims forced the Meccans to lift their siege. In just five years, the Muslims of Medina had demonstrated their military skills and had repulsed the Meccan attacks at least three times. Prophet Muhammad realized that sooner or later he had to capture Mecca for the political stability of Islam. In 630, he marched on Mecca with ten thousand men and entered the city without any resistance. It was a bloodless victory and the declaration of a general amnesty helped to gain the allegiance of most of the Meccans. Kaaba was declared a holy Muslim shrine and all the idols in the Kaaba were destroyed. The Meccans were not forced to embrace Islam but many did embrace the new faith. Few days after the conquest of Mecca, the Prophet returned to Medina which remained the capital and center of the Islamic culture and power. The conquest of Mecca added great strength to the Muslim military might and several tribes sought alliance. In 632, Prophet Muhammad led the pilgrimage to Mecca and delivered his historical speech providing the Muslims with the future directions. Prophet Muhammad had been in poor health for some time and in June 632, he passed away.

The Prophet was not only a messenger of God but also a law giver and society builder. In Medina, he laid out the ways of Islam. Muslims were asked to pray five times a day, fast (from sun rise to sun set) during the month of Ramadan, give alms to the poor and if financial condition allows visit to Mecca for pilgrimage at least once in life. Wine drinking and pork eating, gambling and lending money on interest were prohibited. Issues related to marriage, inheritance, treatment of slaves, appropriation of booty and many social disputes were addressed in fair and practical manner. One of the most important features of the Islamic laws was the rights of the women. Before Islam, in some tribes of Arabia even the birth of a daughter was considered shameful but the Prophet gave women the same rights as men. Under the auspices of Islam, women could inherit and own properties and could file for divorce. Thus a small but growing Muslim community in Medina acquired a unique character due to its own internal discipline and social structure.

After the Prophet, Abu Bakr (632-34) became the first Caliph but he immediately faced rebellion of some Arab tribes and the emergence of many false prophets. Two major military campaigns brought the end of the rebels as well as the false prophets. When Caliph Omar (634-44) took over the reign, a new era of military expeditions began. The military success of the Muslim army was astonishing. Within the next ten years, the whole Arabia, Syria (636), Iraq (637), Egypt (642) and Iran (651) were conquered. The Byzantines were defeated in 636 at the Yarmuk River and the Muslim army marched into Mesopotamia and Asia Minor. The Byzantines and the Iranians had a well disciplined regular army, yet the poorly equipped Muslim army defeated them. Probably the religious fervor, superior mobility and superior military strategy played important role for the Muslim victories. Caliph Omar was assassinated in 644; the assassination was a personal vengeance of a slave against caliph Omar. Caliph Osman (Othman) took over the reign of the caliphate. There was some discontent against his policies and by 656 a civil war like situation erupted in Medina which resulted in the assassination of Caliph Osman. The fourth caliph was Ali (son in law and cousin of the prophet) whose era was marred by political disturbances and civil war. During the time of caliphs Osman and Ali, governor of Syria Muawiya Ibn Sufyan had amassed enough power and support to challenge the central power of the Muslims in Medina. He was Caliph Ali's main rival. The dispute between the two was not resolved and when Caliph Ali was assassinated in 661 in Kufa (Iraq), Muawiya declared himself caliph and the center of power was shifted from Medina to Damascus. Muawiya did not follow the footsteps of the first four caliphs rather started a dynasty, the Umayyads (661-750).

The era of the first four caliphs, Abu Bakr to Ali is considered the 'Era of Caliphate Rashidun (Rightly Guided). These four caliphs lived a very simple and pious life. They did not name their own children or family members as their successor. The companions of the Prophet and the respectable elderly members of the Muslim community in Medina elected these caliphs based on the criteria established by the Quran and the Sunnah. In the seventh and the eighth century Islam, the caliph's position as the political and the religious leader was considered to be very important.

While Umayyads were busy establishing their dynasty, a dissident group in Islam known as the "Shiites" emerged who later became a political force. Shiism is a branch of Islam whose doctrines to some extent differ from those of the orthodox Sunni majority. The roots of Shiism go back to the time of Caliph Abu Bakr. A small group of people in Medina believed that Ali should be the caliph after the Prophet since he was related to the Prophet, was one of the first converts to Islam and was a renowned warrior. Ali became the fourth caliph and after his death, Muawiya became the caliph and started a dynasty. Ali's son Hussain tried to revive the true Islamic spirit by challenging the hereditary rule of the Umayyads. Unfortunately, he could not get the help which the people of Iraq had promised to him and he was killed by Yazid's (son of Muawiya) army in 680 at Karbala (Iraq). This tragic incident and the question of the caliphate of Ali is the highest point of the Shiite history. Both the Sunnis and the Shiites are Muslims as for the most part the Sunni and the Shiite doctrines are similar and both recognize Muhammad as the Prophet.

Despite its hereditary nature, the Umayyad era was an era of prosperity, wealth, pompous, intellectualism and military expeditions. The Muslims have already conquered Herat and Balkh in 651 and in 664 Kabul was taken. By 670 the Berbers of North Africa were subjugated and in 711 an Arab army crossed the Straits of Gibraltar and part of Spain was conquered. In 712, a Muslim army landed in India and captured Sind (712) which facilitated the spread of Islam in India. With the conquest of new lands, the size and the shape of the Muslim Empire were vastly changed. Arabic became the official language during the time of caliph Abd-al Malik (685-705). The wealth and the opportunities drew immigrants and most of them settled in southern Iraq. These immigrants infused their knowledge and experience into the Arab communities. Most of these immigrants were recent converts to Islam and were highly resentful of certain unIslamic practices of the Umayyads and the special privileges given to the Arabs. The Umayyads were corrupt and considered the empire as their private property. They were also worldly and cruel. The Umayyads also found it very difficult to rule over a vast heterogeneous empire and there was widespread belief that their rule is illegal due to its hereditary nature (as Islam does not propagate hereditary rule). Omar Bin abd al-Aziz (717-20) was the only ruler among the Umayyads who was pious and abstemious caliph and he tried to revive the caliphate based on the style of Caliphate of Rashidun but it was too late for the Umayyads. There were many revolts against the Umayyads and by 740 their power all in a sudden disappeared. The Abbasids finally overthrew the Umayyads in 750 and with that a new era of caliphate and Muslim history began.

The first two hundred years of the Abbasid rule is considered the golden age of Islam. Baghdad was the capital and center of power during the Abbasid rule. The social structure under the Abbasids was different than the Umayyads. The non-Arabs were assimilated into the Muslim society and there was no longer any discrimination against them. The pompous and wealth of the Abbasids far exceeded than the Umayyads. An era of scientific discovery and intellectual awakening began and Baghdad became the center of all activities. The Abbasids welcomed the immigrants from different parts of the world who brought their experience and knowledge which immensely benefited the Muslims. Al-Mamun established the 'House of Wisdom' and gathered the scholars from many parts of the world. These scholars translated the scholarly works of Greek, Christian, Jewish, Hindu and Zoroastrian origin into Arabic. This was probably the greatest achievement of the Abbasid period as the translations helped to preserve the works of the many cultures and religions. The Muslim philosophers studied and added to the philosophy of Aristotle and Plato which essentially helped in preserving the Greek heritage. Arabic language, especially prose was refined. The works in medicine, natural sciences, philosophy, literature and art reached to a new height.

The Abbasids were extremely tolerant of other religions and within Islam itself they allowed progressive rational thinking. A group of rationalists known as 'Mutazilites' emerged who analyzed Islam in more rational rather than traditional ways. They argued that the Quran was not eternal and was created in time and its verses were metaphors. They postulated that man was responsible for his action since he was free to choose. Mutazilites reached to great heights during the time of al-Mamun but their intolerance against their opponents and continuous efforts by the orthodoxy against them lead to their downfall. Overall, the Islamic civilization reached its peak under the Abbasids.

By the mid tenth century, the Abbasids remained caliphs only by name, their power and authority were vastly reduced. In 945, Buyids who were Shiites and had settled around the Caspian sea took control of Baghdad, installed a new caliph of their choice, issued decree in the caliph's name and frequently used the ancient Iranian title Shahansha (king of kings). Many other independent dynasties also emerged but they continued to recognize the caliphate of Abbasids. For example, The Seljuks who were of Turkish origin (Oghuz branch) established themselves in Baghdad by 1050, effectively ended the Buyid influence and ruled under the suzerainty of the Abbasids. In 1258, the Mongol invasion of Baghdad brought the end of the Abbasids. The Mongols destroyed Baghdad, killed three-fourth of its population and burned the libraries, mosques and the palaces. The Mongol invasion was a great blow to the Islamic civilization. The disunity, lack of vision and selfishness of the Muslim rulers brought the downfall of the Muslim Empire. Within two years after the destruction of Baghdad, the Mamlukes under Baybars defeated the Mongols but the Mongols had already caused irreparable damage to the Muslim culture and civilization. Ironically, the Mongols were gradually converted to Islam and became a part of the Islamic society.

After the Abbasids ended the rule of the Umayyads (750) in Arabia, an Umayyad prince, Abd al-Rahman fled to North Africa and then to Spain where he declared himself 'emir' and made Cordoba his capital. This was the beginning of a great Muslim empire in the Iberian Peninsula which reached at its peak during the time of Abd al-Rahman III who later proclaimed himself caliph. The Muslim Spain under the Umayyads rivaled that of

Abbasids of Baghdad in every aspect of culture and civilization. Despite the continuous conflict with the neighboring Christian states, the Muslim Spain (al-Andalus) survived with its all might and majesty. The Umayyads in Spain were far different than the Umayyads in Damascus. They were tolerant of other religions and cultures. They were not cruel and worked for the well being of their subjects. The Umayyads developed sea-power and started their imperial expansion towards North Africa at the expense of the Muslim powers rather than the Christians. Scientific discoveries as well as intellectual and philosophical works reached to its peak. The architecture of Muslim Spain produced beautiful monuments, palaces and the cities. The great mosque of Cordoba and the Alhambra palace (Granada) are examples of the monumental architectural works of the Muslim Spain. The glory of the Muslim Spain, however, was over by the eleventh century as the Caliphate of Cordoba broke up into a number of small kingdoms. This allowed the Christian states in the north to march towards south. The complete collapse of the Muslim Spain, however, was prevented by the two Berber dynasties from North Africa, Almoravids (1056-1147) and Almohads (1130-1269). These two dynasties had emerged due to the idea of religious reforms and gained enough power and strength to conquer Muslim Spain and check the advances of the Christian armies. After the fall of Almohads, Muslim Spain once again disintegrated but somehow survived for another two hundred years when finally the Christian army of Ferdinand and Isabella ended the Muslim rule in Spain in 1492 (fall of Granada).

In the early tenth century in Tunisia, the Fatimids appeared. They were Ismailis, an offshoot of the Shiites. The Fatimids moved their capital to Cairo in 973 and proclaimed themselves as caliph. The Fatimids ruled from Tunisia to Palestine, promoted the Shiite beliefs and founded the famous Al-Azhar University. The Fatimids tried to take control of the caliphate in Baghdad but the Seljuks neutralized their political and religious influence. In 1171, Saladin finally ended the Fatimid rule in Egypt.

In the eleventh century, in India the so-called 'Slave Dynasty' established its power and thus began a Muslim rule whose power and roots were in India. After that, many dynasties who were originally Indians ruled over a limited territory but none of these

7

Muslim dynasties could achieve the power and majesty of the Moghuls. Babur invaded India in the sixteenth century (1526) and founded the Moghul dynasty which ruled India for more than three hundred years with its center and power in India. At least for two hundred years (till the death of Aurangzeb in 1705) the Moghul rule over India was of prosperity, expansion, wealth and pompous. The Moghuls gradually became weak and finally the British ended the Moghul rule in 1857.

In the thirteenth century, the Ottomans appeared in Anatolia whose rule lasted for six hundred years (1281-1922). Gradually they built a dynasty and embarked on the mission of expansion and power. By the sixteenth century the Ottoman Empire stretched from the Red sea to the Crimea and from Kurdistan to Bosnia. The Ottomans also defeated the Mamlukes (1517) and took control of Egypt and Syria. Kemal Ataturk ended the Ottoman rule in 1922.

The Safavids, the Shiite rulers of Iran established their power in 1501 under Ismail I. They took the title of shah and ruled over most of Persia. The Safavids came into conflict with the Sunni Ottomans in the west and the Uzbeks in Transoxania. Shah Abbas (1587-1629) was the greatest ruler of the Safavid dynasty but by the mid seventeen century the dynasty started to crumble and was finally ended by Nadir Shah in 1736.

In the Islamic world, the slaves who later became freed men have played very important roles. Some of these slaves amassed great power and became able and exemplary rulers. One such slave dynasty, the Mamlukes began their rule in 1250 in Egypt. The Mamlukes were the military slaves employed by many medieval Muslim rulers and came from the Caucasus or Central Asia. The Mamlukes were the perpetual enemies of the Mongols and they were the first to defeat the Mongols in September 1260. The Mamlukes ruled over Egypt and Syria until defeated by the Ottomans in 1517.

Besides Umayyads, Abbasids, Fatimids, Mamlukes, Saljuqs, Ottomans, Moghuls, Safavids, Almoravids and Almohads, many Muslim dynasties emerged in different parts of the world intermittently with one or two extraordinary rulers but their overall impact was short lived. Mansa Musa of Mali, Muhammad Askia of Gao, Mahmud of Ghazna and Shahab ud-Din Muhammad of

Ghur are few examples of such rulers who produced great impact on their subjects but after their death their empire disintegrated. For five hundred years (from the eighth to the thirteenth century), Islam dominated the world by its cultural progress, scientific discovery and intellectual thinking. By translating the works of the Greek masters, the Muslims preserved the Greek heritage and then advanced the knowledge to pass it to the Western Europe. It is widely believed that the European Renaissance was greatly influenced by the Muslim thinkers.

Before coming in contact with the Muslims, the Latin-Christians despised the Arabs and isolated themselves from the political and cultural progress of the Muslims. This trend however, changed when the Christians came across the Muslims during the Crusades and found many things which were new to them. They brought with them new agricultural and industrial techniques to Europe. New routes of commerce were opened and a new era of cooperation between the Christian and the Muslim merchants began.

The Muslims contributed significantly to the field of astronomy, mathematics, medicine, physics, chemistry, literature, geography, history and philosophy. The Muslim scholars were vastly benefited by the translated works of Greeks, Persians and Indians. This gave the Muslim scholars and scientists an opportunity to read the works of Greeks, Persians and Indians in Arabic and then they revised, corrected and added to the pre-existing knowledge. One of the astonishing things about these Muslim scholars was that they had encyclopedic knowledge. Their expertise was not confined to just one area rather they had mastery in many fields of knowledge.

The Abbasids established observatories where the Muslim astronomers based on their own experience and knowledge refined and corrected the works of Ptolemy and other Greek astronomers. The works of al-Battani, al-Haytham (Alhazan) and Abu al-Wefa contributed significantly to the knowledge of astronomy. Unfortunately, many of these discoveries were wrongly attributed to the western scholars. For example the work of Alhazan on optics immensely influenced the western scientists. His description of the properties of light (e.g. refraction and reflection) was as accurate as we know today but credit goes to Newton as the pioneer of the modern day optics. Long before Newton (in the eighth century), the great Muslim philosopher, al-Kindi, had already described that light travels in a straight line. There is no doubt that the works of Newton, Roger Bacon, Copernicus and Kepler were vastly influenced by the Muslim astronomers, mathematicians and physicists. The sun-dial and the pendulum were invented by the Muslim astronomer Ibn Yunus during the time of the Fatimid caliph al-Hakim (990-1021). The works on astronomy were also conducted in the Muslim Spain but most of these works were lost due to the internal political strife of the Muslims and during the reconquest and the period of religious persecution in Spain.

Algebra was discovered by Musa al-Khwarizmi, a Muslim mathematician. The Muslim mathematicians and astronomers provided the solution of many difficult problems using algebra rather than geometry. Trigonometry is another field which was advanced by the Muslim astronomers and mathematicians. Works of al-Battani, Abu al-Wefa, al-Biruni and Nasir ad-Din Tusi contributed a great deal to the knowledge of trigonometry as the Muslim astronomers used this branch of mathematics to refine the works of Greek and Indian astronomers. In fact, algebra and trigonometry were widely used by the Muslim mathematicians and astronomers as compared to the Greeks who leaned more towards geometry (may be because Greeks did not know algebra and had limited knowledge of trigonometry). The Muslims are also credited for the invention of logarithm in mathematics.

Modern day chemistry owes a lot to the Muslims. They discovered many chemical compounds such as alcohol, sulfuric acid, nitric acid, potassium, silver nitrate, camphor and ammonium salts. The Muslim chemists also developed different techniques such as sublimation, crystallization and distillation which are still used. Jaber Ibn Hayyan (Gaber) the greatest Muslim chemist was also aware with transmutation, a process through which one could make gold from cheap metals.

Medicine was another branch which the Muslims studied and advanced extensively. The works of al-Razi, Ibn Zuhr, Ibnsina, and Ibn Ali Nafis can be considered as monumental. These great Muslim physicians diagnosed and prescribed the cure of many diseases which were not known to the Europeans even several hundred years after their discovery.

Islamic philosophy and intellectualism produced enormous influence on the thinking of medieval Europe. The western scholars mistakenly believe that the Islamic philosophy is handmaid of Greek philosophy. Undoubtedly, the Muslim philosophy is immensely influenced by Greek philosophers, Aristotle and Plato but it has its own Islamic, secular and Arabic flavor.

Islamic philosophy is distinct from Islamic theology, though it originated from its theological background. The Muslim philosophers believed that by using human reasons one can attain the truth. Islamic philosophy is also an effort by the Muslim philosophers to reconcile the religion and the philosophy as both look for the rational inquiry and search for the truth. It should not be however, concluded that the Muslim philosophers only worked within the boundaries of Islam. The secular thinking among the Muslim philosophers and the scientists was widespread till the end of the twelfth century. Some of these philosophers put philosophy above religion and showed that a philosopher can attain the truth by logic, reasoning and practical thinking whereas a non philosopher requires divine help. The Muslim philosophers dealt with the concept of existence, soul, theory of creation and the Active Intellect. Muslim philosophers like al-Kindi, al-Razi, Ibnsina, al-Farabi and Ibn Rushd not only wrote commentaries on the philosophical views of Aristotle and Plato but also corrected them. Ibn Rushd is widely known for his commentaries on Aristotle which earned him the title of 'Great Commentator'. The Muslim philosophers also suffered from criticism by their own, the Muslim theologians who cast doubts about the philosophers, their works and their place in the society. In fact, Ibn Rushd was known, studied and respected more in the western world than in the east. Ibn Rushd is the last great Muslim philosopher and after him the Muslim philosophy came to an abrupt end. The Muslim theologians and orthodoxy were responsible for the downfall of the Islamic philosophy.

Once Arabic became the official language, a great effort was put forward to refine the Arabic prose. Arabic poetry due to its language, lyric and style was always considered spectacular. The work of al-Jahiz brought creativity in the Arabic prose. The works of Ibn Arabi and Ibn Tufyl (Hay Ibn Yakdhan) influenced the

11

works of Dante (The Divine Comedy) and Daniel Defoe (Robinson Crusoe), respectively. The great poets like Sadi, Firdowsi, Omar Khayyam, Hafiz and Rumi wrote in Persian and not only they were master of the language but presented their thoughts in a delicate lyrical quality. In India, Urdu poetry reached to its zenith with the Ghazals of Mirza Ghalib.

Muslim contribution to geography and history is also immense. The great Muslim traveler, Ibn Batuta traveled seventy five thousands miles in his life and the accounts of his journey remains far more fascinating than Marco Polo. The scholarly works of al-Idrisi and al-Biruni provided invaluable geographical information to the west. The Arab merchants discovered the routes to China, India, Sri Lanka and Africa. Vasco de Gama reached India by seeking the help of an Arab sailor. In history, works of Ibn Khaldun, al-Masudi, al-Biruni and al-Tabari are considered extremely valuable, especially Ibn Khaldun made the history writing an art, a style which was followed by the later generation of historians for centuries.

The Muslim architecture and the construction of the cities fascinated the Europeans for centuries. The palaces, mosques and forts of Damascus, Aleppo, Baghdad, Cairo, Samarqand, Delhi, Granada, Cordoba and Istanbul are the masterpieces of Muslim architecture and symbol of prosperity, wealth and pompous. Taj Mahal, built by the Moghul emperor Shahjahan remains one of the Seven Wonders of the World.

The Islamic empire though started declining after the Mongol invasion of Baghdad in 1258, Islam itself continued to expand as a religion. Though the era of discovery and intellectualism in the Islamic empire was over by the thirteenth century, the Muslim dynasties like Ottomans in Europe and the Mughals in India helped in the expansion of Islam. The Muslim missionaries also helped in this expansion, especially in Southeast Asia and West Africa. By the fourteenth century, Islamic intellectualism was greatly reduced and ultimately destroyed by the orthodoxy. In the twenty first century the greatest danger Islam faces is from militants within Islam and the ignorant mullahs. Today Islam remains a religious force but its impact in world politics is relatively of no significance.

Khalid Bin Walid
(Died 642)

Contribution: One of the greatest Muslim commanders during the early days of Islam. His military genius helped the Muslim army to conquer most of the Arabian Peninsula. His victory against the Byzantine troops paved the way for future Muslim conquests in Europe, Africa, and Southeast Asia. The Prophet called him "Saifullah" (Sword of God).

Khalid Bin Walid was a member of the Quraysh, one of the most prominent tribes of Arabia. Very little is known about his early life and achievements. During the early days of Islam, he was one of the opponents of this new faith. In the Battle of Uhud (625 AD, when he was still an opponent of Islam), he converted an imminent Muslim victory into a nightmare by attacking them from behind. Uhud is a hill with a plain stretching in front of it. The Prophet had ordered forty archers to remain on the hill and guard the flank. When the archers saw that the Muslims were at the verge of victory, thirty of them left their position. Khalid who was the leader of the Meccan cavalry found the opening and counter-attacked. Though the Muslim army suffered some casualties but held their ground until the Meccans left the battle field. In 627 AD, Khalid embraced Islam and became one of the leading commanders of the Muslim army. He remained in Medina with the Prophet as Medina at that time was the center of all political and military activities of the Muslims. The Muslims conquered Mecca in 630 AD without resistance and any bloodshed.

After the conquest of Mecca, Khalid was instrumental in extending the authority of Islam in central and southern Arabia. The Prophet sent his messengers to various rulers inviting them to join the banner of Islam. The Ghassanids (Christian Arab allies of the Byzantines) put a Muslim messenger sent to Syria to death. Several other emissaries sent to other tribes in Syria were also attacked and some of them were killed. A Muslim army of three thousand was sent to avenge the death of these emissaries. The combined forces of the Byzantines and the Ghassanids inflicted a defeat on the Muslim army killing many of their commanders. Eventually, the command came into Khalid's hand who organized a safe retreat of the Muslim army. Due to this achievement, the Prophet called him "Saifullah" (Sword of God). Caliph Abu Bakr sent Khalid to northeast to conquer Iraq. After capturing al-Hirah (Iraq), Khalid then crossed the desert to help a Muslim army to conquer Syria. Considering the difficulty of crossing the desert at that time it was a remarkable feat of Khalid.

One of the bloodiest battle, Khalid ever fought was against the false prophet, Muslamah. During the caliphate of Abu Bakr, Muslamah claimed to be a prophet. A Muslim army sent to subdue Muslamah was defeated. Considering the strength of Muslamah, Caliph Abu Bakr sent another military expedition against Muslamah but this time the commander of the army was Khalid Bin Walid. Khalid met Muslamah at Aqrabah and after a fierce battle; Muslamah along with his seven thousand followers was killed. The Muslims also suffered heavy casualties; some of those killed were the companions of the Prophet. This battle is also known as "The Garden of Death" because Muslamah had fortified an orchard and he and his followers were killed inside this orchard. Though many other imitators of the prophet later emerged, Muslamah was the strongest and the most dangerous of these all. With the victory at Aqrabah, a danger of civil war in the Arabian Desert was avoided.

During the time of Caliph Abu Bakr, Khalid remained the supreme military commander of the Muslim army but then Caliph Omar for some unknown reason relieved him from his high position. Khalid, however, remained the commander of the army against the Byzantines in Syria and Palestine. On September 4, 635, Khalid's army annihilated the Byzantine army and captured Damascus. The defeat, however, did not dishearten the Byzantines and in 636 AD, a strong Byzantine army advanced from the north and from the coast of Palestine. Khalid yet attacked and destroyed the Byzantine army at the Yarmuk River in August 636. Almost 50,000 Byzantine soldiers were killed in the "Battle of Yarmuk". The victory at Yarmuk was of immense significance for the expansion of Islam. This victory encouraged the Muslims to advance towards Mesopotamia and Asia Minor. On the other hand, a defeat at Yarmuk would have forced the Muslims to regroup or limit their military expedition. Khalid Bin walid died in 642. Along with Omar Bin al-Aas, Khalid Bin Walid is considered as one of the two greatest Muslim generals of the time without whom the Islamic expansion would have been impossible.

Hasan al-Basri
(642-728)

Contribution: One of the most famous Muslim teachers and preachers of the immediate generation which followed the age of Prophet Muhammad. His religious and political views as well as his piousness made him a towering figure during the early days of the Islamic Empire. At a time when unIslamic practices were making roads into the Muslim society, he preached people to refine their conduct in their daily lives and follow the footsteps of the Prophet and his companions. He also left behind an immense influence on the practices of Islamic mysticism.

Hasan al-Basri was born in 642 AD in Medina. His father of non-Arab origin was brought to Medina as a slave after the Muslim conquest of Iraq. His mother was also a slave of one of Prophet's wife Umm-e-Salma. It is highly likely that Hasan spent his early childhood in the circle of Prophet Muhammad and his companions. Hasan grew up in Medina and by the time he was fourteen, he memorized the Quran. The unfortunate assassination of the third caliph, Osman (Uthman) which Hasan witnessed in Medina as a fourteen year old boy might have shaped his thinking in later years of his life. Hasan's family moved to Basra (Iraq) when he was fifteen years old (657 AD). Basra at that time was a military base from where military expeditions were conducted in the east (Iran). At the age of twenty two he joined the army and took part in some of these military expeditions. At age thirty he became the secretary of the governor of Khurasan. He returned to Basra (hence the surname Basri) at the age of thirty two where he spent rest of his life.

The time in which Hasan lived was the time of expansion and prosperity of the Islamic Empire. Basra was growing in size and population, inhibited by a large number of non Arab Muslims. This influx of people from the lands of Muslim conquest created an enormous influence on the economical, political and religious life of the Muslim society in the Middle East. It was also an era of opportunity, luxury, corruption, wealth and power. The era of the four caliphs known as 'Caliphate Rashidun' (Caliphate of Rightly Guided) was over. In Syria a new political dynasty known as "Umayyads" emerged (661-750). The center of power shifted from Medina to Damascus. The ruling style of Umayyads was mainly directed by self interest and politics was compromised with religion. The opposition to Umayyad rule was quite frequent and the ruling class had to face many revolts in Iraq and the eastern provinces of the empire. The Shiites were emerging as a strong political and religious group with a strong opposition to Umayyads. Even the religious scholars seemed to be affected by the events around them. They were busy promoting the interest of one party or the other.

These were indeed turbulent times for the emerging nascent Islamic Empire. Hasan al-Basri rose to the occasion with an intention to clean the Muslim society from the corrupt and unIslamic practices. Between 684 and 704 AD, his preaching activity was at its peak. Not only he became the most celebrated teacher and preacher in Basra but his fame also grew in the expanding Islamic Empire. The Umayyad caliphs frequently solicited his advice on the matters of policy, ethics and religion. He was considered as one of the most celebrated and eloquent preacher of his time. His life style was another factor which contributed to his fame and drew people to listen to him. He spent a very pious life with no desire for wealth and power. Yet he was generous, whenever he received a gift or donation, he would distribute it to the poor keeping only enough for his immediate needs.

Hasan was an outspoken critic of the Umayyad dynasty but he never undermined their authority. He taught people that they should examine their own act since man is responsible for his own action. In a letter to Umayyad caliph Abd al-Malik, Hasan refuted the widely accepted view that God is the sole creator of man's action. His political views and candid criticism of those in power often landed him into troubled spots. He was forced to go into hiding (705-714) after criticizing the powerful and cruel governor of Iraq, Hajaj Bin Yusuf. In 717, the pious Umayyad prince Omar

Bin Abd-al Aziz took over the reigns of the dynasty. Omar himself was a simple and religious man and the two men established a strong friendly relationship and the caliph sought Hasan's advice on the issues of the empire and tried to model the affairs of the state based on Hasan's teachings. The caliph also appointed him a judge but Hasan gave up the position in a year. Hasan died in Basra in 728 AD. Remarkably he lived during the era of ten Umayyad caliphs (from Muawiya to Hisham).

Despite being a teacher, Hasan al-Basri did not leave any written material. A number of Islamic schools of thought and mystic orders claimed Hasan as their founder. The Sufis and the mystics consider him as one of their foremost spiritual masters. Islamic mysticism evolved as a reaction to the worldliness of the Muslim society, especially against the unIslamic practices of the Umayyad dynasty. The idea of a world of virtues, belief that by abandoning the worldly possessions and repetition of the name of God in prayer may purify the heart and may help to move closer to God was gaining momentum which gave birth to many Sufi orders. Hasan's pious life and the practice of religious self examination left great influence on the ascetic and mystical practices in Islam.

Muhammad Bin Qasim
(695-715)

Contribution: Islam's youngest military commander. At the age of seventeen, he led a military expedition to India which later proved to be a significant mission. His military victory at Sind not only helped in spreading Islam but also laid the foundation of a future Muslim empire in India. It also helped Arabs to understand rich Indian cultures and traditions.

Before the arrival of Islam in India, both Hinduism and Buddhism prospered under the patronage of regional rulers and had broader appeals to the general masses. The Hindu religion prospered better in the south, whereas Buddhism flourished more in the north-west. Hinduism, however, remain the predominant religion of majority of Indians till today.

Islam arrived in India in the eighth century through Arab merchants who landed on the western coasts of India. These Arab merchants frequently used to travel between Ceylon (now Sri Lanka) and India. Dahir was then Hindu ruler of Sind (now in Pakistan). His army regularly intercepted these merchant ships and not only confiscated the merchandise but also enslaved the Muslim families. In one such incident, Dahir's army captured a ship of pilgrims who were on their way to Mecca, killed and enslaved the occupants of the ship. In response to the aggression of Dahir's army, Hajaj Bin Yusuf, the governor of Iraq, sent a military mission to Sind led by his nephew and son-in-law, Muhammad Bin Qasim. At the age of 17, this young commander marched towards Sind with a small army and in 712 AD won the battle against Raja Dahir's army. This military expedition led by Muhammad Bin Qasim to India was both of political and religious importance.

The victory at Sind was of great significance for the spread of Islam in the Subcontinent. A fairly good number of local people embraced Islam and undoubtedly most of the credit goes to this young commander whose kind gesture and humble attitude won the hearts of many. Probably, never before the local people had witnessed such a polite and fair treatment of a conqueror. Therefore, this generous attitude of a victor - yet so young but matured in thinking and vision- later paved the way for the Muslim missionaries to spread Islam beyond the corners of Sind. After taking Sind, Muhammad Bin Qasim then marched towards northward and captured Multan, which later became the seat of Muslim preachers and scholars. Unfortunately, the family feud and court intrigue resulted in the recall of Muhammad Bin Qasim to Iraq where he was accused of treason and was sentenced to death. Muhammad Bin Qasim lived only twenty years but in this short life he established a name for himself and left behind a legacy.

Muhammad Bin Qasim was not only a brilliant military commander at a very young age but also had the vision in the affairs of the state. Before leaving India, probably he knew his fate, yet he obeyed the orders of the caliph and returned home rather than being labeled as a 'rebel' who might have caused civil unrest and disobedience. Muhammad Bin Qasim in the end sacrificed his life for the principles he believed and for the stability of the state. Muhammad Bin Qasim is considered the youngest military commander among all time great conquerors. Probably, he was also one of the greatest martyrs of Islam.

The victory at Sind by the Arabs led by Muhammad Bin Qasim was not only significant from religious point of view but it also had cultural and economical impact. Though the Arab merchants and missionaries frequently visited India, there was no central base where they could stay permanently. An Arab establishment in Sind opened the doors for the Arab Muslims to understand the rich Indian culture and enhanced the trade and ideas between India and the Muslim world. This indeed proved beneficial to both the Indian Subcontinent and the Islamic world.

Abu Hanifa
(699-767)

Contribution: Muslim jurist and theologian. He was the founder of the Hanafi School of Islamic laws. He provided the Muslims a systematic and applicable system of laws. With time Hanafi doctrines gained enormous popularity and were used by the majority of Muslim rulers in different parts of the world. Even today, it is widely followed in the Subcontinent, Central Asia and many Arab countries.

Abu Hanifa was born in Kufa (Iraq) in 699 AD. His ancestors may be of Iranian or Afghan origin. It is believed that his grandfather, Zuta was brought as a slave (probably from Afghanistan) and became a possession of Thalaba family. Reasons best known to Thalaba family, Zuta and his descendants were set free. Abu Hanifa's father established a business and became a successful merchant. Abu Hanifa followed his father's footsteps and he himself became a wealthy merchant dealing in silk trade. He became reputed as an honest and generous businessman. His wealth provided help to poor and needy and many students benefited from his generosity. Soon Abu Hanifa turned his attention from business to scholarship. He was a man of logical mind and systematic thinking. He studied theology and focused on human ethical, legal and equity issues. He believed that ethical and legal frameworks have been provided to man by God through the Quran. Abu Hanifa worked for eighteen years with reputed Muslim jurist, Hammad Ibn Ali Suleiman. Extensive traveling, the heterogeneous society of Iraq and his friendship with Jafar al-Sadique, the founder of Shiite sect helped him a great deal to advance his knowledge in jurisprudence and theology. After the death of Hammad (738), Abu Hanifa became a leading legal

21

thinker in the Muslim world and devoted his entire life to teaching and research.

Abu Hanifa's personal wealth made him independent and he did not need any patronage or financial help from the royal, private or government sources. His independence and financial security proved to be a boon to him as he could entirely concentrate on teaching and research leading to the Muslim laws.

Abu Hanifa's teachings revolved around the teachings of Quran and Hadith (sayings of the prophet). However, the interpretation of these was complex and not without controversy. He argued that in making decisions, a judge has to use his own knowledge, experience and intelligence and analytical skills. He advocated the use of analogy and logical thinking in discussions and extrapolation from known to unknown based on experience and rational thinking. As a legal thinker he believed in the opinion of the majority. He himself never wrote any treatise or book but his students recorded his teachings. As a teacher he was the founder of the Islamic law and the Hanafi School of Jurisprudence.

During the time of Abu Hanifa, Islamic law had become unsystematic, without any direction and fundamental principles. The individual judges used their discretion to give their verdicts which on many occasions were conflicting. Abu Hanifa's greatest contribution in this regard was that he established a systematic doctrines of laws based on reasoning and logical thinking rather than decisions made based on the situations and occasions. He examined a vast number of legal writings of his time and laid out the standards which could be applicable regardless of time and place. His legal theories were based on several principles, such as, he viewed the law to be systematic rather situational, rational than empirical, and moderate rather extreme.

During his time, the Muslims were also debating if they should be led by the descendants of the Prophet Muhammad or by caliphs who were not directly related to the Prophet. This was a serious political problem and despite the fact that Abu Hanifa avoided political involvement, he had to deal with two rival Caliphates (Umayyads (661-750) and Abbasids (750-1258)). He had no liking of either of these dynasties and tried to be neutral, yet he was arrested and imprisoned. The circumstances surrounding his death are not clear. He died in Baghdad in 767 either while in prison or shortly after he was released.

Hanafi School of Law, founded by Abu Hanifa became the most famous of four schools of Sunni Islamic laws. In his system of Islamic jurisprudence, Abu Hanifa, tried to give judges the liberty to exercise opinions based on the logic and natural law (finding of reasons based on physical and social sciences). His legal system is liberal and tolerant than the other three Schools of Islamic Laws (Hanbalis, Shafis, and Malikis).

In short, in his doctrines, Abu Hanifa, emphasized on the systematic and technical legal considerations rather administrative convenience. His doctrines were carefully formulated based on actual problems and then extrapolated to solve the future problems. This approach considerably enlarged the area of the legal systems. His works made the law universally applicable by reasoning and refinement. He was a great jurist of the Muslim civilization but his legal philosophies can also be embraced by other communities.

Abd al-Rahman I
(731-788)

Contribution: Emir of Islamic Spain. He was the founder of the Umayyad dynasty which ruled the Iberian Peninsula for more than three hundred years. A capable administrator and a military commander, he fought on many fronts to establish a stable Umayyad rule in Spain.

After the assassination of the fourth caliph, Ali Ibn Talib (661 AD), the Islamic world to some extent was in chaos. Muawiya Ibn Sufyan came to power in 661 and with that the era of Caliphate of Rashidun (Caliphs of Rightly guided) came to an end. Muawiya was the founder of the Umayyad dynasty which remained in power till 750. The Umayyads expanded the Muslim rule beyond the Arabian Peninsula. The Arabs landed in Spain in 710 AD and created a kingdom which reached as far as north of the Iberian Peninsula. With time the Umayyad power declined and the Abbasids ended the Umayyad caliphate in 750 AD. The Abbasids also hunted down the members of the Umayyad family and slaughtered many of them. One of the Umayyad princes, Abd al-Rahman, fled towards North Africa and later established the Umayyad dynasty in Spain.

Abd al-Rahman was the son of Umayyad prince Muawiya Ibn Hisham and a Berber woman of Nafza tribe from Morocco and a grandson of caliph Hisham. After traveling across North Africa, Abd al-Rahman finally sought refuge in his mother's tribe. Here in Morocco, he realized that Spain could be a suitable ground for his political ambitions. The Arabs in the Iberian Peninsula were divided among the tribal lines and were weak. There had been fighting between different groups of Arabs and Berbers in Spain. There were also many Syrian immigrants who had settled within the territory of Muslim Spain and were loyal to the Umayyads. These loyalists and some Arab tribes in Spain thought that the presence of an Umayyad prince among them would be politically helpful to them. When Abd al-Rahman landed at Almunecar in August 755, the Syrian immigrants immediately acknowledged his leadership. After gaining the support of some Arab and Berber tribes as well as former family loyalist, Abd al-Rahman attacked and defeated the governor of Muslim Spain, Yusuf al-Fihri. Abd al-Rahman made Cordoba his capital and on May 15, 756 he was proclaimed Emir (ruler).

For the next 32 years, Abd al-Rahman ruled Spain but faced numerous revolts and opposition. He faced the opposition from both the Berber and the Arab clans. Many of these uprisings were supported by the Abbasids. One of the serious threats came from Charlemagne, the Frank king, who on the request of some Arab Chiefs, besieged Saragossa in 778 but part of his army was destroyed in the Pass of Roncesvalles by the Basques. With the passage of time, Abd al-Rahman crushed all opposition and maintained a firm grip on the power.

Abd al-Rahman's success drew thousands of Umayyad supporters and loyalists towards Spain. They brought administrative skills with them and soon Abd al-Rahman's administrative system resembled the Umayyad administrative system in Syria. Abd al-Rahman centralized the government operations in Cordoba. Before his death in 788, he had stabilized the Umayyad rule in Spain. He did not try to avenge the deaths of his family members by the hands of the Abbasids rather his focus was to establish an Umayyad rule in the Iberian Peninsula. He left behind an administrative system on which his descendents consolidated their power and built a great empire in Spain which for centuries remained the center of Islamic culture and civilization.

Jabir Ibn Hayyan
(721-815)

Contribution: The greatest chemist of Islam. Though his training was in medicine, his reputation is due to his works in chemistry. His works in chemistry exerted considerable influence in the development of modern chemistry, especially due to many techniques he developed for the purification and separation of chemical moieties.

Jabir known as 'Geber' (Latin of Jabir) to the west is considered the father of modern chemistry. Jabir was born in Tus (Iran) in 721. His father, Abu Musa Jabir Ibn Hayyan was a Shiite apothecary in Khurasan (Iran). He was also a supporter of the Abbasid family who were preparing to overthrow the Umayyad dynasty. When Jabir was still a child, his father was captured and killed by the Umayyad's agents. Jabir was then sent to southern Arabia where he learned the art of Alchemy and medicine. Jabir also became interested in Sufism and learned a great deal from the Sufis. They taught him the hidden meaning of numbers and letters. Jabir was also a member of the Shiite sect and was a close friend of the sixth Shiite Imam Jafar Ibn Muhammad. When Abbasids finally came into power, Jabir became a court physician of Harun Rashid and made a great name for himself as a chemist and astrologer. He was a close friend of Barmakids (a powerful political family during Abbasid's period). When Barmakids were accused for plotting against the caliph, they were persecuted and Jabir also fell from the caliph's favor. He moved to Kufa where he died in 815. Two hundred years after his death, his laboratory was accidentally discovered in Kufa. Besides being a chemist and a physician, Jabir also contributed to philosophy and logic.

The fact that he was a physician by training did not stop Jabir from pursuing his scientific curiosity. His fame lies in his work of alchemy. The term 'alchemy' comes from medieval Latin alchimia derived from Arabic al-kimia. The original alchemists were probably members of a secret cult who were involved in some form of chemical works, probably trying to make gold from cheap metals by chemical means. The basic concepts of alchemy pivoted around the transmutation of metals. In other words alchemies believed that one can convert base metals such as lead and iron into expensive metals like gold. The techniques of alchemy reached to Arabia through the Arabic translation of the works of Greek alchemies. Probably many Arab individuals practiced alchemy though with little success. The man who, however, gained reputation in this field was Jabir Ibn Hayyan.

Greek philosophy, especially the views of Aristotle seemed to have a great influence on Jabir. Jabir like ancient Greeks believed that every object in the universe is composed of fire, earth, water and air. When these four elements are combined together in different proportions, two new substances, mercury and sulfur are formed. According to this belief, both mercury and sulfur are basic elements for metals and different kinds of metals can be obtained by combining mercury and sulfur in different proportions. Jabir probably also knew how to make gold by using different proportions of mercury and sulfur. This secret art of making gold remained a fascination among alchemies for generations to come and produced great influence on the progress and understanding of early chemistry.

Jabir also believed the Hellenistic idea that basically all metals are same substance but have different amount of impurities. Therefore, he focused on finding method(s) which can transmute base metals into gold. He also developed numerological system which was important in the process of transmutation. Mizan or balance was one of the key elements of Jabir's work on chemistry. Astrology also played an important role in Jabir's system of classification of chemical substances.

The alchemies believed that the transmutation of ordinary metals into gold requires a catalyst known as 'elixir' or philosopher's stone. Before Jabir, the Alchemists used inorganic materials to make this elixir, whereas Jabir used vegetable and animal sources to make this elixir.

In chemistry, Jabir is credited for his discoveries of acids, potassium, arsenic and silver nitrate. His discovery of nitric acid is probably one of the pioneering works in chemistry which opened the door for the synthesis of many chemical compounds. The process of distillation and sublimation was extensively used and described by Jabir as important techniques for the separation of chemical substances. He described his experimental processes clearly and in minute details. He also improved the techniques of dyeing and glass-making. Indeed, his works produced considerable influence on the process and development of modern chemistry and on the chemists round the globe.

Ibn Mahbub al-Jahiz
(776-868)

Contribution: Muslim intellectual and littérateur who contributed significantly to the Arabic language. In his Arabic prose, he employed innovative style and creativity to free the language from the limitations of religious themes. His intellectual capability was far reaching and he touched a wide variety of subjects such as theology, politics and natural sciences. His writings revolved around human nature, its low and high points presented in an eloquent style and manner. He also wrote zoological treatise.

Al-Jahiz was born in Basra (Iraq) in 776 AD to a family of immigrants, probably of Ethiopian origin. His family though of slave origin was completely Arabized and was living on a modest income in Basra. Al-Jahiz took his early education in his native city and then went to Baghdad for higher education. His intellect, wit and wisdom earned him acceptance in the scholarly and high society of Basra. He began his career as a clerk or a copyist in the government. His writing style caught the attention of the high officials and caliph al-Mamun asked him to write a commentary justifying the uprooting of Umayyad dynasty and taking control of power from them by the Abbasids.

Al-Jahiz's intellectual capabilities were of highest order which led him to write on a wide variety of subjects. Besides literature, he touched subjects like politics, theology and natural sciences.

During the eighth century, a group of Muslim thinkers emerged who called itself Mutazilis or Mutazilites (those who keep themselves apart). The Mutazilites were progressive thinkers and believed that truth could be attained by using reasons and logical thinking. They also believed that the Quran was created. Al-Jahiz was a member of the Mutazilite school of thought and took part in many public debates defending Mutazilite views despite the fact that sometimes these views were not very popular among the masses. Though Mutazilite School of thought was supported by al-Mamun and his successor al-Mutasim (833-42) but by the time al-Mutawakkil (847-61) became caliph, Mutazilites were losing grounds. Although caliph Mutawakkil was not a patron of Mutazilite School of thought he did not deprive al-Jahiz from royal favor. During this time al-Jahiz wrote essays about the government and its policies. In his essays known as Manaquib al-Turk (Exploits of the Turks), he wrote about Turks who were predominantly in the military and the government policy very much depended on them. He described their military qualities and praised their virtues. Using jokes and anecdotes, al-Jahiz also tried to unveil the corruption in the government.

The Arabic language spread with Islam, though in Iraq and Syria Arabic was a spoken language even before the conquest of these territories by the Arab Muslims. Even in Iran where Persian was a well established language, Arabic became the language of religion and legal learning. With the Arab conquest, Arabic crossed the Arabian Peninsula and reached as far as Spain and Morocco. However, the use of Arabic in prose remained rigid, inflexible and unimaginative. Mostly the Arabic prose was confined to the religious matters, life and achievements of the Prophet and his companions and the historical evens related to the Arab conquests. On the other hand, Arabic poetry which was famous for its high language continued to flourish during the Umayyads and the Abbasids reign. In fact the Quran was written in Arabic and was expressed in the high language, the language of the poetry of the earlier times.

During the Arab conquest, the immigrants of non-Arab origins flocked in many Arab cities, especially in Basra, Kufa and Baghdad which were literary centers of the time. These immigrants learned Arabic and used it in their daily life. By this time Arabic prose also began to take shape. The interaction among the caliphs, their courts, high officials and the social elites changed and expanded the outlook of the Arabic prose. The artistic prose which emerged due to the themes taken from other cultures and languages gave birth to a new kind of Arabic prose, known as 'Adab' or high culture. The Adab which was developed during Abbasid period demanded certain mannerism and style of expression. It was also developed to focus on the moral and spiritual aspects of life as well as for entertainment.

Considering the fact that Arabic as a language was not used as its full capacity for prose writing, al-Jahiz's contribution to the Arabic prose is immense. He showed that Arabic is a literary language and can be used to express a wide variety of subjects in a very effective manner. Without al-Jahiz, Arabic secular writing would not have been possible.

Al-Jahiz was fluent both in Arabic and Greek. In his writings he cited Aristotle and other Greek intellectuals. Most of his treatises on theology and politics have been lost but his Arabic prose have survived. In his book Kitab al-Bukhala (Book of Misers) which is a collection of stories about the Persian middle class, he described their lack of generosity as compared to the Arabs. This book is a hallmark of effective language presented by stylistic flair filled with witty comments and anecdotes. His work Kitab al-Hayawan (Book of Animals) is a zoological treatise and is an attempt by al-Jahiz to systematically classify the living organisms. Kitab al-Bayan wa al-Tabiyn (Elegance of Expression and Clarity of Exposition) is his another work which reflects al-Jahiz's mastery of Arabic language, style and expression.

Al-Jahiz was a devout Muslim (though not orthodox) who was deeply disturbed by the corruption in the government as well as in the literate class. In his writings he emphasized on exemplary behavior and revealed the moral qualities of human beings showing its both positive and negative sides (love, friendship, sincerity, pride, hatred, jealousy, greed, ego and treachery). As a scholar and a littérateur, al-Jahiz had left an indelible mark on the Arabic prose, hence on the Arabic language itself. His chief contribution to the Arabic prose was that he broadened the themes and subject matters. Before him, Arabic prose appeared to be a slave of religious stories and historical events of religious background. Not only he introduced a wide variety of topics in his writings but also used the language with style, clarity and expression. Muslim Spain was also highly influenced by his writings and for several centuries his writings inspired the Muslim Spanish writers. Al-Jahiz died at Basra in 868 AD.

Ahmad Ibn Hanbal
(780-855)

Contribution: Theologian, jurist and the compiler of the Traditions of Prophet Muhammad. His views and religious beliefs helped in initiating and formulating the Hanbli School of Law. He was willing to sacrifice his life for his strict traditionalist Islamic beliefs. His doctrines influenced many Islamic reform movements as late as the nineteenth century.

Ibn Hanbal was born in Baghdad in 780 AD. He belonged to an Arab tribe, Banu Shayban, which had played an important role in the conquest of Khurasan. His father died when Ibn Hanbal was an infant. He began to study the Traditions of Prophet Mohammed (Hadith) at the age of 15. In quest of knowledge, he traveled to Kufa and Basra in Iraq, Yemen and Syria. He visited Mecca and Medina not only for pilgrimage but to learn about the Hadith. During this period he came across and befriended with a number of scholars specialized in Islamic laws and history. These contacts proved to be a great influence on his life. He was married twice and had eight children. He led a very simple life and was devoted to the principles he taught. He often fasted and prayed at length during the morning and evening hours.

The Muslim jurists followed the teachings of the Quran, Sunnah and Hadith to settle the disputes of law. Some jurists, however, formulated opinions on matters where precedents or texts were lacking. Abu Hanifa (699-767) founded the first school of law which allowed the legal reasoning and was influential in Iraq and Syria.

With the emergence of Mutazilis in the mid eighth century, a debate between these progressive thinkers and traditionalist began. The most important question was whether human acts are the act of a free human choice or these acts are dictated by God? The Mutazilis believed that God is all powerful and all knowing, but man is responsible for his action and will be judged for his acts. The Mutazilis were rationalists and believed that the Quran was created in time and was not eternal. They argued that God has no human attributes (a pure Essence) therefore; the Quran can not be his spoken words. The truth can be reached by using reasons without revelation. They also believed that the judicial issues should be reviewed by the state. On the other hand there were traditionalists who believed that the word of the Quran should be the basis for the faith. The Quran is regarded uncreated and eternal word of God. The reconciliation of these two statements became a matter of debate.

The Quran and the Sunnah of the prophet show that God is all powerful and just. This line of thinking was formulated by Ahmad Ibn Hanbal. This was the reign of Caliph Mamun who had adopted the views of Mutazilis mainly to combat dissention and external challenge to his government. The Mutazili beliefs that reasons and logic should be used to answer different questions of theology, created a political episode known as mihnah (inquisition or trial). Ibn Hanbal refused to accept the Mutazilite doctrine. The inquisition lasted from 833 to 848, involving the reign of four caliphs. During this inquisition, Ibn Hanbal was subjected to torture (chained and beaten) and was imprisoned for two years. After the death of Mamun, al-Mutasim and then al-Wathiq continued with the inquisition. The advisors of these two caliphs, on the political grounds, wanted to persecute Ibn Hanbal but the mounting anger of the public forced them not to take any harsh action against him. During the reign of al-Mutawakkil, the inquisition was carried out for two years but then he brought an end to it in 848. Ahmad Ibn Hanbal showed great patience, courage and determination during the inquisition. He held his grounds without relinquishing his opinions regarding the Quran and the Sunnah.

Ibn Hanbal's works became the basis for the Hanbli School of Law. His most extensive and well known work is 'Musand' a collection of traditions. His writings also include his views on religion, faith, prayer and politics.

Hanbli School of Law is the last but most rigid School of Laws (the other three School of Laws are: Hanafis from Abu Hanifa, Malikis from Malik and Shafis from al-shafi). For centuries,

Hanbli doctrines were taught in Baghdad, Damascus, Egypt, Syria, Palestine and Iraq. However, due to its rigidity, its appeal to the masses declined with time. The Wahhabi movement in the eighteenth century borrowed its principles from the doctrines of Ibn Hanbal. Salafiyyah reform movement in Egypt was also influenced by Hanbli doctrines.

Ibn Musa al-Khwarizmi
(780-850)

Contribution: Astronomer, mathematician and geographer. Al-Khwarizmi was the first to use Indian numeral to develop new forms of mathematical calculations. His concept of algebra and Hindu-Arabic numerals became an important source into the mathematics of medieval Europe especially for the inclusion of decimal numbers.

Al-Khwarizmi, the father of modern day algebra, a mathematician and astronomer was born in Khwarizm (or Baghdad) in 780 AD. His place of birth is controversial. Though some historians believe that he was born in Baghdad, his name suggests that his family might be of Persian origin. Very little is known about his early life. In Baghdad he rose to great heights as a scholar and a scientist in the courts of Caliphs al-Mamun and al-Mutasim.

During the eighth and the ninth century, Muslim intellectualism as well as science and philosophy were greatly influenced by the Greek ideas. The Indian influence, especially in mathematics also made its way into the Muslim world. The initial efforts by the Muslims were to preserve the Hellenistic heritage. Caliph al-Mamun had established 'Baitul Hikma' (the House of Wisdom), a world class center of learning. In this center, he had gathered scholars as well as translators from different parts of the world. The primary job of these translators was to translate the Greek, Persian and Sanskrit scientific works into Arabic. These translations contributed to a great deal in bringing Greek, Iranian and Indian traditions together and probably for the first time in history, science and scholarly works became international. The fusion of Greek, Persian and Indian ideas stimulated new scientific discoveries among the Muslims.

Al-Khwarizmi was appointed by al-Mamun as the chief of the House of Wisdom. It is believed that while in Al-Mamun's court, al-Khwarizmi actively took part in the calculation of the length of a degree of latitude. This work was probably a joint effort of various scholars and scientists present in the court. Al-Khwarizmi died in Baghdad in 850 AD.

Al-Khwarizmi, the founder of Analytical Algebra wrote a comprehensive book on this subject known as 'Kitab Al-Jabr wa Al Muquabla' (the book of Integration and Equation). This book is the origin of the term 'Algebra'. This book provides the solution of linear and quadratic equations as well as elementary geometry. This book also provided the solution of inheritance problems (deals with the distribution of wealth according to proportions). The method for surveying plots of lands has also been described in this book. 'Kitab Al-Jabr wa Al Muquabla' was translated into Latin in the 12th century.

Al-Khwarizmi classified numbers into three types and its operation into six types. His classification of numbers is roots, squares and numbers. His algebraic examples were repeated for centuries and were so deeply rooted in algebra that the subsequent mathematicians did not bother to acknowledge his works as the source.

Al-Khwarizmi introduced logarithm into numbers. He also introduced Hindu numerals and surveyed Greek and Indian sciences. He revised the Hindu astronomical tables for the calculation of positions of heavenly bodies. His treatise on Hindu numerals describes the use of decimal digits and gives methods for four basic mathematical operations. His treatise on mathematics has survived in Latin rather than Arabic.

Al-Khwarizmi compiled astronomical and trigonometric tables (sine and tangent). His astronomical tables were used for time keeping. From his work 'On the Construction and Use of Astrolable', times of midday and afternoon prayers can be determined by measuring the length of shadows. These techniques to determine time were widely used for centuries. He also created a table to determine the direction to Mecca. This is important from Islamic point of view because the Muslims face Mecca when they pray.

Al-Khwarizmi's another important contribution is in geography. His book 'Kitab Sura al-Ard (Shape of the Earth) consists of a world map and a list of coordinates of known important locations of the time. Al-Khwarizmi's descriptions of geography differ from the geography of Ptolemy and are more accurate than Ptolemy.

Overall, al-Khwarizmi's work produced immense influence on the European mathematics. Three of his works, the Algebra, Astronomical tables and the treatise on the Hindu numerals were translated into Latin in the 12th century. He introduced the Hindu-Arabic numerals which were adopted in Europe at the end of the 16th century. Karpinski described al-Khwarizmi's contribution in mathematics as follows:

No other writer from the time of the Greeks to Regiomontanus (the German astronomer and mathematician; 1436-1476) has influenced mathematics as did Muhammad Ibn Musa al-Khwarizmi.

Abdallah al-Mamun
(786-833)

Contribution: Seventh Abbasid caliph and one of the most liberal caliphs of the dynasty who supported the views of the rationalists known as 'Mutazilites'. He made an all out effort to end the sectarian rivalry in Islam. He was also a great patron of arts, philosophy and science.

Mamun, son of the legendary caliph Harun Rashid and one of his Iranian concubines was born in 786 AD. Mamun grew up with his half-brother Amin whose mother Zubayda Khatoon was of Arab origin and the legitimate wife of Harun Rashid. Mamun, however, was more intelligent and skilled than his brother and served as the governor of the eastern provinces of the empire with his capital at Merv (current Turkmenistan). In 802, Harun Rashid announced Amin as his successor but Mamun retained absolute sovereignty over the eastern provinces. Though in his father's life Mamun acknowledged Amin as the successor to the caliphate in Baghdad but an armed conflict soon developed between the two brothers after the death of their father, Harun Rashid (809 AD). Backed by the Iranian politicians and military commanders, Mamun not only captured Western Iran but also parts of Iraq and Arabia. In September 813, after more than a year of siege, Baghdad finally fell to Mamun's army and against the orders of Mamun, Amin was killed. With the accession of Mamun to the throne, a long and bloody civil war thus ended. After becoming caliph, Mamun remained in Merv, though there were disturbances in Iraq, Syria and Egypt. In order to gain support from the Shiite group, Mamun designated Ali al-Rida his successor, one of the descendants of Caliph Ali. Mamun also gave his daughter to Ali Rida as a wife. This political approach of Mamun, however, failed and resulted in a revolt in Baghdad. Mamun's uncle Ibrahim was proclaimed caliph but Mamun moved swiftly and in 819 crushed the revolt. Mamun's success, however, in crushing the revolt in 819 did not bring peace to him. For rest of his life, he remained busy in suppressing disorders in various parts of the caliphate. Nevertheless, he maintained a firm control on his ministers and provincial governors. Ali Rida meanwhile died in Meshed. With passage of time Mamun also abandoned his policy of reconciliation with the Shiite Muslims.

A major political development during Mamun's reign was the rise of semi-independent hereditary dynasty. A Persian military general Tahir was main architect behind Mamun's success against his brother. In 821, Tahir was appointed governor of the troubled province Khurasan. After his death in 822, his son Talha was appointed governor and in 828 his brother succeeded as governor. This was the beginning of the emergence of independent dynasties which were appointed by the caliph and were loyal to him but with time such independent dynasties became very powerful and the caliphs were left with no real power.

In 830, Mamun began military expeditions against Byzantines and during one of such expeditions he died in August 833 at Tarsus.

During the reign of Mamun, despite internal troubles, trade and culture flourished and the Abbasid caliphate was at its zenith of prosperity and progress. Mamun had a great interest in Greek philosophy and encouraged the study of Greek thoughts. He founded Baytul Hikma (House of Wisdom) an institute for translating books in Arabic from foreign languages such as Greek, Persian and Sanskrit. In this institution, Mamun had collected the scholars from different parts of the world with several religions and cultural background. The Arabic translation of Greek and Indian scholars' works were of great help to the Arab scholars as they could read their works in Arabic. The great al-Khwarizmi, the founder of analytical algebra, was the director of the 'House of Wisdom'.

Mamun also had interest in science. He established an observatory at which Muslim scholars and mathematicians studied astronomy. The great Muslim astronomer-astrologer, al-Farghani played an important role in building the observatory. Here

Farghani wrote his treatise on Ptolemic astronomy and provided the new estimate of the circumference of the earth.

During Mamun's reign, a group of rationalists known as 'Mutazilites' emerged. This group had liberal views (compared to the norms of the time) though its base was still very Islamic. They believed in the freedom of the will and that the Quran was created rather than the words of God. Several members of this group were prominent at the court of Mamun and he was very impressed by the philosophical and political views of this group. In 827, Mamun publicly adopted the Mutazilite doctrine and ordered the judges and governors to enforce the Mutazilite doctrine. Mamun also established the inquisition or Minha. The inquisition forced the high level officials to confess publicly that the Quran was created. Most of the officials made the declaration but there was also resistance especially from religious groups. One of the most prominent opponents of the Mutazilite doctrine was renowned theologian and jurist, Ahmad Ibn Hanbal. Ibn Hanbal was imprisoned and tortured but survived due to sudden death of Mamun at Tarsus in 833. Ibn Hanbal continued his opposition to Mutazilite doctrine and finally in 848, caliph Mutawakkil ended the inquisition.

Overall, Mamun's reign was full of events. As an intelligent and open minded ruler, he tried to reform the political arena around him with his personal ideas which in turn ended in failure. His efforts to reconcile Sunni and Shiite Muslims were not successful though credit must be given to him for taking such an attempt which could have resulted his overthrow and anarchy in the empire. His greatest achievement was facilitation and encouragement of the scientific knowledge. The translation of books into Arabic from foreign languages served generations of Muslim scholars and scientists to improve the knowledge handed down from the ancient times. In the end, however, Mamun tarnished his own image by imposing an unpopular doctrine on his subjects and setting the inquisition or trials for those who resisted his beliefs.

Yaqub Ibn Ishaq al-Kindi
(800-873)

Contribution: Muslim philosopher known as the 'Philosopher of the Arabs'. Al-Kindi developed and interpreted philosophical concepts of Greek thinkers. His works exerted great influence on the philosophy and intellectual development of Western Europe in the thirteenth century.

Unfortunately very little is known about the life of this outstanding philosopher of Islam. Al-Kindi was born at Kufa (Iraq) in early 9th century where his father was governor. Al-Kindi was educated at Basra and Baghdad. At that time Baghdad was cultural and political capital of Islam. Abbasids were in power and encouraged the Muslim intellectuals and the philosophers of the time to attain as much knowledge as possible. The Arab world was getting familiar with the scientific and intellectual works of Greeks and Indians through Arabic translation. The works of Indian and Greek philosophers were translated into Arabic by way of Persian and Syriac, respectively. Al-Kindi was a court scholar under the Caliphs al-Mamun (reigned 813-833) and al-Mutasim (reigned 833-842). Al-Kindi, while working in the court translated many works of Greek and Indian scholars and philosophers, especially he improved the Arabic translation of 'Theology of Aristotle'. Al-Kindi was also the tutor of al-Mutasim's son. Though he belonged to the rationalist group of Mutazilites, he believed that certain aspects of faith can not be explained by reasons. Under the conservative Caliph al-Mutawakkil (reigned 847-861), al-Kindi's philosophical views were condemned and he fell from favor and lost his court position. Very little is known about his later life though he continued working as a private citizen and scholar. Al-Kindi also known as the 'philosopher of the Arabs' died in Baghdad in 873 AD.

The origin of Islamic philosophy can be found in Greek philosophical works. The Abbasid Caliphs encouraged the translation of the scientific, philosophical and intellectual works from other languages. In this way Greek and Indian philosophical works made their way into Arabic. The Islamic philosophy however, does not disagree with the truth of Islam rather it evolves from its theological background. Philosophy and Islam are related as both pursue the truth and rational inquiry. The Muslim philosophers learned and understood the philosophy of the ancient thinkers. These Muslim philosophers then wrote their commentaries and developed their own doctrines related to the issues of revelation, prophecy and divine law. With this background in mind it is not surprising that al-Kindi's philosophy pivots around reconciling and combining the views of Plato and Aristotle (Neo-Platonism). Al-Kindi believed that all humans can achieve knowledge by learning logic and mathematics as well by analyzing the experiences and knowledge of earlier thinkers and scholars. In his opinion, both prophets and common human beings can achieve enormous knowledge, though they achieve it by two different means. God may provide this knowledge to his prophets by giving them his guidance and inspiration which then prophets communicate to general masses in a comprehensible form. Al-Kindi termed this knowledge as 'Divine Knowledge' which is only reserved for prophets and is achieved by the revelations of God. On the other hand ordinary people can achieve this knowledge without divine aid though this knowledge may not be as complete and convincing as the divine knowledge of the prophets.

Al-Kindi did not believe that the world has been created for eternity rather he maintained that the world was created from nothing by a divine creator and at some future time at the will of the divine creator, will dissolve into nothing again.

Al-Kindi's important and well known works are,'On the Intellect and What is Understood', 'Introduction to the Art of Logical Demonstration', 'On Sleep and Vision', 'On the Five Essences' and the 'Theory of the Magical Arts'. His most important work is 'On the Intellect and what is Understood' which elaborates the views of Aristotle by differentiating between the intellect which receives the knowledge and the intellect that causes the knowledge (Active Intellect). The Active Intellect, according to al-Kindi may be spiritual and different from the ordinary human beings. This active intellect may evolve from God and may be reserved for prophets. His book al-Tibb al-Nujum is an attempt to establish a relationship between astronomy-astrology and medicine. Al-Kindi also explored the field of optics. He described that light travels in a straight line (surprisingly the credit for this discovery goes to Newton). He attributed the blue color of sky as the effect of particles of dust and vapor.

Besides philosophy, al-Kindi was familiar with Hellenistic sciences as well as Indian mathematics. He was also well versed in medicine, astrology, optics, geometry, politics, music and mathematics. One of his principle works deal with geometry and philosophy. He believed that doxology (a hymn or form of words praising the glory and majesty of God) is a mathematical art. He did not believe in the art of alchemy as he maintained that it was not possible to transmute base metals into gold by chemical means. At least five musical works (determination of pitch and description of rhythm) were compiled by al-Kindi.

He wrote more than 300 treatises most of which are unfortunately lost. Most of his works however, have survived in Latin rather than Arabic. Al-Kindi laid the foundation of natural philosophy which later helped other great Muslim philosophers (e.g. Ibn Rushd) to think, revise and comment not only on al-Kindi's works but also the Aristotelian philosophy. Al-Kindi exerted great influence on the Western European philosophers in the thirteenth century.

Ibn Muhammad al-Junayd
(830-910)

Contribution: One of the most famous early mystics or Sufis of Islam. He is an important figure in the development of Sufi doctrine; especially he is credited for the development of "sober" mysticism as compared to "God-intoxicated" mysticism. Al-Junayd is widely respected and is known as "Sultan" or "Syed" (lord) of the Sufis.

From the very beginning of human existence, there was a desire to purify one's soul. This desire of purification gave birth to ascetic practices. Initially, the Hindu, Buddhist and Christian monks were on the forefront and practiced asceticism. The idea behind these practices was to establish a relationship between God and man. In this relationship, man obeys God's will out of love and respect for Him and desires to draw nearer to God. With the passage of time, these practices became widespread and crept into every religion. Islam was not immune of these ideas either.

In the early days of Islam, strict observance of the Divine Law or Sharia was considered to be only way to purify oneself. With time, a different kind of theory emerged. Those who adopted this theory believed that salvation can be achieved by prayer and renunciation of worldly pleasure. Especially after the Muslim conquest of Syria and Iraq, the newly converted Christians and Jews brought their ascetic thoughts and practices into Islam. Those who believed that abandoning the worldly possession and repetition of the name of God in prayer will draw them nearer to God and put this theory into practice are known as 'Sufis'.

By the ninth century, the Sufi masters began preaching practices different than the Divine Law. These masters believed that the Divine Law itself was not sufficient to attain truth and

44

salvation. These Sufi masters also developed their own system of spiritual journey called Tariqa or path. Among the Sufis, in the eleventh century, a new trend emerged. The followers of a given Sufi master identified themselves as a single spiritual family adopting the same path as taught by their spiritual master. These followers of a particular "order" carried their master's teachings or paths over a wide area. In such a way many orders emerged but they differed in their views. The followers of one order believed that due to the experience of union with God there is a divine presence around them, therefore, they should live a life of solitude and abandon all worldly possessions and pleasure. These believers also developed the poetic expression of love between human and God, especially in Arabic and Persian languages. The desire towards the union of God affected the emotions, minds and souls of these believers. The behavior and attitude of these Sufis earned them the title of "drunken" or "God-intoxicated" Sufis. On the other hand, one order believed that after the mystical vision, the believer should return to the world and continue with his day to day activities. Such an order known as "sober" order was first given by Abu al-Qasim Ibn Muhammad al-Junayd.

Al-Junayd was of Persian origin but lived and taught in Baghdad. Very little is known about his early life and family background. As was the custom of the time, he first learned the Quran by heart and then studied law and Hadith (Traditions of Prophet Muhammad). He learned mysticism from his uncle who was a Sufi. Al-Junayd's mystical career was more of a sober nature; this might be due to his sound training in the orthodox Islamic sciences. After finishing his training under his uncle, al-Junayd began teaching in Baghdad and soon found many disciples. He formulated a sober and systematic doctrine of mysticism. He was an advocate of integration of mysticism in daily life. He believed that a Sufi or mystic should live a life of a normal person rather as a wandering dervish running away from the world. The true or sincere believer may lose his existence for a moment due to the meeting with the Divine but this ecstasy of seeing God face to face is only for a moment. After that the believer should return to the world carrying with him the memory of the moment and then indulge into normal daily life and live within the boundaries of the Sharia. Al-Junayd also believed that the mystic knowledge is not for every body rather it is for a selected few. In order to follow the path of mysticism one requires a skilled guide and inner devotions.

Al-Junayd did not leave behind any book but his teachings came to the public knowledge from his disciples, his letters and the writings of other Sufis. Besides being a mystic and a teacher, al-Junayd was also a reputed jurist and a merchant who kept a shop in Baghdad. He died in Baghdad in 910.

Mansur al-Hallaj, the famous God-intoxicated Sufi was one of al-Junayd's students. Later he broke away from al-Junayd and became much more ecstatic. Al-Hallaj's provocative statements and mystical experiences led to his execution.

Muhammad Ibn Jarir al-Tabari
(839-923)

Contribution: Historian and scholar. He was the author of early Islamic history and Quranic exegesis. His chief contribution is to condense the extensive historical knowledge of the preceding generations of Muslim scholars and to present these historical events without any personal opinion or bias.

Al-Tabari was born in Amol, Tabaristan (now in Iran) in 839 AD. As a child, he demonstrated extraordinary capabilities and it is mentioned that he memorized Quran by the time he was seven years of age. He took his early education in Amol and continued his higher education in Raay and Baghdad. After spending few years in Northern Iran, he traveled to Baghdad with an intention to learn jurisprudence under Ahmad Ibn Hanbal. Unfortunately, Hanbal died before Tabari's arrival in Baghdad. Tabari, however, stayed in Baghdad for a brief period and then went to Syria to learn Hadith. Tabari visited Iraq and traveled to Egypt in 867 AD, both being the major centers of learning at that time. From the libraries of these countries he collected materials which he later used in his works. He returned to Baghdad in 872 and devoted rest of his life to teaching and writing. He gained enormous fame as a teacher, writer and scholar. Despite his fame, Tabari endured extreme poverty in Baghdad mainly because he refused to accept positions in government or in the court and remained financially independent. Al-Tabari died in Baghdad in 923 AD.

The era in which al-Tabari lived was marked by social crisis, political disorders and philosophical-theological controversy. Though the socio-religious movement was directed against the Sunni orthodoxy, al-Tabari chose a moderate path. He neither accepted the extreme theological positions of these opposition movements nor embraced the views of ultra-orthodox Sunni faction.   Al-Tabari tried to form his own school of Muslim Jurisprudence that resulted in hostility from the Hanbali School which was dominant in Baghdad.   Hanbalis attacked his home and prevented others to attend his lectures.   His school of legal doctrines, however, did not survive long.

Al-Tabari wrote on many disciplines. These included history, religion, ethics, jurisprudence, mathematics and medicine.   He devoted enormous amount of time to gather Hadith.   Al-Tabari's major works are 'Commentary on the Quran' and the 'World History'. His commentary on the Quran which was completed in 883 or 884 was compiled from different regions of Islam to make it a standard work. In his commentary, al-Tabari mainly concerned himself with the language and grammar rather than inserting his own opinions on religion or historical issues. His works on Hadith and the commentary on the Quran provided great insight of the evolution of the Muslim thinking during its rise to power.

The most important work of al-Tabari is his World History which was completed in 915. His book is known as 'Tarikhul Rasul Wal Muluk' (History of Prophets and Kings). This is an enormous work and consists of thirteen volumes. This book became so popular that Samanid prince Mansur Ibn Nuh got the book translated into Persian in 963. Al-Tabari's book on world history is not simply the history of Islam. It begins with the creation, accounts of prophets and ancient rulers, followed by the history of Sasanian kings (226-637).   Then came the era of Prophet Muhammad and the first four caliphs (571-661), followed by Umayyad dynasty (661-750) and finally the Abbasid's era in Baghdad.   The coverage of the historical events ended in 915.

Before Islam, the Arab tribes used to keep their own records of the heroic achievements of their ancestors and were either transmitted orally from one generation to the other or were depicted either in verses or in prose, generally narrated by the storytellers.   With the rise of Islam and its growing powers it became important to record historical events, especially the Prophet's life and teachings, the role of early caliphs, the Muslim conquest and the structural and functional aspects of Muslim communities.   These historical events were recorded and transmitted by the scholars. Unfortunately, sometimes due to the political and theological controversies, these events were changed or even concocted. These events were further corrupted by the storytellers and with the passage of time many different kinds of conflicting historical events emerged.

The tradition of history writing reached to its zenith in the ninth century, when historians like al-Masudi, al-Baladhuri and al-Tabari appeared on the scene with broader scope and greater power of understanding. Al-Tabari is the most reputed among these historians. He introduced a style of history writing which was an attempt to provide the readers with the facts rather than fiction. The sources of al-Tabari's historical accounts come from both written as well as oral accounts. It is interesting to note that al-Tabari mentioned the same events from number of sources and as a result these accounts are conflicting. Although al-Tabari has not provided his own commentaries on these historical events or attempted to isolate facts from fiction, he has provided his readers biographical information about the people of his source. Thus he leaves it to his readers to decide about the authenticity of an historical event. Though for a general reader this style of history writing may be confusing but it was of great importance to the scholars (since little genuine information are available on the first century Muslim history). Al-Tabari's style of history writing was later adopted by many Muslim historians. Unfortunately, al-Tabari's other works are lost with the exception of some minor treatises.

Ibn Sinan al-Battani
(858-929)

Contribution: Astronomer and mathematician. He improved and added to the knowledge of trigonometry. His contribution to spherical trigonometry is outstanding. He determined the obliquity (a slanting or sloping direction) of the ecliptic and corrected the astronomical theories of Ptolemy. His calculations of planetary motion are astonishingly accurate.

Al-Battani (known to the west as Albatenius), was probably the best known Muslim astronomer and mathematician in Europe during middle ages. Al-Battani was born in Haran (Syria) in 858 AD. When he was a child his family moved to al-Raqqah on the Euphrates River. His family belonged to Sabian sect whose members practiced mixed Christian and Islamic principles. Al-Battani however, followed the Islamic beliefs in his life and gained his fame as a Muslim astronomer.

Very little is known about the educational background of al-Battani. It is not clear whether he was educated in a religious setting or in a secular scientific background. It appears that at some point of his youth, he became interested in science and got an opportunity to read about the works of Ptolemy.

Al-Battani studied astronomical theories of Ptolemy, a second century Alexandrian astronomer. Al-Battani worked in the observatories constructed by Abbasid Caliph Al-Mamun in Baghdad, at Darul Hikma and at al-Raqqah in Iraq. Al-Battani died near Samarra (Iraq) in 929 AD.

Al-Battani's fame lies in understanding and improving the knowledge of 'Trigonometry'. Trigonometry deals with the specific functions of angles and is applied to calculations in geometry. Trigonometry is combination of arithmetic, algebra and geometry. In the early days of its development, trigonometry was intimately associated with astronomy but became an independent subject in the thirteen century. Early Hindus and Greeks who were interested in astronomy contributed to trigonometry but their works are not extant. It is now well known that the Hindu mathematicians prepared the tables of sine and knew about the half cord of the double arc. Ptolemy of Alexandria (probably died after 161 AD), was an astronomer and contributed significantly to the knowledge of trigonometry. The astronomical calculations of Ptolemy are based on the geometrical approaches. Al-Battani used algebraic rather geometric methods to carry out his calculations. He introduced trigonometry to refine Ptolemy's calculation as well as for his own astronomical experiments. His knowledge of trigonometry helped him to criticize and correct Ptolemy's astronomical views. He refuted the concept of Ptolemy that solar apogee (an apogee is a position most distant from earth in the orbit of a satellite) is immobile. He proved the mobility of solar apogee and the variation of the apparent angular diameter of the sun. He also corrected Ptolemy's precession of the Equinoxes (a westward shift of the equinoctial points due to the earth's rotation).

Al-Battani introduced the law of Cosine for oblique spherical triangles and provided the solution to the problems of triangular equations. He added the function of Sine for the chord into the work of Ptolemy. He further explored and expanded the relevance of Sines. He explained the use of Tangent and Cotangent functions and constructed a table for these trigonometric functions. He was also familiar with the Indian Sine or half chords.

On the astronomical side, al-Battani refined the existing values for the length of the year and the precise duration of the four seasons of the year. He used the horizontal and vertical sun dials to calculate cotangents and tangents, respectively. He also mathematically demonstrated that the sun can undergo for annular eclipse. After numerous calculations and observations, Al-Battani described how to determine the time of the visibility of the moon. His descriptions of lunar and solar eclipse were regularly used by the European astronomers for centuries to gather information regarding eclipses.

Al-Battani's major written work is 'Kitab al Zij', a book of astronomical tables. This book was translated into Latin in 1169 and in Spanish in the 13th century. Al-Battani's contribution to trigonometry is tremendous. He believed that trigonometry can be effectively used to achieve greater precision in already known methods of astronomical calculations.

Abu Bakr al-Razi (Rhazes) (865-925)

Contribution: Islam's greatest physician. He contributed substantially to philosophy and chemistry. Razi advanced the knowledge, ethics and practice of medicine to a new height. The impact of his experiences and observations in medicine still exists. His treatise on small pox and measles are still considered classics in medicine.

Al-Razi known as "Rhazes" to the west was a renowned philosopher, chemist and one of the greatest physicians of the Islamic world. Razi was born in Raay (Iran) in 865 AD. In his youth, Razi was interested in music but gave up this interest in his adulthood. He became interested in medicine after visiting a sick home in Baghdad. At that time Baghdad was the center of culture, scientific knowledge and intellectualism. It is exactly not known where did Razi study medicine? It is likely that he learned the art of medicine in Baghdad though some scholars believed that he studied medicine in Iran. He also studied philosophy, mathematics, astronomy and chemistry. After spending sometime in Baghdad, he returned to Raay and served as a chief physician in a public hospital. Razi's reputation as a great healer resulted in his appointment as a chief physician in a Baghdad hospital during the time of al-Muktafi (reigned 902-907). Due to his compassion for the sick and his contributions to medical ethics he is compared to Hippocrates. In later years of his life, Razi's eye sight was hampered by cataract but he repeatedly refused surgery mentioning that he has seen enough of the world. He distributed his wealth among his poor patients and died almost in poverty in Raay in 925 AD.

Razi's fame lies in his works in medicine. His practice of medicine is based on the concepts of Hippocrates as both these notable physicians based their diagnosis on the course of the disease. His book al-Judari wal-Hasbah (A Treatise on the small pox and measles), which is the first clinical account of small pox is an example of Razi's brilliant observations and diagnostic capabilities of diseases. In this book he has described the type of people who can become susceptible to small pox and measles. He described the seasons in which one may become the victim of these diseases. He described the symptoms of small pox and measles as well as provided the remedies and the prevention of the secondary effects of these diseases.

His books 'Kitab al-Mansuri' and 'Kitab al-Hawi' are considered authentic books on medicine and about the practices of medicine of his time. Kitab al-Mansuri is dedicated to Mansur Ibn Ishaq, governor of Raay. This book is a concise handbook of medical science and was part of medical curriculum in European medical schools till the sixteenth century. Kitab al-Hawi, a 24 volume encyclopedia, known as 'Comprehensive Book' is survey of Greek, Syrian, Arabic and Indian medicine practices as well as accounts of Razi's experiences as a physician. It was first translated in 1279 into Latin and had considerable influence on the Latin West. Since in Islam the dissection of human body is prohibited, most of the anatomical and surgical knowledge described in this book come from the experiences of Greek physicians Galen and Hippocrates. Razi described his own experiences with surgery related to diseases of intestinal obstruction, hernia, tracheotomy and cancer. Interestingly enough his views on cancer was similar to the modern day views. He described that simply removing cancerous tissues may not be appropriate rather attempts should be made for complete eradication of cancer from the body.

Razi challenged the old views of medicine and provided new and thoughtful insight for the generations of the physicians to come. His treatise on the small pox and measles remains an authentic book till present time and has been translated into Latin, Greek and various modern languages.

Though Razi is renowned for his works in medicine, his philosophical works are of no less important. His works on philosophy were neglected for generations and renewed interest in his philosophical works began in the twentieth century. His philosophical views can be found in 'Kitab al-Tibb al-Ruhani' (The Book of Spiritual Physick) and Sirat al-Faylasfaf (The

Philosopher's way of life). He believed that every human being possess the capacity of thinking and reasoning and does not need continuous teaching by religious leaders. He challenged and criticized the authority and the religious beliefs of the religious figures. He stated that only by questioning, testing and reasoning one can improve the knowledge and the progress can be achieved. In this respect, Razi's philosophical views are different than such great Muslim philosophers like al-Farabi, Ibnsina and Ibn Rushd (Averroes).

Razi's metaphysics is based on five principles: the creator, the soul, matter, time and space. He did not believe that the world was eternal. Metempsychosis (transmigration of soul from one human or animal to the other) was the central theme of Razi's philosophy. He maintained that the soul is liberated from the body by the creator who gives intelligence to the soul and once all souls are liberated from the bodies, the end of the world will come. Razi also believed that the highest form of living is the life of a philosopher, who like the creator should treat men with justice and kindness. He wrote that there was no reconciliation between philosophy and religion. Philosophy, he maintained was a way of life and religion was the cause of wars. Such radical views put Razi in conflict with both the Muslim philosophers and theologians. His views, thus created opposition by the religious leaders and orthodox Muslim scholars and they tried to discredit his medical works.

Razi as a chemist published a book called 'Kitab al-Asrar' (The Book of Secrets) which was translated into Latin in 1187 and remained a source of chemistry and chemicals for 300 years. Many regard Razi as the Socrates (as a philosopher and teacher) and the Hippocrates (as a physician) of the Muslim world. Razi established ethical, clinical and scientific standards and modern day medicine owes a great deal to him. Till today Razi remains a captivating figure in the world of medicine and his experiences and commentaries have vastly benefited the modern medicine.

Abu Hasan al-Ashari
(873/74-935/36)

Contribution: Muslim theologian who integrated the method of rational discourse into the framework of orthodox Islam. He maintained that the literal interpretation of the Quran can be justified by reasons but only up to a certain point, beyond which it should be simply accepted. He was the founder of a theological school which produced such greats like al-Ghazali and Ibn Khaldun.

Al-Ashari was born in Basra in 873/874 AD. He may be the descendent of Abu Musa al-Ashari who was one of the companions of the Prophet Muhammad. Abu Musa also served as the governor of Kufa during the time of Caliph Ali. Very little is known about early life of al-Ashari but it is believed that his father was an orthodox wealthy Arab-Muslim and educated his son on the traditional Islamic lines. Al-Ashari studied the Quran, Traditions of the Prophet, canon law (Sharia) and scholastic theology. Basra at the time of al-Ashari's youth was the center of Islamic intellectualism but also center of religious controversy. Basra was the home of some of the most famous teachers of the Mutazilites (rationalists), among them Abu Ali Muhammad al-Jubbai was the most famous and head of Mutazilite doctrines. The Mutazilites who were rationalists, argued regularly with the fundamentalists on the issues of Islam and Sharia.

Early in his life, al-Ashari joined the Mutazilites and became a student of Abu Jubbai. Till the age of 40, al-Ashari remained a member of Mutazilite school of thought. During this time he wrote Muqualat al-Islamiyin (Theological Opinions of the Muslims) in which he presented the wide variety of opinions of the Muslim scholars related to the Islamic theology. The book is important not only for its record of Mutazilite doctrines but also presents the early history of the Muslim theology.

By the age of 40, al-Ashari was well known for his written works and was considered an expert in theology. Then came a change of heart and mind and al-Ashari abandoned the Mutazilite doctrine and joined the ranks of the fundamentalists. He publicly announced his conversion to orthodox Islam and the rest of his life he maintained his orthodox views of Islam. What made him change sides is still unknown. After embracing the orthodox Islam, al-Ashari started attacking Mutazilite doctrines and even refuted the teachings of his teacher Abu al-Jubbai. After breaking from Mutazilites, he wrote Kitab al-Luma (The Luminous Book). In this book he defended Islam by the use of dialectical theology based upon the principles of logic.

One of the most crucial theological arguments of the time was whether or not the Quran was created. The Mutazilites argued that since only God is eternal, the Quran can not be eternal therefore, it was created by the Prophet. The general Muslim belief is that God through angel Gabriel dictated the contents of the Quran to the Prophet. Al-Ashari argued that since the Quran is the literal speech of God, therefore, it can be eternal and hence uncreated.

Around 915 AD, al-Ashari moved to Baghdad where the followers of Ibn Hanbal were practicing and propagating a strict Islamic code of life. In Baghdad, he wrote Ibanah un Usul al-Diyanah (Elucidation of the Principles of Religion). The book provides the outlines of the principles of Islam.

Al-Ashari was an avid writer. His theological works revolve around the exegesis of the Quran and the Traditions. He also wrote several philosophical articles. His polemics against heretics and non-believers are well known. He also wrote several pamphlets which were his response to the theological and philosophical questions raised by the contemporary religious scholars. In his writings, al-Ashari emphasized the use of reasons and criticized those orthodox thinkers who opposed the reasoning in religious matters. Unfortunately, most of his writings are lost and only five treatises have survived.

While in Baghdad, al-Ashari laid the foundation of a new school of theology which was different from both the Mutazilites and the Hanbalis. The theological movement, al-Ashari led produced a great influence on the Muslim sects. It gained its foothold in Iraq and then spread to Iran, Syria and Egypt. Ibn Tumart (Berber spiritual and military leader who was the founder of the Almohad dynasty in North Africa) introduced al-Ashari's theological views to North Africa which then became the official doctrines of Almohads. His theological school produced numerous remarkable thinkers; one of them was al-Ghazali. These thinkers systematically formed a body of doctrine which is still acceptable to the Islamic world.

Al-Ashari's fame in the Muslim theology lies in the fact that he was first to use dialectic method to defend orthodox Islamic doctrines. He provided the scholars of orthodox Islam with the same tool which the rationalists used, that is the reasoning and proof. Thus al-Ashari provided with an intellectual need to the leaders of orthodox Islam to defend their positions.

Al-Ashari reconciled both faith and reasoning and managed to establish a school of thought, whereas the Mutazilites who took the same path failed to accomplish this task. The failure of the Mutazilites and the success of al-Ashari in reconciling the faith and reasons are difficult to assess. It appears that the Mutazilites tried to explain every aspect of the religion by reasoning and logic which was not very popular among the masses. On the other hand, the fundamentalists accepted religion as a whole without questioning even though they could not understand many aspects of it. Al-Ashari, successfully reconciled both faith and reasoning in a way that it was acceptable and appealing to people with moderate views. Al-Ashari's views, however, were not universally accepted as both Hanbalis and Shafiis opposed to it. Al-Ashari believed that power to act comes from God and human being can seek his guidance. Al-Ashari died in Baghdad in 935 or 936 AD.

Abu Nasr al-Farabi
(878-950)

Contribution: Renowned Muslim philosopher. He is considered 'The Second Teacher', the first being Aristotle. His great contribution to the world is that he preserved the Greek heritage. Besides philosophy, Farabi contributed to logic, metaphysics, ethics, mathematics and political science. He also contributed to music by inventing two musical instruments and writing a comprehensive book on music. As a philosopher, Farabi was rated by Ibn Khaldun above Ibnsina and Ibn Rushd.

Very little is known about the life of this great Muslim philosopher who was probably of Turkish origin. He was born in Turkistan at Wasij in 878 AD. He received his early education in Farab and Bukhara. His training in philosophy came from Abu Bishr Mata Ibn-Yunus, a very prominent member of the school of Christian Aristotelians in Baghdad. Besides philosophy, Al-Farabi studied mathematics, physics, logic, medicine and music. He joined the court of Saif ad-Dawlah, the ruler of Halab (Aleppo) in 942 and remained there till the time of his death in 950.

In the ninth century Islamic world, the greatest challenge to philosophy was to reconcile faith with Aristotle's theory that matter exists for eternity and by using right kind of logic and reasoning, man can achieve some knowledge about the universe. The Islamic belief was that knowledge to humans comes from the revelations of God. Farabi attempted to show that religion and philosophy are not contradictory. In his opinion, philosophy and religion are similar in the sense that the idea of a true prophet law-giver is the same as that of a true philosopher king. In this respect, Farabi's philosophical views are not in agreement with al-Kindi or al-Razi. Al-Kindi believed that the philosophers and the prophets have separate ways and means to achieve the highest truth whereas al-

Razi believed that philosophy is the only way to attain this highest truth.

Farabi's philosophy is based on the teachings of Aristotle and Plato and he skillfully blended the philosophy of these two with Islamic flavor. In his writings, Farabi adopted a style which can be easily comprehended by different groups of people. Farabi argued that philosophy is not for everyone. The philosopher due to intellectual capabilities can attain the truth by reasoning but non philosophers may not attain the truth directly. The enlightened man can live by philosophy whereas common people should live following Sharia or religious laws. Farabi's view that philosophy is not for everybody, created a distinction between the intellectual elite and the general masses. Though the philosophy continued to exist in the Islamic world but was mainly pursued by the scientists or by some physicians as part of personal interest or activity.

Farabi's concept of metaphysics is based on Aristotelian views but his concept of an ideal state has been borrowed from Plato. His concept of ideal state described in his book 'Al Siyasat-al-Madaniyah (Political Economy) is based on Plato's Republic and Aristotle's Politicia. The main theme of Farabi's political goal is to find an ideal state where the citizens and the rulers are virtuous. The ideal ruler is both philosopher and prophet. The philosopher has the highest level of theoretical intellect, whereas prophet receives inspiration from God. Since it is difficult to find such an ideal ruler (combination of philosopher and prophet), Farabi is content if the ruler has the qualities of a philosopher. Therefore, he argued that the philosopher should run the state as the philosopher is a perfect kind of man. Farabi maintained that man's happiness can be permanent, provided he frees himself from matter and enjoys the society of pure spirits. He also maintained that man as a social being requires the company of other man for the pursuit of happiness.

Farabi believed that God is the creator of the world and all other existence proceeds from God. He also believed that world is eternal. His concept of emanation gave birth to the 'Active Intellect' whose ultimate product is man who has a body and soul. Farabi developed the doctrine of intellect and elevated the philosophy at the highest levels and put the religious laws and revelations under it. He prepared the ground for future towering

Muslim philosophers, such as Ibnsina and Ibn Rushd. He constructed the theory of 'Divine Inspiration' and determined the line of Islamic philosophy which counterbalanced the philosophical movement of the orthodoxy.

In his theory of prophecy, he tried to explain how the prophet received the Quran from God. Farabi blended philosophy, psychology, logic, physics, mathematics and politics into a political theology and tried to establish a relationship between philosophy and the religion.

Besides his contribution to philosophy, Farabi also contributed to music. He invented two musical instruments called 'Rabab' and 'Qanun'. He also wrote a comprehensive book on music known as Mausiqui al-Kabir (Grand Book of Music).

Farabi was criticized by al-Ghazali but was highly acclaimed by Ibnsina and Ibn Rushd. Farabi wrote commentaries on Plato's Republic and the Laws. His works were translated into Latin and Hebrew in the medieval period.

Abu al-Hussain al-Masudi
(890-956)

Contribution: Arab historian, geographer and explorer. He traveled extensively and gathered information which helped in correcting old geographical views of Ptolemy and other Hellenistic writers. Al-Masudi's original and versatile writing contributed to understanding not only Muslim civilization but also other religions and cultures. He is known as 'Herodotus of the Arabs'.

Al-Masudi was born in Baghdad probably in 890 AD. His roots were Arab and he was a descendent of Abdullah al-Masud, a prominent companion of Prophet Mohammed. Very little is known about al-Masudi's early life and education. It is believed that he had an excellent memory and thirst for knowledge and learning. He studied a wide variety of subjects but history and geography were his major interest. His enormous knowledge and observations seems to come from his extensive travel. Though exact dates of al-Masudi's journeys are not known but most of his travels occurred between 915 and 930 AD. During this period he traveled to India, Ceylon (modern Sri Lanka), Zanzibar, Oman, Aleppo, Yemen, Tikrit, Kerman (Iran) and Palestine. From Baghdad he traveled across Iran to the south shore of Caspian Sea. He then sailed to Armenia and also visited Turkistan. He sailed westward across the Mediterranean to Spain and North Africa. His longest sea voyage was from the South China Sea westward across Indian Ocean. He visited Multan (Punjab) and Mansura (Sind), the cities which were the centers of Islamic learning and civilization in India at that time. During the last period of his life he settled in al-Fustat (Egypt). While in Egypt he traveled as far as Nubia. Al-Masudi died at al-Fustat in 956 AD.

More than 20 book titles are attributed to al-Masudi but unfortunately with the exception of few, his works have been lost. His major work Akhbar az-Zaman (The History of Time) which was on 30 volumes has been lost. As an abridgment of Akhbar az-Zaman, he wrote another book known as Kitab al Awsat (Book of the Middle) which has also been lost. His book which has survived and made him a reputed historian is Muruj adh-Dhahab (Meadows of Gold and Mines of Gems). This book was translated into English in 1841. The book consists of 132 chapters. The first half of the book describes pre-Islamic history of the world. It begins with the creation, description of Biblical stories, and the history of non-Arab nations (India, Greece and Rome) as well as the history of Arabs before the advent of Islam. In this book, al-Masudi has vividly described geography (climate, oceans, solar system etc), social life, religion and the customs of various nations. The second half deals with the Islamic history. It begins with Prophet Muhammad, the four caliphs down to al-Masudi's own time.

In his another famous book Kitab al-Tanbih W'al-Ishraf (Book of Indications and Reviews), which has survived, al-Masudi laid out his philosophy of history and in this book he also updated and corrected his previous history works.

In Islam, the tradition of history writing reached to its zenith in the ninth and the tenth century with the arrival of several outstanding historians such as al-Tabari, al-Masudi, and al-Biruni. Though the Islamic history was their subjects, these authors in details described the pre-Islamic history covering many religions and cultures. Al-Masudi considered seven ancient nations who had a real history: the Chinese, Indians, Egyptians, Greeks, Turks and Chaldaeans (Chaldaea was an ancient region in the lower Tigris and Euphrates valley. Chaldaeans are the Semitic people of Chaldaea who conquered Babylon from the Assyrians in the seventh century BC). The style of history writing, however, varied from historian to historian. For example, al-Masudi did not question his sources or chain of witnesses about a certain historical event, whereas al-Biruni was careful and critical. Al-Masudi's style of presentation of historical events was different than contemporary historians. He organized the historical events around dynasties, ethnic groups and important rulers rather than in chronological order. His style was original and his focus was mostly on social, economical, religious and cultural issues of the nations. He showed great interest in all religions and kept his mind open while describing the customs and practices of different religions. This style of presentation and open mindness led to belief that al-Masudi belonged to the rationalist Mutazilite school of Islamic thought.

Besides history, al-Masudi was also quite well versed in geography. He described in details about the Indian Ocean and the countries surrounding it. He contradicted the erroneous notion that the Caspian Sea and the Aral Sea were connected. Based on his own exploration he provided his account that they are two separate seas.

Al-Masudi also demonstrated his skills in geology. Based on his intuitions and remarkable analytical observations of the geological changes, he described the dry lands which were seabed. He also described the nature of volcanic activity. Remarkably his descriptions of the nature of geological changes have been proven correct by the modern scientific theory.

Al-Masudi undoubtedly was one of the greatest historians of the Islamic world. One of the characteristics of his history writing was that he covered history beyond the boundaries of Islam and created an intellectual curiosity to learn and describe the other cultures, customs and religions. He was a unique historian in the sense that he combined both history and geography in his monumental work of world history (Meadows of Gold and Mines of Gems). He certainly exerted a great deal of influence on the later generations of Muslim historians. Ibn Khaldun, the great fourteenth-century historian described Masudi as a leader and inspirer to the historians.

Abd al-Rahman III
(891-961)

Contribution: First caliph and the greatest ruler of the Umayyad dynasty in the Muslim Spain. He consolidated the Muslim power in Spain and brought prosperity to his people. His was a tolerant reign and both Christians and Jews enjoyed religious freedom.

The Abbasids ended the Umayyad rule in 750 AD and started persecuting the Umayyad family members. Abd al-Rahman I, one of the Umayyad princes in Syria fled to Spain where he found opportunities to gain power. He took advantage of the rivalries of the Arab factions in Spain and with the help of the mercenaries and some Arab groups he defeated the governor of al-Andulus and chose Cordoba as his capital. Despite unfavorable conditions surrounding him, Abd al-Rahman I managed to establish the authority and the rule of Umayyad dynasty over Cordoba and its surroundings. This was the beginning of eight hundred years of the Muslim rule over Spain but the man who consolidated the Umayyad rule, brought prosperity and paved the way for future Muslim rule in Spain was Abd al-Rahman III.

Abd al-Rahman III was born in Cordoba on January 7, 891 AD. He was the son of Prince Muhammad and his Christian wife. He spent his youth in the palace of his grandfather Abdallah who was the Emir of Cordoba. Abd al-Rahman's strong character and intelligence made him an obvious choice for the throne. In October 912 at the age of 21, Abd al-Rahman succeeded his grandfather as Emir of Cordoba. Spain during the time of Emir Abdallah was without any political unity. The Arab and Christian aristocrats and Berber tribes had gained enormous power and strength to ignore the central authority. The economical condition of Spain was also deteriorating. Though the Christians and the Muslims were in conflict in Spain, the nature of conflict was rooted in power, politics and economy rather than religion (Abd al-Rahman's mother, grandmother and great grandmother were all Christians). Abd al-Rahman was very well aware of his mixed background and used this background to exploit the situation(s) in his favor. When Abd al-Rahman assumed the throne, his authority extended only to the area around Cordoba. Immediately after assuming the throne, he put forward two major objectives in front of him; (i) the unification of his kingdom and, (ii) the promotion of economical growth in Spain.

For the first twenty years of his rule, Abd al-Rahman was engaged in crushing the rebels and neutralizing the military powers of Berbers. He established a standing army which was composed of slaves and the inhabitants of the Mediterranean. He led several campaigns against the Christian rulers of Leon, Castile, Navarre, Bobastro and Galicia. In 913, Ordono II, the Vassal king of Galicia and later king of Leon sacked the city of Evora and massacred its Muslim population. Abd al-Rahman led a campaign in 920 against combined armies of Leon and Navarre inflicting a crushing defeat to the Christian armies. In 924, he led another campaign into Navarre and captured the capital Pamplona. These two campaigns helped him to secure his frontiers with Christian Spain. In 933, Toledo fell to Abd al-Rahman and with that a major center of resistance against Cordoba disappeared. In 932, Romiro II, ascended the throne of Leon and began attacking Muslim territories. He proved to be a formidable foe to Abd al-Rahman. In 939, Romiro II defeated a Muslim Army led by Abd al-Rahman and for time being Abd al-Rahman halted his military expeditions. After the death of Romiro in 950, a civil war broke out in the Christian territories which helped Abd al-Rahman to recover his lost lands from the Christians. By 958, all major Christian strongholds were subdued and they agreed to pay tribute to Abd al-Rahman.

In 937, Abd al-Rahman started a campaign against the westward expansion of Fatimids based in Tunis. Though Abd al-Rahman extended his authority over Western Algeria and Morocco, the struggle with the Fatimids for the control of North Africa continued throughout the tenth century.

In 929, Abd al-Rahman declared himself as caliph of Islamic Spain and assumed the title Nasiruddin Allah (He who fights for God). Though he was heavily engaged with his military campaigns, Abd al-Rahman gave serious attention to improving the economy of Spain. He improved the irrigation systems which resulted in increased agricultural products. The growing of grapes and making wine became an important business in Spain. Wheat, olives and grains were traditional Spanish agricultural products. The Arabs introduced rice, peaches. oranges, cotton, sugar, figs and saffron in the list of Spanish agricultural products. As agriculture became the backbone of Spanish economy, the introduction of industrial establishments further boosted the economy. Leather, steel, olive oil and paper became important industrial products. In order to safeguard the Spanish trade against the attacks of Normans, Abbasids and Byzantines, Abd al-Rahman expended and improved his navy. In the end his navy and the merchant ships dominated the Western Mediterranean.

In 936, Abd al-Rahman launched the construction of a royal city, Madinat Al-Zahra, named after his wife Al-Zahra. It took 10,000 workers, 300 animals and 25 years to complete the city. Cordoba which was Abd al-Rahman's capital became the greatest metropolis of Western Europe, rivaling Constantinople and Baghdad.

Abd al-Rahman died in 961 AD at the age of 70. He was succeeded by Al-Hakam, his son by his Christian wife. As a ruler Abd al-Rahman demonstrated a high degree of administrative, political and military skills. He expended and stabilized his kingdom and refined the cultural and economical plight of Spain. In reality he established the most magnificent and powerful kingdom in Europe. In Cordoba he built palaces, libraries, paved and well lit roads, baths, schools and mosques. He founded the University of Cordoba which attracted students and scholars from many parts of the world. Abd al-Rahman also showed enormous religious tolerance. He established a center for Jewish theological studies in Cordoba. His personal physician, Hasdai Ibn Shaprut was a Jew who was educated at the University of Cordoba. Abd al-Rahman established a kingdom which lasted for many centuries. He stabilized and glorified Muslim Spain by his courage and wisdom. Muslim Spain never again saw a ruler of Abd al-Rahman's stature and magnificence.

Abul Quasim Firdowsi
(940-1020)

Contribution: Persian poet of highest order in the long history of Persian culture. A poet of extraordinary talents, Firdowsi wrote 'Shahnama', the Persian epic. Shahnama is history of Persia described in verses and in a language which transformed the Persian language into a coherent force to be used as court language for most of the Eastern Islamic world. Shahnama also served as a source of preserving Persian cultural identity.

Very little is known about the early life of Firdowsi. Many legends have been woven around this Persian poet. Some reliable information about Firdowsi's life comes from Nezami-Ye-Aruzi's account who visited Firdowsi's tomb about a century after his death. Firdowsi was born in Tus (modern Mashed) in 940 AD. His original name was Mansur Bin Hasan. He studied philosophy, astronomy, poetry and astrology. Firdowsi was probably a landowner with a comfortable income. Firdowsi spent most of his time either in Iran or Afghanistan, though it is believed that he also visited Baghdad.

Persia at the time in which Firdowsi grew was under the influence of Arab-Islamic culture. The Muslim Arabs had conquered Iran in the seventh century and the Arabic culture was still somewhat foreign to the Iranians. Firdowsi began writing Shahnama (Book of Kings) at the age of 40, though the accounts of the reasons for Firdowsi's writing of Shahnama vary. According to Aruzi, Firdowsi wrote Shahnama in order to raise money for the dowry of his daughter. The other reason may be that Firdowsi wanted to revive the ancient glory of Iran. Shahnama is mainly based on a previously written prose of the same name. Originally the idea of narrating Iran's history in verses came from Daqiqi, a poet at the court of Samanids. Daqiqi could only finish a small portion of the work as he was assassinated (cause of assassination is not known). Using his imagination and an epic prose written in the ancient Iranian language Pahlavi as the source of his historical information, Firdowsi took up the task.

Firdowsi's Shahnama consists of nearly 60,000 couplets. Shahnama covers nearly four thousand years of Iranian history narrated in verses. The work was divided into several parts, describing the history of four dynasties; the Pishdadian, the Kayanian, the Ashkanian and the Sassanian. The description of the first two dynasties is based on mythology and the last one is based on the actual facts whereas the third one is a mixture of mythology and historical facts. Shanama was completed in 1010 and was dedicated to Sultan Mahmud of Ghazna. Firdowsi anticipated a large sum for his work (believed to be one dirham for a verse) but received only 20,000 dirhams from the Sultan. Firdowsi was disappointed and showed his dissatisfaction and annoyance by dividing the money between a bath keeper and a sherbet (a nonalcoholic drink) seller. This act which was an insult to Sultan Mahmud forced Firdowsi to flee Ghazna. He went to Herat then to Tus and Tabristan. After ten years of wandering he finally found refuge in the court of Sephabad Shahreyar. There he wrote a long romantic poem ' Yusuf and Zulaikha', the love story of Potiphar's wife for Yusuf. He dedicated this work to Shahreyar. Some scholars now believe that ' Yusuf and Zulaika' was composed more than one hundred years after Firdowsi's death. Firdowsi also wrote a satire on Sultan Mahmud and inserted it in the preface of Shahnama. Firdowsi died in Tus in 1020 in relative reclusion.

There are wide speculations about sultan Mahmud's refusal to give Firdowsi the kind of reward he wanted. The speculations are:

Sultan Mahmud had no interest in poetry.

Mahmud was Sunni whereas Firdowsi was Shiite.

Mahmud was insulted by the verses composed in Shahnama as he was of Turkish origin and the description in Shahnama was about the splendors of Persia.

The fact(s) may never be known but considering Mahmud's interest in arts and literature and his liberal tolerant views about other religions, it is highly unlikely that Firdowsi was deprived of the reward he was seeking based on his religious belief or Mahmud's lack of interest in poetry. There might be some court intrigue involved or it is also possible that Mahmud never knew the amount of reward Firdowsi was anticipating. Many years later, however, Mahmud did send Firdowsi 60,000 dinners.

Firdowsi was a poet of extraordinary skills. His narration of history is a touch of romance and sentiments which he described with clarity and eloquently. The language used in Shahnama is based on Phalavi with only slight admixture of Arabic. Iranians consider Firdowsi as the greatest of their poets along with Jami, Hafiz and Sadi. However, Firdowsi differs from these poets that his theme was neither religion nor mysticism. Shahnama always held a special place among Iranians and Shahnama indeed is a masterpiece in Persian literature and over the centuries its influence on the Iranians has not subsided. The epic also became well known among the general population due to the recites. The recitation of Firdowsi's Shahnama generally used to take place on festive occasions such as weddings and before the era of television and radio served as entertainment in the villages and teahouses.

Abu al-Wefa al-Buzajani
(940-998)

Contribution: Astronomer and one of the greatest Muslim mathematicians. He contributed significantly in the field of trigonometry. His role in the development and understanding of sines and cosines is significant. He used the knowledge of trigonometry to correct classical astronomical calculations.

Abu Wefa was born in 940 in Iran during the reign of Abbasid caliph al-Muttaqi. Though very little is known about his early life, it is possible that his early education and his interest in mathematics emerged from his family's interest. One of his uncles (Amr al-Mughazili) was trained in mathematics by renowned mathematicians of the time. At the age of nineteen, Abu Wefa moved to Baghdad. At that time, the Islamic world was booming with cultural and intellectual activities, especially Baghdad was the center of all these activities. Mathematics and astronomy were highly respectable and widely recognized subjects of the Islamic civilization. The atmosphere in Baghdad proved to be a great learning place for Abu Wefa. In a short time, he mastered many technical fields. Though there were political turmoils in Baghdad, the Islamic culture and civilization was still flourishing. The Persian Buyid dynasty (a family of military leaders) had taken over the Abbasid court and the power and authority of the Abbasid caliphs were drastically reduced. The Buyids were favoring young Persian talents. The Buyid Emir, Saraf al-Dawlah had great interest in astronomy and had built his observatory near his palace and gathered scholars from all regions of the Empire. One of the elite groups was the group of mathematicians and astronomers who carried out many experiments on astronomy. Abu Wefa was the member of this group. Here in this observatory, Abu Wefa built the first wall quadrant to observe the stars. He translated and wrote commentaries on the works of Greek mathematicians Diophantus and Euclid.

Abu Wefa's fame lies in the field of trigonometry. Trigonometry is the study of triangles and trigonometric functions. Trigonometric functions represent periodic phenomenon such as the motion of pendulums or the analysis of alternating-current electricity. There are many applications of trigonometry in our daily life. Lengths and heights of many objects can not be measured directly, therefore, trigonometry is used to measure the heights of the mountains, distances across lakes and countries, navigators use it to find latitudes, longitudes and directions.

Astronomy was of great interest to the Hindus and the Arabs, especially to find a solution of spherical triangles, which ultimately led to the development of spherical trigonometry. Astronomers use spherical trigonometry to find the time of day, directions of motion and in locating the positions of bodies (planets and stars) in the sky. Abu Wefa gave a new and accurate method for computing sine tables. He also established the generality of the sine law for spherical triangles. He also introduced the secant and cosecant functions in trigonometry.

The second century Greek astronomer and mathematician Ptolemy had provided an approximate method for calculating sines which he described as 'chords'. Though unknown to Ptolemy, the Hindu mathematicians had also made tables of sines and the half chord of the double arc. Abu Wefa, using this Indian concept of trigonometry, views of al-Battani (858-929) and by algebraic rather geometric manipulation, improved Ptolemy's chords. He developed the half-chord, which proved to be very useful in surveying and navigation. Abu Wefa's tables of sines were extremely useful in astronomy which he used to make corrections in the classical astronomical calculations.

Abu Wefa also studied the variation in the longitude of the moon. Though his theory of the 'third inequality of the moon' was later proved to be partly incorrect, his work remained pioneering and original in this field.

Not all of his works have survived. His commentaries on Diophantus, Euclid and al-khwarizmi have not survived. A book on astronomical tables entitled Zij al-Wadih (that which is clear) is also not extant in the original. His books which have survived and partially translated are: Kitab fi Ma Yahtaj Ilayh al-Kuttub Wal-Ummal Min Ilm al-Hisab (book on what is necessary from the science of arithmetic for scribes and businessmen) and Kitab fi ma yahtaj ilayh al-sani min al-amal al-handasiyah (book on what is necessary from geometric construction for the artisan).

The time in which Abu Wefa lived was the time of intellectual and scientific progress in the Islamic world. Baghdad was crowded with highly intelligent and skilled people of different backgrounds: Arabs, Persians, Greeks and other minorities. In this very competitive background, Abu Wefa excelled which shows his brilliance. His works in trigonometry are still used.

Al-Hasan Ibn al-Haytham (Alhazan)
(965-1039)

Contribution: One of the greatest scientists of Islam. His scientific works involve physics, astronomy, mathematics and medicine. His works on 'Optics' exerted a profound influence on physicists to understand the characteristics of light and the function of eye.

Abu Ali al-Hasan Ibn al-Haytham (also known as Alhazan to the Western world) was born in Basra in 965. Though his early education was based on the traditional Muslim education, Alhazan, kept his mind open about the variety of religious beliefs and sects. He searched for the truth in sensible and rational doctrines. This search led him to the writings of Aristotle and to philosophy and mathematics. Soon his reputation grew and he became famous for his knowledge of physics. The Fatimid ruler of Egypt, al-Hakim, asked him to regulate the flow of the Nile. Alhazan failed in his attempt and went out of favor. He went to seclusion for some time and after the death of al-Hakim, resumed his activities as a copyist of mathematical manuscripts and very soon once again became reputed. He continued pursuing his scientific studies and wrote on mathematics, physics, metaphysics, astronomy and medicine. He published a large number of original works (25 books on mathematics and 44 on physics and metaphysics). He also wrote commentaries on the works of Aristotle and Galen (Greek physician).

Alhazan's reputation lies in his works on optics. His book on optics is 'Kitab al-Manazir', which was translated into Latin in the thirteenth century known as 'Optica Thesaurus Alhazeni libri VII'. Alhazan described the properties of light, phenomena of reflection and refraction, spherical and parabolic mirrors, theories on vision and anatomy of eye, binocular vision and the rainbow lenses.

According to Alhazan, light exists in an essential form in self-luminous bodies such as the sun and the stars, and in an accidental form in the bodies which use an outside source for their luminosity such as moon and the planets. The accidental light is however, weaker than the essential light.

Alhazan modified the traditional view that visual rays are emitted from the eyes. He argued that light affects the eye as one experiences pain by directly looking at the sun or staring at fire. From these observations he concluded that light rays proceed from the visible objects to the eye and are accompanied by color. The eye though receives the rays of light and color; it is the mind which dictates the pattern produced on the glacial humor. He further postulated that glacial humor may be responsible for the sight in the eye as the injury to the humor leads to the vision impairment.

Alhazan also investigated the phenomena of reflection and refraction. Reflection is rebounding of light rays from a surface. The laws of reflection as described by Alhazan are that incident and reflected rays are in the same plane and incident and reflected angles are equal. This property of reflected light helped him to explain the formation of an image in a plane mirror.

The 'Optics' consists of seven books. The fifth book contains the famous 'Problem of Alhazan': For any two points on the plane of spherical reflecting surface, find a point where a ray of light emitted from one point will be reflected to the other point. Alhazan solved this problem geometrically by the intersection of an equilateral hyperbole with a circle. Today the algebraic solution of this problem is a fourth degree polynomial equation.

Alhazan also explored the phenomena of refraction. He described that light travels with great speed in a transparent medium (air or vacuum) but slows down in dense medium such as water or glass. The denser medium however, cannot stop the movement of light completely but forces the light ray to change its direction. This phenomenon of bending light waves when they pass from one medium to another is termed refraction. This theory of Alhazan still holds true.

His works on astronomy do not equal to those of optics but his clear explanation of the motion of the heavenly bodies showed his mastery on the subject. In his book, 'On the Structure of the world', he attempted to correspond the astronomical system to the true movements of heavenly bodies. In order to explain the motion of heavenly bodies, Ptolemy used imaginary points moving on imaginary circles. Alhazan described the motion of heavenly bodies based on the physical reality rather than Ptolemy's abstract astronomical system. His explanation was that heavenly bodies are in a series of concentric spherical shells and their rotations are interconnected. He explained the increase in size of heavenly bodies near the horizon and provided the thickness of the atmosphere.

As a mathematician his fame lies in giving the geometrical solution of various optical problems. He dealt with the quadrate problem (the condition in which the phase angle between two alternating quantities is in 90 degrees. For example, the electric and magnetic fields of electromagnetic radiation are in space quadrate meaning that these are at right angles in space). He also described the properties of conic section (a curve formed by the intersection of a plane with various parts of a cone).

Al-Hazen's work on optics will keep his name alive for centuries to come. His scientific works not only influenced the later generations of the Muslim scientists but also had great impact on the scientists in the western hemisphere. His works were widely studied in the west and had great influence on the thinking of such greats like Roger Bacon and Johannes Kepler.

Mahmud of Ghaznavi
(971-1030)

Contribution: Ruler of Ghaznavi (Ghazna) and the first Sultan of Ghaznavid dynasty in Afghanistan. He is famous for numerous attacks on India (altogether 17 attacks), plundered wealthy Indian Temples and used the wealth to modernize and improve Ghaznavi. His attacks opened the door of commerce between India, Afghanistan and Iran and also promoted cultural interaction among these countries.

Popularly known as 'Mahmud Ghaznavi' (Ghaznavi is a city in Afghanistan known as Ghazna to the western world) was born in 971 AD as Abul Quasim Mahmud Ibn Subuktagin. Mahmud was the Sultan of 'Kingdom of Ghazna' from 998 to 1030 AD. Mahmud was the eldest son of a Turkish slave Subuktagin who assumed the throne of Ghazna in 977. Subuktagin gained his throne by defeating Sumanids, an Iranian dynasty in Bukhara. From an early age, Mahmud was by his father's side and learned the art of military warfare from him. It is mentioned that Mahmud was instrumental in his father's success in gaining the kingdom of Ghazna. After Subuktagin's death, Mahmood became the ruler of Ghazna in 998 at the age of 27. Mahmood was an intelligent and ambitious ruler. He annexed Khwarizm in 1017 and asserted his rule over Ghur, Qudsar and Baluchistan. During his conquest of Northern India and parts of Iran he proved his military genius. He invaded India 17 times and amassed enormous wealth from those attacks. The first attack took place in 1001 and the last was in 1026. His first attack brought him into the Punjab where the local ruler (Raja Jaipal) fought bravely but Mahmud's military skills gave him the much needed victory despite the fact that he was outnumbered in number and equipment. Another great resistance came from Anandpal (son of Raja Jaipal) who had gathered a great army by appealing to the Indian rulers. Anandpal lost the battle at

Peshawar despite putting up a heroic fight. This victory helped Mahmud to advance further into India. In 1024, Mahmud attacked famous Indian city of Somnath which was his last expedition in India. He finally returned to Ghazna in 1026. Mahmud died in Ghazna in 1030.

After becoming the ruler of Ghazna, Mahmud started building educational institutions, gardens, palaces and mosques and patronized scholars, artists and literary figures. During his time famous Iranian poet Firdowsi (author of poem Shahnama) and the great Muslim philosopher, mathematician and historian ' Al-Biruni' settled in Ghazna. Mahmud also transferred the city of Ghazna into a center of art and culture. Though he was an independent ruler, for political reasons he sought allegiance with the Abbasid Caliph in Baghdad. In turn, the Caliph recognized him as the new ruler of the lands which Mahmud had conquered and bestowed on him the title of 'Yamin-ad-Dawalah' (the right arm of the state).

Some historians (particularly some Indian historians) regard Mahmud as a fanatic Muslim ruler whose main purpose behind his Indian expeditions was to amass wealth, especially hidden in the Hindu Temples. The fact of the matter is that he remained open minded to his Indian subjects and did not impose Islamic laws on them. No attempt was made to convert non-Muslims into Muslims. Mahmud maintained a large contingent of Hindu troops led by Hindu commanders. These non-Muslim troops proved to be beneficial to Mahmud in his expedition in India.

Mahmud's expedition to Northern India brought many cultural and economical advantages to both the people of India and Afghanistan. The exchange of trade and ideas were enhanced between India and the Muslim world. The Indian culture was introduced into different parts of the Islamic world and this opened the door for a large number of Muslim scholars, writers and intellectuals to visit India and many stayed behind.

Firdowsi's Shahnama made Mahmud immortal but ironically Mahmud refused to pay Firdowsi 60,000 gold pieces he promised. In anger and bitterness, Firdowsi wrote a satire about Mahmud. Mahmud was also a hero of many legends, especially the way he treated his slave Ayaz (he gave lot of respect to Ayaz and treated him as his equal).

Abu Rayhan al-Biruni
(973-1048)

Contribution: Historian, astronomer and mathematician. He was one of the greatest scholars of his time. He compiled the cultural and scientific traditions of ancient cultures. Al-Biruni was called by his contemporaries as 'The Master'.

Al-Biruni, perhaps the most learned man of his time, was born in Khwarizm (now part of Uzbekistan) in 973 AD. Very little is known about his childhood. He learned astronomy and mathematics at his early age and was heavily involved with astronomy. Before, Mahmud of Ghazna conquered Khwarizm (1017), Biruni visited the Sumanid court at Bukhara and the court of Ispahbad of Gilan. During this period he continued learning and gathered enormous information about ancient Europe and Asia. In 1017, after conquering Khwarizm, Mahmud invited Biruni to Afghanistan. Biruni went with Mahmud to Ghazna where he eventually settled. Mahmud appreciated the scholarly talents of Biruni and offered him a position in his court as an astronomer/astrologer. Al-Biruni served as a historian in the court of Mahmud of Ghazna and his son Sultan Masud. Mahmud attacked India 17 times and during these expeditions to India, Biruni got the opportunity to learn some Sanskrit, Indian astronomy and social customs and traditions of India. Biruni died in 1048 in Ghazna.

Al-Biruni was conversant with Persian, Arabic, Sanskrit and Turkish languages. His talents were not limited to only one discipline rather he was equally brilliant in astronomy, mathematics, physics, history and medicine. To-date in each of these disciplines he remains a towering figure. Almost half of his life he traveled in quest of knowledge. He traveled to India and learned Sanskrit and studied Indian culture and religions.

Considering the tremendous amount of knowledge he acquired during his life, al-Biruni is probably one of the greatest scholars of all time. Even to-day it is difficult to imagine a man with so much talent in so many disciplines. His most famous works include: The Chronology of Ancient Nations, Elements of Astrology, A history of India and The Masudi Quanoon.

In 'A history of India' he has described the intellectual and socio-economic conditions in the Subcontinent. This is an outstanding work since it is a great attempt by a Muslim writer to go beyond the boundaries of Islam and describe the cultural traditions of non-Muslims. In this book, al-Biruni has described the straightforward accounts of Hindu culture in India. He pointed out that in religious matters the beliefs of Hindus were similar to Greeks at least before the advent of Chritianity. He however, made a clear distinction between the Muslims and the Hindus. He described Hindu caste system as a class distinction among human beings as compared to Islam where all human beings are created equal. 'A history of India' remains of enormous value even to modern day scholars. While in India, he shared his Greek, Persian and Islamic knowledge with Indian scholars and religious figures.

The Masudi Quanoon which is dedicated to Sultan Masood (son of Mahmud of Ghazna and heir to the throne) is significant work on astronomy. This book consists of al-Biruni's mathematical and geographical experiences. His other important work is 'The Chronology of Ancient Nations'. This book consists of calendars and a periodical account of history of ancient nations and their cultures. The book also deals with mathematics, astronomy and geography.

Al-Biruni described the rotation of the earth on its axis and provided the accurate measurements of latitude and longitude. He also constructed tables for trigonometric functions such as cosine and tangent. Al-Biruni also contributed to chemistry/physical sciences. He described the nature of liquid pressure and invented a method to calculate the specific weight of elements. His approach provided accurate estimation of specific weights of at least 18 elements. He has left behind more than 100 works in history, geography, medicine, astronomy and mathematics.

Al-Biruni probably was the 'scholar' among the scholars and he remains a fascinating figure in many disciplines of arts and sciences. Al-Biruni's immense knowledge and writings have provided inspiration to the generations of scholars and scientists irrespective of their religion, culture, language and nationality. Though some compare Biruni with Leonardo De Vinci (probably one of the most underestimated geniuses), Biruni was simply called by his students and contemporaries as 'The Master'.

Abu Ali Abdallah Ibnsina (Avicenna) (980-1037)

Contribution: Philosopher, physician, lawyer and administrator. He diagnosed and described the causes of many illnesses and proposed remedies. He presented Aristotle and Plato's philosophy with Islamic traditions.

Ibnsina known to the western world as 'Avicenna' is one of the most famous and influential Muslim philosopher-scientist. Ibnsina was born in Bukhara (Iran) in 980 and received his early education in Bukhara under the direction of his father who was governor of Balkh (now Afghanistan) under the Samanids dynasty. By the age of 10, Ibnsina had memorized the Quran and was well versed in poetry. He studied logic and metaphysics at an early age and by the age of 21 he was a reputed physician. He learned the Indian system of calculation and the use of zero in mathematical computation from an Indian surveyor. His early training in philosophy came from a well known philosopher of the time Abu Abdallah al-Natili. Ibnsina served as an administrator when the Samanids dynasty was in power in Iran. Samanids were defeated by Mahmud of Ghazna and with that Ibnsina's life took a sharp turn. He wandered for many years in different cities of Khurasan, finally moving to Qazvin where he started practicing medicine to earn his livelihood. In these cities he did not find enough social and economical opportunities as well as peace to continue his intellectual works. Therefore, he decided to move to Hamadan (west-central Iran). Shams Ad-Dawlah, the ruler of Hamadan, gave him a warm welcome. Ibnsina became a court physician and also got involved into administrative issues. He was twice appointed Vizier. Unfortunately, court intrigue and jealous courtiers incited Shams Ad-Dawlah and Ibnsina fell from favor. He was forced into hiding and was also imprisoned for some time. In 1022, after a difficult time that included imprisonment, Ibnsina decided to move to Isfahan (Iran). The last 15 years of his life were relatively peaceful. He settled in the court of Alaad-Dawlah, the ruler of Isfahan. While accompanying Alaad-Dawlah on a campaign, Ibnsina fell ill and died in Hamadan in 1037 AD.

Ibnsina like Galen, Rhazes and Hippocrates can be regarded as one of the most dominant figures in medicine. In the east, Ibnsina was titled as 'the leading wise man' and in the west he is called 'prince of physicians'. His two most famous books are 'Kitab Al Shifa' (Book of Healing) and 'Al Quanun Al-Tibb' (The Canon of Medicine). Kitab Al Shifa is a philosophical and scientific encyclopedia which deals with logic, psychology, geometry, astronomy, arithmetic and metaphysics. Al Quanun Al-Tibb is probably one of the most famous books in the history of medicine in both eastern and western world. This book became a medical authority and was used as a text book for several centuries in the medical schools of the western hemisphere. This book is based on the Greek, Roman and Arab works in medicine as well as Ibnsina's own experiences and observations.

Ibnsina remains one of the most influential Muslim figures in the western world. His most two famous books, Book of Healing and The Canon of Medicine, were translated into Latin. These translations of his works spread his name all over the western hemisphere. His philosophical as well as scientific works probably helped a great deal in initiating the European Renaissance. In the east his influence in medicine, philosophy and theology still exists.

Ibnsina identified many diseases and prescribed remedies of these diseases. He identified tuberculosis and proposed that some illnesses like meningitis and some inflammatory diseases may be caused due to degeneration of the nervous system. He understood the rhythm of the pulse and used this knowledge as a tool to diagnose illnesses. He wrote about preventive medicine and described the effects of climate on human health. He introduced the medicinal herbs for the treatment of many illnesses and was well versed with the properties of these herbs and shrubs.

On the philosophical front, Ibnsina's ideas were influenced by Greek philosophers, particularly by Aristotle and Plato. The Muslim philosopher who exerted a great deal of influence on Ibnsina was al-Farabi. Ibnsina adopted al-Farabi's concept of divine essence and existence. Though Ibnsina's philosophical views are based on the existence of God, he negates the creation of the world as viewed by the religion and disputes the immortality of the soul. The world emanates from God as the consequence of His self-knowledge, Ibnsina writes. The self-knowledge of God results in the existence of one intellect which then multiplies to form other intellect. The second intellect follows the same pattern of multiplication until it reaches to the last intellect (the ninth intellect down to the sphere of the moon), the active intellect. Ibnsina believed that the number of intellects should be at least equal to the number of heavens. The human soul and the knowledge emanate from the active intellect, hence the body receives the soul and the soul receives the knowledge. The human soul is individual, immaterial and indivisible and does not exist as an individual prior to the body (the concept of transmigration does not exist in Ibnsina's theory). In short, soul is not a material or a substance, rather it is created with the body but not 'imprinted'on it. Soul uses the body to perfect itself through the knowledge it has attained. Though the body is perished, soul exists and retains all good and bad qualities of the body, hence either is rewarded or punished. Using this line of philosophical thinking, Ibnsina reconciles philosophy and the faith. He also argues about the presence of essence in everything but God, since God's existence is unique. In his book 'Kitab Al Isharat wa Attanbihat (Book of Directives and Remarks), Avicenna describes the mystic's spiritual journey. Mystic is motivated by faith, love and desire which lead him to perform spiritual exercises. Such practices bring the mystic to a stage where he can have uninterrupted vision of God.

Ibnsina is also a symbol of courage and perseverance. Despite the fact that there were so many turmoil in his life mainly due to the socio-political situations surrounding him he somehow managed to survive. He suffered from financial troubles and lack of mental peace, yet produced two marvelous books which will keep his name alive for centuries to come. During day Ibnsina, served as an administrator and a physician in the court and at night along with his students compiled many scientific and philosophical works. Kitab Al Shifa is probably the largest work of its kind ever written by a single person.

Ibnsina belongs to the school of such great Muslim philosophers as al-Kindi, al-Farabi, Ibn Rushd (born almost one hundred years after Ibnsina's death) who studied the philosophy and works of Aristotle and Plato, modified and presented it by reconciling religion and philosophy. Though Ibnsina was criticized by the orthodox Muslim theologian al-Ghazali, Ibnsina's influence remained substantial on the medieval Europe.

Abu Muhammad Ibn Hazm
(994-1064)

Contribution: Celebrated theologian, littérateur, historian and jurist of the Muslim Spain. He wrote on a variety of subjects such as philosophy, history, logic, jurisprudence and theology. His most important work is a comparative religious history. He was one of the leading scholars of the Zahiri (literalist) school of jurisprudence.

Ibn Hazm was born in 994 AD at Cordoba (Spain). His great grandfather probably belonged to a family of Iberian Christians who abandoned his Christian beliefs and embraced Islam. His father was a devout Muslim and a learned man who held a high post (probably vizier) under Emirs al-Mansur and al-Muzaffar. His father's position helped Ibn Hazm to move in the high society of the Muslim Spain and provided him with an excellent opportunity of education. Al-Muzaffar died in 1008 AD and with that the Muslim Spain plunged into anarchy and civil war which continued till 1031. When the civil war was over, the Caliphate was abolished and many small states emerged with no centralized political structure left within the Muslim Spain. In 1012, Ibn Hazm's father died and after Berbers destroyed many of his family palaces, he left Cordoba and lived a quiet life in Almaria. Since his loyalty to Umayyad was well known, he was imprisoned for many months. When al-Murtada (Abd al-Rahman IV) was declared caliph of Valencia, Ibn Hazm went there and became his vizier. He fought along with al-Murtada at Granada, was taken prisoner but released after some time. When al-Mustazhir (Abdur Rahman V) became caliph of Cordoba (1024), he chose his friend Ibn Hazm as his vizier. Unfortunately, within few months, caliph al-Mustazhir was assassinated and Ibn Hazm once again found himself in the prison. At the age of 32, he decided to give up politics and spend his life in scholarly works.

Muslim Spain was dominated by Malikis but Zahiris (literalist) for a short time became strong in Spain. Their teachings were based on the literary meaning of the Quran and the Hadith, hence the name literalist. Initially Ibn Hazm was a follower of Shafiie School but later he changed to Zahiri School of legal interpretation and as a jurist became a strong advocate of them. His outspoken opposition of predominant Maliki School of legal system landed him into trouble and attempts were made to silence him. Ibn Hazm finally retreated to his family estate in Manta Lisham where he died in 1064.

Ibn Hazm was an avid writer and 400 works spread over 80000 pages are attributed to him. In his writings, whether prose or poetry, he used the Arabic language skillfully. His well known book, Tawq al-Hamamah (Ring of the Dove) is an example of his command of the Arabic language. The book is about the art of love and its psychological and ethical aspects. Most of Ibn Hazm's literary works were, however, devoted to theology. His most important work is the 'Book of Religions and Sects'. The book is a comparative religious history which examines Judaism, Christianity, Zoroastrianism and Islam. This work was among the earliest of such comparative studies on religion and is held in high esteem for its careful historical details. As a jurist, he maintained that the legal conclusions not based on revelation and tradition should not be accepted. Ibn Hazm also wrote historical treatise, especially the 'History of the Fatmids was highly acclaimed by Ibn Khaldun. In his treatise on logic (now lost), he disregarded Aristotle's position and tried to reconcile logic with theological concepts which did not meet with appreciation and approval.

In his theological writings, Ibn Hazm's tone is fanatical and immoderate. He showed no respect to the esteemed religious authorities of the past or of his time. His charges of heresy against such well respected Muslim theologians like al-Ashari, Abu Hanifa and Malik made him highly unpopular among the theologians. His pen was regarded as the sword of Hajjaj (governor of Iraq known for his cruelty).

Ibn Hazm's writings and teachings were attacked after his death. His books were banned or left unstudied; this may be one reason why his books and works are lost. His books were also publicly burned in Seville during his life.

Nizam al-Mulk Tusi
(1018-1092)

Contribution: Persian vizier of the Seljuk sultans. He was an administrator of remarkable capabilities and vision. He consolidated the power of Seljuks under two great rulers. He is the author of 'Seyasat-Namah', a book of practical advice on statecraft for the rulers. As a great patron of education, he established higher institutions of learning in Iran and the Middle East.

Nizam al-Mulk (in Arabic means Regulator of the Kingdom) was born as Abu Ali Hasan Ibn Ali in Tus (Khurasan, Iran) on 1018 AD. Probably Nizam al-Mulk received his early education in Neshapur (Iran). His father was a treasury official for the Ghaznavid dynasty and owing to his father's position, Nizam al-Mulk moved among high Persian social class. When the Seljuks invaded Iran, his father moved to Ghazna (Afghanistan). For a brief period, Nizam al-Mulk also served the rulers of Ghaznavid dynasty. When the Ghaznavids were forced out by the Seljuks in 1040, Nizam al-Mulk switched sides and went into services of Seljuks. He was employed by the governor of Balkh (Afghanistan). Nizam al-Mulk quickly proved his prowess, moved to Khurasan and joined the services of Seljuk governor of Khurasan, Alp-Arsalan. Nizam al-Mulk's administrative capabilities impressed Alp-Arsalan and he appointed Nizam al-Mulk as his vizier.

After the death of Sultan Toghral Beg in 1063, Alp Arslan also became the ruler of the territories left behind by his uncle but a feud over succession began. Al-Kunduri, the vizier of the late Sultan tried to block the accession of Alp-Arsalan on the throne. Nizam al-Mulk played a vital role in bringing Alp-Arsalan into power. In the end, Alp-Arsalan succeeded his uncle to the throne and Nizam al-Mulk became the grand vizier of the new Sultan. Al-Kunduri was imprisoned and eventually executed.

With time, Nizam al-Mulk became responsible for the entire civil administration of the empire. He maintained close ties with the Ulemas (religious scholars). He appointed them in the religious courts to maintain the Sharia (religious laws). For the next 30 years, Nizam al-Mulk was the grand vizier of two great Seljuk rulers, Alp-Arsalan and his son Malik Shah. During this period, Nizam al-Mulk gained confidence of both rulers and assumed enormous power. His vision and skills guided the Seljuk empire which stretched from Amu Darya to Khwarizm in the east and the central Anatolia in the west. Besides showing his skills in civilian administration, Nizam al-Mulk undertook many military campaigns along with Alp-Arsalan and also conducted independent military operations.

Nizam al-Mulk was a devout Sunni Muslim and contributed significantly in the revival of Sunni Islam. At the beginning of the eleventh century, the Fatimids of Egypt who were Shiite Muslims began spreading Shiite doctrines in the areas which were under their control (Egypt, part of North Africa, Syria and Palestine). In order to counter the Shiite influence, Nizam al-Mulk decided to establish madrasas or religious schools in different parts of the empire. As a great patron of learning, he established higher educational institutes at Neshapur, Baghdad, Khurasan, Iraq and Syria. He founded Nizamiyah college in Baghdad in 1066 which was one of the best learning seats in the world. Al-Ghazali, the famous Muslim philosopher, theologian and mystic was one of the rectors of this college.

At the request of Sultan Malik Shah, Nizam al-Mulk began writing his political views and experiences in a book known to world as Seyasat-Namah (Book of Government or Rules for Kings). Seyasat-Namah was probably of great interest to those bureaucrats who exercised the power in the name of ruler(s) and served one dynasty after another. The book provides advice to the rulers on the art of statesmanship and also educates the princes who would be the rulers. The book advised them on different aspects of royal duties and conduct, such as the selection of the officials for the administrative positions, preventing bureaucrats from abusing their power, management of the Sultan's household and to recruit soldiers and slaves and to maintain their loyalties etc.

After Alp-Arsalan's death, his son Malik Shah became the new king. Nizam al-Mulk remained the grand vizier of Malik Shah but the relationship between the two became strained with passage of time. Nizam al-Mulk tried to act as an experienced and a wise mentor to the young Sultan who was only 18 years old. With time Malik Shah, however, grew suspicious and resentful of his vizier's power and wealth. Nizam al-Mulk had appointed his relatives and protégés to the key positions in the administration. This led to corruption, abuse of power and unpopularity of Nizam al-Mulk. In the end his downfall was brought by one of the wives of Sultan Malik Shah, Terkhan Khatun. She wanted her son as the successor whereas Nizam al-Mulk supported Sultan's older son by another wife. This disagreement between the two caused the dismissal of Nizam al-Mulk as the grand vizier though he was still part of Sultan's entourage. While traveling with the Sultan, from Isfahan to Baghdad, Nizam al-Mulk was stabbed to death on October 14, 1092. It is widely believed that Nizam al-Mulk was assassinated by an Ismaili cult known as 'Assassins', though the role of Malik Shah or Terkhan Khatun in the murder of Nizam al-Mulk can not be ruled out.

Nizam al-Mulk was an administrator of highest order who probably single handed built up Seljuk power with the Sultan at the center of this power. He was a shrewd statesman with an appetite for power and used all his skills and ruthlessness necessary to be in firm control. Probably he shaped himself after the Barmakids, the powerful family of viziers to the Abbasid Caliph Harun al-Rashid.

Alp Arslan
(1030-1072)

Contribution: Second Sultan of the Seljuk dynasty. He established the great Empire of the Seljuks by expending his kingdom beyond the borders of Persia. He defeated the Byzantines, a victory which paved the way for a Muslim state in Asia Minor (Turkey). He also revitalized the Muslim rule in the declining days of the Abbasid Caliphate.

Seljuks were originally one of the Turkmens tribes who in the tenth century founded dynasties in Persia, Mesopotamia, Syria and Asia Minor. Seljuks were the ruling family of Oghuz branch of Turkey that had settled in Bukhara and embraced the Sunni faith. In 1055, Tughral Beg, a grandson of Seljuk, entered Baghdad and was greeted by the Abbasid caliph, al-Qaim. Tughral Beg was seen as a liberator of the Abbasid Caliphate from the domination of Persian Shiite dynasty Buyids. The caliph bestowed on Tughral Beg the title of Sultan. Despite the fact that the Abbasid Caliphate was dependent on them, the Seljuks ruled under the suzerainty of the Abbasid Caliphate and never claimed to be caliphs rather used the title of Sultan.

Alp Arslan, the second and the most famous sultan of the Seljuk dynasty was born around 1030 AD in Khurasan (Persia). The Arabic name of Alp Arslan was Adud al-Dawla Abu Shuja Muhammad Ibn Daud. In Turkish Alp Arslan means courageous lion. Alp Arslan was a great grandson of Seljuk, the leader of Oghuz Turkmens. His father, Chaghri Beg was brother of Tughral Beg. Chaghri Beg was a Quasi-independent ruler of Khurasan and after his death in 1060, Alp Arslan succeeded his father. He established himself a formidable ruler of Khurasan. He appointed Nizam al-Mulk, as his vizier, who later proved himself not only as a shrewd administrator but also a remarkable statesman. In 1063, Tughral Beg died and Alp Arslan also became the ruler of the lands left behind by his uncle. Though Tughral Beg himself was childless, he had designated Suleiman, one of the other sons of Chaghri Beg as his heir mainly under the influence of his powerful vizier al-Kunduri. Soon an internal struggle began between Alp Arslan and Suleiman. Suleiman, however, was no match for Alp Arslan and in the end Alp Arslan established his rule. Al-Kunduri was executed on the orders of Nizam al-Mulk. Alp Arslan also faced internal opposition from Quatlumush, a son of his granduncle and his own brother Qavrut. He defeated Quatlumush and reconciled with his brother. While he was still suppressing the internal opposition, Alp Arslan in 1064, raided Georgia and Armenia. The Georgian king acknowledged Seljuk Suzerainty. The following year Alp Arslan marched into Transoxiana (Bukhara, Samarqand and Western Farghana). In 1070, he took Aleppo and with that he extended his rule from Central Asia to Mediterranean.

Though the Abbasid caliph al-Qaim had recognized Alp Arslan as the Sultan, Alp Arslan declined to visit Baghdad or get involved into the political treachery of the Abbasid Caliphate. Nevertheless, he kept a close eye on the political developments in Baghdad. His main goal was to augment the influence of the Fatimid dynasty based in Cairo on the affairs of Baghdad. Nizam al-Mulk worked closely with the viziers of the Abbasid Caliphate to make sure that the Shiite influence in Baghdad did not grow beyond the acceptable proportions. Alp Arslan also established relationship with al-Qaim by marrying one of his daughters to the designated heir al-Muqtadi.

Alp Arslan's reputation as one of the greatest medieval Muslim rulers rose from his success against the Byzantines in 1071. The independent Turkmens were invading deep into Byzantine territory and in order to protect their frontiers, the Byzantine emperor, Romanus IV Diogenes had reinforced four major outposts; Malatya, Diyarbakar, Antioch and Odessa. Since Alp Arslan was planning to attack Fatimid stronghold in Syria, he had signed a peace treaty with the Byzantine emperor. Unfortunately, the Turkmens who were not under the control of Alp Arslan continued to plunder the Byzantine territory. This provoked the emperor and he assembled a huge army and marched towards Armenia, north of Lake Van. Alp Arslan considered this move as a breach of treaty, abandoned his military expedition against Fatimids in Syria and moved to stop emperor Romanus further advances. On August 26, 1071, the two armies met at Manzikert (modern malozgirt). A great battle was fought but the Byzantine army was completely destroyed and emperor Romanus was captured. Alp Arslan treated the emperor honorably, released him in exchange of ransom, promises of tribute and the cession of some territory. The emperor, however, did not keep his promises on his return to Constantinople. The battle of Manzikert was a significant battle between the Muslims and the Christians. It very much changed the course of history in Europe. The Byzantines lost many provinces and territories which in turn resulted in loss of revenues and financial losses. The Turks became the ruler of Anatolia and later Asia Minor became Muslim Turkey.

In 1072, Alp Arslan ordered the execution of a Mamlukes commander. The Mamlukes considered this as an injustice to him broke loose from the Sultan's escort and stabbed Alp Arslan to death.

Alp Arslan extended and stabilized the territory ruled by Tughral Beg. With the help of his able administrator, Nizam al-Mulk, Alp Arslan not only succeeded militarily but politically he also gained vast grounds. His victory at Manzikert changed the course of history in Asia Minor resulting in the Islamization of the region. Alp Arslan was a brave soldier and a magnanimous ruler who treated his enemies with respect and leniency.

Omar Khayyam
(1048-1131)

Contribution: Persian poet, mathematician, philosopher and astronomer. Though he has contributed significantly to mathematics and astronomy, his fame lies in his poetry. He is widely known for his Rubayaat (quatrains), popularly known as 'Rubayaat of Omar Khayyam'.

Omar Khayyam was born in Neshapur (Iran) on May 18, 1048. He received his early education in Neshapur and showed enormous interest in science and philosophy. He studied in Balkh (Afghanistan) and went to Samarqand where he wrote a treatise on algebra and made a name for himself as a mathematician and astronomer.

There is a legendary story described by the historian Rashid ad-udin al-Tabib, known as 'The Tale of Three School fellows'. According to al-Tabib, Nizam al-Mulk, Omar Khayyam and Hasan al-Sabbah were class fellows at Neshapur. They promised to each other that if any one of them succeeded in life he would help others. When Nizam al-Mulk became the Vizier of Seljuk Sultan Alp Arsalan, he gave al-Sabbah an important post. Due to his intrigue, al-Sabbah was forced to flee and later founded the 'Assassin Sect' at Almut in Northern Persia. Nizam al-Mulk also invited Omar Khayyam to join the court of Seljuk Sultan Jalaluddin Malik Shah. The authenticity of this story, however, remains clouded.

During the eleventh century, Suljuks were gaining power and in 1055, when Toghrul Beg took control of Baghdad, the Seljuks became the powerful rulers of the Islamic world. Soon Omar Khayyam's reputation as an astronomer reached to the Seljuk Sultan, Jalaluddin Malik Shah, who invited him along with eight other scholars to build an observatory in Isfahan. The Sultan also asked Omar Khayyam to reform the existing Persian solar calendar. Based on his astronomical observations, Omar Khayyam devised a new calendar called Maliki (named after Malik Shah), which was more accurate than the Gregorian or Julian calendar. He also compiled an astronomical table called the 'Zij Malik Shah'. In 1092, Sultan Malik Shah died and unfortunately the subsequent Seljuk rulers did not give Omar Khayyam as important positions as Sultan Malik Shah did. In 1092, Omar Khayyam left for Mecca to perform Hajj. He returned to Neshapur and spent his time either teaching or occasionally advising Seljuk Sultans. During this time, Omar Khayyam mastered philosophy, history, astronomy and mathematics. Very little is known about Omar Khayyam's life after his return to Neshapur from Mecca. He died in Neshapur in 1131.

Omar Khayyam's contribution to mathematics has not been well recognized. In his treatise on algebra (Treatise on Demonstration of Problems of Algebra and Almuqabla), Omar Khayyam classified equations of the first degree and provided the algebraic and geometric solution of the cubic equations. Omar Khayyam also wrote commentary on Euclid's Elements known as 'The Difficulties of Euclid's Definitions'. Omar Khayyam attempted to resolve the problems of irrational numbers (numbers which can be approximated as closely as desired by rational numbers. For example, $(2)^{0.5}$ is not a rational number) and their relations to rational numbers (numbers which can be expressed as the ratio of two integers. For example, $2 = 2/1$). He also discovered the set of numbers which later became known in the West as Pascal's triangle.

Omar Khayyam's reputation lies in his Rubayaat, popularly known as 'Rubayaat -e- Omar Khayyam'. Rubayaats were popular in Persia since the ninth century. A rubai is a quatrain consisting of four lines. The first, second and the fourth lines are rhymes, the third one is free. Omar Khayyam's Rubayaat came to the West through the translations of Edward FitzGerald (1809-1883). However, FitzGerald distorted the original theme of Omar Khayyam's Rubayaat and presented it in more Victorian era style. Initially 1200 Rubayaats were attributed to Omar Khayyam but a research by A. J. Arberry, who used a thirteenth century manuscript, indicated that there are no more than 250 Rubayaats which are originally written by Omar Khayyam. Ali Dashti in 'In

Search of Omar Khayyam' concluded that there are only 102 Rubayaats which are authentic.

A close examination of Omar Khayyam's authentic Rubayaats reveals many aspects of this highly talented man. Each of Omar Khayyam's Rubbayats is related to a particular occasion or incident which ultimately results in a complete poem. In his verses, Omar Khayyam appears to be a thoughtful and observant man. His Rubayaats are not merely love stories laced with beautiful language and abstract thinking rather he questions the existence of God, relationship between man and God, uncertainty of life and immortality of soul. He was also disturbed by man's ignorance and inability to think in broader terms. In the end, however, Omar Khayyam failed to find outright answers of his perplexing questions and chose to be content with his surroundings, e.g. the material world.

Though Omar Khayyam is known for his Rubayaats, his contribution to mathematics and astronomy can not be neglected and he should be remembered not only as a poet but as a mathematician and an astronomer.

Muhammad al-Tusi al-Ghazali
(1058-1111)

Contribution: Muslim theologian and mystic. Most of his works were in the field of jurisprudence and theology. For his role, Ghazali is considered by some as a Mujaddid (renewer), a role many Muslims believe to be filled by one figure at the turn of every century.

Known in Europe as "Algazel", al-Ghazali was born at Tus in 1058 AD. He came from a family which was reputed for its knowledge of Sharia. His father was a businessman with modest means. Ghazali received his early education in Tus and then went to Neshapur for higher education. There his teacher was al-Juwani, the Imam of Mecca and Medina. At Neshapur, Ghazali acquired an in-depth knowledge of Islamic theology and law. He was also initiated into the philosophical speculation of al-Farabi and Ibnsina. After al-Juwani's death in 1085, Ghazali was invited by Nizam al-Mulk Tusi, the powerful vizier of Suljuk Sultans (Alp Arsalan and Malik Shah) to teach in Nizamiyah College (established by Nizam al-Mulk in 1066). In 1091, Nizam al-Mulk appointed Ghazali the rector of Nizamiyah College. The college was a world famous seat of learning and drew students from all over the world. While teaching at Nizamiyah College, Ghazali became familiar with the Neo-Platonist philosophies of Al-Farabi, al-Kindi and Ibnsina. He also realized that external observance of Sharia is not enough and he began his search for right path in life. He studied philosophy, theology, law, mysticsm and the thoughts of various schools of his time. With time he also became troubled with the corruption associated with Sharia. He wrote against the Ismaili cult of the 'Assassins', a political-religious terrorist group who was responsible for the murder of many intellectuals and administrators (presumably Nizam al-Mulk Tusi was also assassinated by this group). In 1095, Ghazali suffered from a nervous illness and he abandoned his career at Nizamiyah college, disposed his wealth and became an ascetic. His illness may not be a physiological illness rather he suffered from spiritual and intellectual crisis and decided to change his direction. He lived in solitude performing mystical rituals. He stayed for some time in Damascus and Jerusalem, visited Mecca in 1096 and then returned to Tus where he was joined by Sufi disciples. Ghazali finally settled with mysticism. He described his arrival at the truth not by reasoning or proofs but by a flash of light which God sent into his soul. In 1106, he started teaching in Nizamiyah College at Neshapur at the request of the Suljuk vizier, Fakhr al-Mulk. He remained there till 1110, returned to Tus and died on December 18, 1111 at Tus.

The main theme of Ghazali's philosophy was that Muslims should observe the laws derived from the Will of God as described in the Quran and Hadith. His greatest work is Ihya Ulum ad-din (Revival of the Religious Sciences). The theme of this book was that the human beings should obey the Will of God in a way that brings them nearer to God leading to the higher stages of Sufism or mysticism. The book also explains how life according to Sharia can contribute to human salvation. He believed that virtues and good character could be achieved by individual efforts and strengthened by right action. According to al-Ghazali, purification of soul can not be achieved in a single day as well as a single sin does not deserve eternal punishment. One abstention from virtue leads to another and gradually the soul degenerates until it looses its direction and nobility.

He wrote a critical book on Neo-Platonism entitled: Tahafat al-Falsifa (Incoherence of the Philosophers). He criticized the philosophy of al-Kindi, Ibnsina and al-Razi almost declaring their philosophical views as unIslamic. Al-Ghazali neither believed in the eternity of matter nor in the immortality of soul. In his opinion the way philosophers look at God is not the God of the Quran, speaking to every man, judging him and loving him.

In his book, Mishkat al-Anwar (The Niche for Light), he described his mystical experiences with other forms of cognition. In another book, al-Munqidh min al-Dalal (The Deliverer for Error), he described the reasons for his abandonment of his career at Nizamiyah college and adoption of mystical life (this book should not be considered Ghazali's autobiography).

Ghazali promoted the devout life based on Sharia and personal faith and advocated to maintain certain standards in social and political life. There was a tradition among the 'Ulema' (religious scholars) to keep distance from the rulers. Ghazali pointed out that the Ulema should not visit the unjust rulers but can visit just rulers without subservience. Ghazali, however, also mentioned that even a ruler is unjust or impious; he should still be obeyed so that law and order could be maintained. According to Ghazali, the tyranny of a ruler for hundred years causes less harm to a society than one year's tyranny exercised by the masses against one another. In other words, Ghazali favored the law and order over anarchy but does not hesitate in saying that revolt against a ruler is fully justified if he went against the command of God or His prophet.

Ghazali was a staunch critic of classical Neo-Platonism doctrines of Farabi and Ibnsina. He criticized the theologians for using arguments based on universal consent and the Muslim philosophers for not explaining their own position rather continuing in the traditions of Greek philosophers. He favored the mystics and believed that by going through a period of visions and revelations, the mystic can come closer to God. He believed that the mystic is real heir to the Prophet as he is capable of getting the direct Divine knowledge and is authority on the Islamic doctrine.

Ghazali's abandonment of a brilliant career and adoption of a monastic life won him followers as well as critics. Western scholars were extremely fascinated by his account of spiritual development, though in reality al-Ghazali was more than just a mystic.

Ghazali is regarded as the greatest and the most influential theologian in the Islamic world. In Islam, the collision between the rationalistic thought and the sciences of theology began as early as the eighth century. Both the rationalists and the orthodoxy claimed to be authentic and right. His greatest achievement is that he combined different disciplines (mysticism, theology, philosophy and law) as an integral part for the progress and stability of a society. In modern time one may not agree with his preferences as he put mysticism in the center. His writings certainly induced a sense of unity and harmony among different schools of thought in Islam.

Ghazali's writings and teachings ultimately provided the theologians with a triumph over rationalists mainly due to the popular religious feelings of the masses and systematic anti-intellectualism propaganda. Ghazali's distrust of human reasoning became standard tool for Muslim theologians for the centuries to come. It is, however, difficult to assess how much the later generations of Muslim theologians have distorted Ghazali's real teachings in order to achieve their own objectives.

According to a Hadith, at the beginning of every century, God will send a renewer who will bring people back to the faith. Many consider Ghazali as the "Renewer" (Mujadid) of his age (twelfth century).

Ghazali's works were translated into Latin by the middle of the twelfth century. Many Christian and Jewish theologians were influenced by al-Ghazali's works. His impact on Islamic theology has been compared to that of Saint Thomas Aquinas on Christian ideology and thinking.

Yusuf Ibn Tashfin
(Died 1106)

Contribution: The greatest Almoravid ruler who created the first Berber empire in North Africa and Spain. He was an excellent military commander, sound administrator and devoutly religious who inspired his people by example.

Almoravids (1056-1147) were the Saharan Berbers who built an empire in Northwest Africa and Spain in the eleventh century. Almoravid dynasty originates from a religious movement led by Abd Allah Ibn Yasin and Yaha Ibn Abrahim. Their followers from Lamtuma and Gadala Berbers of Mauritania moved to south-and-northward to spread Islam. First they established themselves in North Africa and soon they were needed by the Muslim Spain to defend them against the advances of the Christian armies. When the Umayyad rule in Cordoba collapsed, many small kingdoms emerged from the ruins of Cordoba. The Christian states which have survived in the north of Spain began expending southwards. Their advances were checked by Almoravids when in 1086 they defeated the Castilian Christians near Badajaz. With this victory Almoravids ruled all Muslim Spain except the Christian kingdom of Valencia.

Very little is known about Yusuf Ibn Tashfin's early life except that he belonged to a Berber family. His place and year of birth is also obscure. He was a cousin of Abu Bakr Ibn Omar who had succeeded Ibn Yasin. In 1061, Abu Bakr went to Morocco on a military campaign leaving Ibn Tashfin behind as his deputy. Ibn Tashfin first consolidated his power in Morocco by establishing the city of Marrakesh which became his capital. In 1063, he began a campaign against Zenata Berbers in central Morocco which finally ended in 1069 with the conquest of Fez. By 1083, he had conquered all of Morocco and western Algeria.

Meanwhile in Spain, the Muslim rule was in decline. The rulers of Muslim Spain were divided and weak to defend themselves against Christian attacks led by Alfonso VI of Leon and Castile. The Christian armies were conquering the land they had hold before the arrival of the Muslims in Spain. In 1085, Toledo fell to the Christian armies and the rulers of Muslim Spain invited Ibn Tashfin to come to their rescue. In 1086, Ibn Tashfin crossed into Spain and decisively defeated Alfonso at the battle of al-Zallaque. He returned to Morocco but the rulers of Muslim Spain did not take any lesson and failed to patch their differences. In 1088, Ibn Tashfin returned to Spain but was defeated by a Christian army. Realizing the corruption, greed and weaknesses of the Muslim rulers of Spain, in 1090, he again returned to Spain, led a campaign against them in an attempt to unite them. He finally captured the Muslim Spain and by 1097, the southern half of Iberian Peninsula was under Yusuf's control. He adopted the title of Amir al-Muslimin (Leader of the Muslims) though as a token he accepted the authority of the Abbasid Caliphs. He tried to reform the Andalusian courts by bringing orthodoxy. Yusuf Ibn Tashfen died in 1106 after 45 years of rule. Before his death, he was the ruler of modern Algeria, Morocco, Western Africa and half of the Iberian Peninsula. This was the apex of the Almoravid dynasty.

Though the Almoravid rule lasted for another forty years after Ibn Tashfin's death, overall, the empire was in decline. The rise of the Almohads in the south and the Christian threat from the north, threatened the power of Almoravids. There was always a cultural and racial animosity between the Berbers and the Muslim Spain that also forced the Almoravids to withdraw from Spain, yielding power to weak and divided rulers of Muslim Spain. In 1147, Almohads defeated Almoravids bringing the end of the dynasty.

The Almoravid dynasty, though, did not last even one hundred years, it had a lasting impact on the Berber culture, politics and the history of North Africa. During his 45 years of rule, Ibn Tashfin, united North Africa and Muslim Spain under one Berber rule. His empire stretched across Southern Iberia, Valencia and North Africa from the Atlantic to Algiers. His greatest contribution to the Islamic world was attempt to unite the Muslim Spain (which was again fragmented after his death) and halting the advances of the Christian armies, thus preventing an early demise of the Muslim rule in Spain.

Muhammad Ibn Tumart
(1077-1130)

Contribution: Celebrated North African religious reformer, known as the 'Mahdi' of the Almohads. He founded the Almohad movement which ended the Almoravid rule in North Africa. He organized and unified the Berber tribes of North Africa who ruled over Morocco and Spain for almost 140 years.

The Almoravids (1056-1147), who ruled North Africa and Spain, started to decline in less than one hundred years after assuming power. The moral decay and the lack of intellectual capabilities in Almoravid society resulted in a quick fall of the dynasty. The intellectual and independent thinking were prohibited. The books of al-Ghazali were burned and the verses of the Quran were taken literally. Under these circumstances, a reform minded Berber, Ibn Tumart, began a religious rebellion which ultimately toppled the Almoravid dynasty in 1147.

Ibn Tumart was a Berber from the Masmuda tribe in the Atlas Mountains in Morocco. His exact date of birth is not known but it is speculated that he was born between 1077 and 1088. His family belonged to one of the most important tribes of Atlas Mountains, Iserghin. Ibn Tumart, as a young man distinguished himself from the others as a piety, industrious with a remarkable thirst for knowledge. He used to visit mosques regularly and burned so many candles that he was given the nick name 'Asafir' (fire-brand).

In pursuit of knowledge, Ibn Tumart left home in 1105 and went to the east visiting important cities of the Islamic empire. He began his journey by traveling to Spain where Ibn Hazm's writings produced significant influence on him. He then traveled to the east, though the chronology of his travel is uncertain. From Spain, he probably went to Alexandria. Soon he left Alexandria and visited Mecca for pilgrimage and then he studied in Baghdad and probably in Damascus. While in Baghdad, he came across al-

Ghazali's writings and was highly influenced by his views. In 1118, he returned to Morocco with a passion and ideas of reforms. He began preaching the sailors and the passengers of the ship on which he was coming back home. He mainly focused on reforming morals and religious beliefs. He started preaching in towns and villages, denounced drinking of wine, playing musical instruments and the appearance of the women in public places without veil. His criticism of the Almoravid regime and some of the prominent theologians of the time led his banishment from Marrakesh, the Almoravid capital. Unfortunately his religious beliefs were becoming fanatic and occasionally violent. He threw the sister of the Almoravid prince Ali from the horse for not wearing the veil. Prince Ali, showed great restrain and patience and spared Ibn Tumart's life. Ibn Tumart, then fled to his birthplace, Aghmat, in the Atlas Mountains, started preaching and recruiting disciples from Masmuda tribesmen.

In 1125, Ibn Tumart declared himself as 'Mahdi' (according to the Muslim belief a divinely inspired leader who would bring righteousness and justice to the mankind). His major objectives were to unite the Berber tribes under the umbrella of Islam, the adoption of the Quran and the Hadith (the Traditions of the prophet) and to restore justice by overthrowing the Almoravids. Ibn Tumart's rising power and strength alerted the Almoravid rulers and in 1125, they tried to crush the movement forcing Ibn Tumart to retreat to Timmel, a mountain village which was even more inaccessible than Aghmat. For the next five years, Ibn Tumart was busy teaching the Masmuda Berbers the Quran and the Islamic laws as these tribesmen were nominally Muslims and were quite unfamiliar with the basic tenants of Islam. Meanwhile he also recruited warrior disciples and attempted to unify the Berber tribes, hence the name Muwahhiden (Unifers). By 1130, Ibn Tumart had organized and gathered enough disciples to launch a military campaign against the Almoravids, led by his most trusted lieutenant, Abd al-Mumin. The campaign, however, was proven to be a disastrous. The Almoravids inflicted a crushing defeat on the Almohads and they retreated to their mountain fortresses. Shortly after this unsuccessful campaign, Ibn Tumart fell ill and died in 1130 AD. His death was kept secret for the next three years and finally Abd al-Mumin took over the reign of the Almohads. The hiding of Ibn Tumart's death from his followers was probably necessary due to the political and the psychological reasons. This also indicates the influence and charisma of Ibn Tumart on his followers. He did not live to see the victories of his followers in North Africa and Spain. By 1149, the Almohads controlled North Africa as far as the Libyan Desert. In 1170, the Muslim Spain was conquered by the Almohads and Seville became their capital, though eventually they returned to Morocco to rule from Marrakesh. In 1195, the Almohads defeated the Spanish Christians at the Battle of Alcaros which marked the height of the Almohad's political power.

Though the Almohad's rule lasted only for 140 years, its impact on the people of North Africa and Spain was immense and all these would not have been possible without the religious inspiration and sociopolitical organization of Ibn Tumart. His grave still exists in Timmel but history and people have forgotten his name and the achievements.

Abd al-Malik Ibn al-Zuhr
(1090-1162)

Contribution: One of the greatest physicians/surgeons of Muslim Spain. He described the surgical procedures for removing the kidney stones and for the excision of cataracts. He developed a procedure known as 'tracheotomy' to relieve obstruction to breathing.

Known as 'Avenzoor' in the western world, Ibn Zuhr is one of the most practical and influential physicians of Muslim Spain. Ibn Zuhr was born in Seville (Spain) in 1090 AD and learned the art of medicine from his father, Abul-Ala Zuhr. He was a court physician for Almoravids. Ibn Zuhr died in 1162 in Seville.

Ibn Zuhr compiled his medical knowledge and experience in his book ' Kitab al-Taysir Fil Mudawat Wal Tadbir' (practical Manual of Treatment and diet). This book was translated in Latin and Hebrew.

Ibn Zuhr's knowledge of human body and the functions of many organs are astounding. He described the inflammation of membranous sac surrounding the heart, medically known as 'pericarditis'. He also identified an abscess known as 'mediastinal abscesses' which affects the tissues of thoracic cavity above the diaphragm but does not affect the lungs. He also described the process of contraction and dilation of the pupil in details.

Ibn Zuhr also demonstrated his surgical skills by describing the surgical methods for removing the kidney stones and the method for the excision of cataracts. He outlined a procedure called 'tracheotomy' in which a hole is made in the 'trachea' through the neck to relieve obstruction to breathing.

Ibn Zuhr left behind an indelible mark on medicine. His knowledge and understanding of diseases and the management or cure of these diseases was remarkably accurate as compared to the knowledge of modern day medicine.   He remained a towering figure in medicine and provided mentoring to many physicians for centuries to come.   The great Muslim philosopher Ibn Rushd (Averroes) was a student of Ibn Zuhr from whom he learned his medical skills.   Ibn Zuhr had also great influence on the physicians of medieval Europe.

Abd al-Mumin
(1094-1163)

Contribution: Founder of the Almohad Empire in North Africa and Iberian Peninsula. He was considered a highly skilled administrator and military commander. Under his leadership an era of commerce and artistic creativity began in North Africa and Mediterranean.

Almohads were a Berber dynasty that ruled over Morocco, Algeria, Tunisia and Southern Spain during the twelfth and the thirteenth century (1130-1269). It began as a religious movement by Muhammad Ibn Tumart (1077-1130). This movement was initiated as a reaction to Puritanism of the Almoravid dynasty and a belief of Ibn Tumart that many pagan practices have crept into Islam.

Abd al-Mumin was born in Tagra (Algeria) in 1094 AD. His father was a member of Berber Zanata tribe and a potter by profession. Abd al-Mumin received his early education in Tagra and in the Algerian city of Tlemsen. He showed extraordinary brilliance in learning and understanding the materials. In 1117, he had a momentous meeting with Ibn Tumart at Mallala (Algeria) which changed the course of his life.

In 1117, Ibn Tumart landed in Tunisia and began a journey towards his native country, Southern Morocco. Ibn Tumart's journey was more of a preacher. He preached about the oneness of God and the practice of Islamic laws. Abd al-Mumin was extremely impressed by Ibn Tumart's preaching and became his disciple. Ibn Tumart, then first went to Marakesh where he initiated opposition movements against Almoravid regime. Ibn Tumart, then moved to Atlas Mountains, founded Almohad state and in 1125, declared himself as Mahdi. Abd al-Mumin became a trusted lieutenant of Ibn Tumart and helped him in spreading his doctrine, organizing Almohad society and fighting against the

Almoravid regime. Ibn Tumart launched several military attacks on Almoravids. In one of such attacks, his second in command Al-Bashir was killed. Ibn Tumart, then appointed Abd al-Mumin his second in command and successor. In August 1130, Ibn Tumart died and Abd al-Mumin became the leader of Almohads. For three years, the death of Ibn Tumart was concealed because some Almohads questioned the succession of Abd al-Mumin. By 1133, however, Abd al-Mumin's leadership was established.

After taking over the reign of Almohad movement, Abd al-Mumin continued in the footsteps of Ibn Tumart. The struggle against the Almoravids continued. In the next 15 years, using guerrilla tactics and sheer military genius, Abd al-Mumin took control of the High and Middle Atlas mountains and the Rif region (mountains of eastern Algeria and northern Tunisia). In 1145, Abd al-Mumin defeated the Almoravids and in 1147, he captured Marrakesh and with that the Almoravid dynasty came to an end. The last Almoravid ruler was executed and Lemtuma Berbers were massacred in Marrakesh. Abd al-Mumin now became the ruler of Northwest Africa, retaining Marrakesh as his capital. In 1151, declining Hammadid kingdom surrendered to Abd al-Mumin, thus he annexed Algiers and Bougie (Hammadid capital) into his rule. In 1152, the Hilalians joined a coalition of powerful Arab tribes to push Almohads but were decisively defeated by Abd al-Mumin after a four-day battle. Though he treated the defeated Arab tribes with leniency but used them as needed to suppress his opponents. After consolidating his base in Morocco and Western Algeria, he turned his attention towards Tunisia and Spain. Southern Spain was taken from Almoravids in a series of campaign between 1146 and 1154 and Algeria was annexed in 1151. The Muslims in Tunisia sought Abd al-Mumin's help in repelling Norman influence in North Africa. In 1151, Abd al-Mumin led an expedition against Normans in Tunisia. On January 22, 1160, his navy defeated the Normans. After some negotiations, Normans were given a safe passage to Sicily, thus ending the Norman rule in Africa. By 1160, Abd al-Mumin had built the largest Berber empire, united by religion and political beliefs, who ever ruled North Africa and Southern Spain.

Abd al-Mumin also had to deal with internal opposition to his regime. In 1155, Ibn Tumart's two brothers staged a military rebellion against him and besieged Marrakesh but were defeated and executed. On the suspicion of fomenting treason, Abd al-Mumin also executed many chiefs of Hargha tribe.

Abd al-Mumin ruled for 30 years which was significant for the propagation of Ibn Tumart's teaching and for the establishment of a unified Berber empire in North Africa and Southern Spain. Abd al-Mumin not only conducted military expeditions but also organized his state. Between 1152 and 1159, he devoted most of his time in establishing law and order in the territories he had conquered. He assumed the title of 'Caliph of Ibn Tumart' and also became Amir al-Muminin (Leader of the faithful). He built his state around the teachings of the Quran and the traditions of Prophet Muhammad. He established a tax system based on geographical survey, declaring that only two-thirds of the land is fertile, therefore, tax should be based only on the fertile land. He set up an organization to promote Almohad doctrine and established a central administration, an idea that he had borrowed from the Muslim Spain.

Abd al-Mumin was a great patron of architecture. The Kutabia mosque at Marrakesh and the mosques at Taza and Timmel are examples of combined architecture of local, the east and the west (Moorish Spain). He also built a fortress known as Ribat al-Fath. Abd al-Mumin died on May 2, 1163 and was buried near Ibn Tumart at Timmel.

Abd al-Mumin's greatest achievement was to convert a small spiritual/religious movement into a powerful empire which lasted almost one and a half century He united and mobilized the Berber tribes from the mountains and desert fringes of North Africa. Arts also flourished in Morocco and Spain under him and his successor. He introduced a new simple architectural style which when combined with the Spanish and Moroccan architecture produced a magnificent and impressive form of architecture. The era of his son (1163-84) and grandson (1184-99) is considered the golden era of Berbers. They opened the commerce, built the most sophisticated navy in the Mediterranean and the urban life thrived under their rule. In 1212, after the defeat against Christian Spain at Las Navas de Tolosa, Almohads began to decline and by 1269 the empire was disintegrated. Like Almoravids, Almohads decline was also hastened due to their rigid and uncompromising principles. This rigidity caused much unnecessary opposition to Abd al-Mumin but overall, his achievements were remarkable. He single handed wrote one of the most glorious chapters in the history of Berber North Africa.

Ibn Bajjah (Avempace)
(1095/1106-1138)

Contribution: Spanish Muslim philosopher who exerted a great influence on Ibn Tufyl and Ibn Rushd. In Spain he represented the Arabic Aristotelian-Neo-Platonist philosophical tradition.

Ibn Bajjah, known to medieval Europe as Avempace was born in Saragossa, Spain. His exact date of birth is not known. His family background, his childhood and source of education are also obscured. It is believed that he studied mathematics, astronomy and medicine. He served as a minister to the Emir of Mauracia. He wrote number of poems, a treatise on botany and a commentary on Aristotle. His philosophical writings include treatise on logic, On the Contact of the Intellect with Men and a treatise on the soul. His commentary on Aristotle's physica might have helped Galileo to formulate his laws of falling bodies. Ibn Bajjah's fame, however, lies in his philosophical views presented in 'Tadbir al-Motawahhid' (The Rule of Solitary). The book remained incomplete due to his sudden death probably at the age of 32 or 43. The work remained obscure for a long period of time and was only known through a detailed analysis in Hebrew by Moses of Norbonne (in the fourteenth century) who analyzed Ibn Bajjah's work while writing a commentary on Ibn Tufyl's work 'Hayy Ibn Yaqdhan'. The original work in Arabic is now in the Bodleian Library at Oxford, England.

In the 'Rule of Solitary', Ibn Bajjah attempted to show that the human soul could unite with the Divine. This union, however, is achieved through many stages. The human intellect which consists of form and matter can gradually rise to spiritual forms (gradual decrease in matter as the spirit then gradually evolve from the forms of matter) where it can unite with the Active Intellect (God).

Ibn Bajjah based his philosophy on the theoretical sciences and the intuitive knowledge with a radical interpretation of al-Farabi's philosophy. According to Ibn Bajjah, the philosopher's life should be of a solitary individual. The rule or discipline a solitary man (philosopher) seeks is vital to be a member of a Perfect City or an Ideal State. Ibn Bajjah also emphasized that the Ideal state could only be built by social reform not by a political coup. The philosopher should not associate with the non-philosophers and their ways of life and thinking. The common people live a life which consists of many layers of darkness and reason alone cannot free them from this darkness. Therefore, the divine law has been formulated which enables them to know the dark region. The philosopher's goal should be to seek the light of the Intellect, ultimately being transformed into the light which unites him with the Intellect. To Ibn Bajjah, philosophy was the only way to reach the highest point of the Intellect. Unlike, Farabi, Ibn Bajjah believed that a philosopher could achieve or see the light even in the absence of the Perfect City or the Ideal state.

His silence about theology led to believe that Ibn Bajjah was an atheist, probably an incorrect view. In his philosophy he did mention about the union of human soul with the Active Intellect or God. Ibnsina in his writings made clear distinction between theoretical and practical sciences but Ibn Bajjah showed little concern for the practical science. Ibn Bajjah was also not a proponent of imaginative representation of philosophy. In reality, Ibn Bajjah's writings and views differ from al-Farabi and Ibnsina.

Al-Hammudi al-Idrisi
(1100-1165)

Contribution: Arab geographer. He entered into the services of Norman king of Sicily, Roger II and became a leading map maker and scientific consultant to the court of Palermo. He designed the first map of the world that was similar to those made by modern geographers. His works served for several centuries as a model in geography.

Al-Idrisi was born in Sabath (now Ceuta in Morocco) in 1100 AD. He was a descendent of Hammudid dynasty who ruled in Spain and North Africa for almost 42 years (1016-1058). After the fall of Malaga (Spain) in 1057, his ancestors fled to Ceuta. They ruled over Ceuta and Tangier till 1084. In his early age, al-Idrisi traveled to North Africa and Spain. He studied in Cordoba and visited Portugal, Southern England, French Atlantic coast and Asia Minor.

The Arabs had conquered Sicily in 902 AD and ruled effectively for almost 200 years, before Sicily fell to the Normans. Roger II (1095-1154) was crowned as the king of Sicily in 1130 AD. Roger made Palermo his capital which soon became a major meeting place for the Christian and Arab scholars. Roger himself had a keen interest in geography. In 1139, he had established a commission for world geography to be based on Greek, Latin and Arab geographical literature. Roger's interest in geography may be due to his desire of expansion and trade as well as to further his political goals. Hearing al-Idrisi's reputation as a scholar, Roger invited him to join his court. Al-Idrisi accepted the offer and in 1145 went to Sicily and soon became a leading member of Roger's commission. Roger gave al-Idrisi a lot of respect and honor. It was in his court that al-Idrisi established himself as a geographer and cartographer. Al-Idrisi spent rest of his life (with the exception of the last few years) in the court of Palermo where his achievements made him famous. Those days it was considered a taboo for a Muslim to enter into the court of a Christian king. What led to his entry into the court of Roger is not exactly known. Al-Idrisi might have been forced to take such a position for his own safety due to his background as a descendent of Hammudid dynasty. His life might have been in danger from assassins hired by the rivals of his family or religious factions.

Al-Idrisi's three major geographical works can be summarized as follows:

1. A silver celestial sphere or globe on which a map of the known world was depicted.

2. A world map consisting of 70 sections in a disk form also made of solid silver (1.5-by-3.5 meters). Al-Idrisi's world map is a monumental work in geography. Al-Idrisi divided the map into seven horizontal climactic zone of equal width and described each zone in details moving from west to east. Each zone was divided vertically into 11 sections to create a grid to accurately describe the location of a place. Though his maps were correctly drawn for the time, they were not drawn mathematically.

3. A geographic text based on which the globe and the map were constructed.

The world map depicted on the silver and the globe is lost but the book and the seventy sectional maps have survived.

In his concept of the world, al-Idrisi was more influenced by Ptolemy than the Arabs. Al-Idrisi's works heavily relied on the works of the Muslims and the Greeks. He also sought help from the travelers and the eye witnesses. Al-Idrisi with the help of Roger selected people skilled in drawing and sent them to different parts of the world. When these men returned they provided their accounts of journey which al-Idrisi incorporated into his text. He also relied on his own recollections of his journeys.

Al-Idrisi's famous work of descriptive geography is known as 'Kitab Nuzhat al-Mushtaq Fi Ikhtiraq Al-Afaq', also known as Al-Kitab Al-Rujari (The Book of Roger) and was completed in 1154. This book remained as a reference book on geography for almost 300 years in Europe. The complete version of the Book of Roger does not exist in any language but an abridged version first appeared in Rome in 1592 and was later translated into Latin in 1619.

Roger died in 1154 but al-Idrisi continued to work for his son and successor William I. Al-Idrisi produced a geographical treatise for William which is lost. Disheartened due to anti-Muslim riots in 1161, al-Idrisi left Sicily for Morocco. Not much is known about his later life in Morocco where he died between 1164 and 1166.

Though uncharacteristic of the time, al-Idrisi's works represent Muslim-Christian collaboration in geography. In his maps, al-Idrisi applied scientific methodology and precision based on the accounts of travelers and eye witnesses. Before al-Idrisi, geography was an imaginary art which he transformed into a real art. His cartographic works provided a practical map of the world based on geographical facts rather than scriptural teachings. His works laid the basis for the modern navigational maps.

Al-Idrisi also had knowledge about pharmacology. He wrote a book known as 'Book of Simple Drugs' in at least 12 languages. He also wrote some poetry which indicates his knowledge of Arabic literature.

Abu Bakr Muhammad Ibn Tufyl
(1110-1185)

Contribution: Spanish Muslim philosopher and physician. He wrote a philosophical treatise in the form of a story, a highly celebrated and acclaimed work of Ibn Tufyl.

Very little is known about the early life of Abu-Bakr Muhammad Ibn Tufyl, known to medieval Europe as Abubacer. He was born in Guadix (Spain) in 1110 AD. His family background and the source of his education are not known. Though by training he was a physician, early in his career he was involved with the government. He served as the secretary to the governors of Granada, Ceute and Tangier. He practiced medicine in Granada and later served as a court physician and vizier to the Almohad sovereign Abu Yaqub Yusuf. Abu Yusuf was an intellectual ruler and had a great interest in philosophy. He asked Ibn Tufyl to write a commentary on Aristotle's work with clarity. Ibn Tufyl, on the pretext of old age, recommended a young Spanish philosopher named Ibn Rushd (Averroes), who took this responsibility and later himself became one of the most celebrated philosophers of the world. Ibn Tufyl died in 1185 AD at Marrakesh (Morocco).

With the exception of a number of medical treatises and some writings on astronomy, little of Ibn Tufyl's work has survived. Fortunately, his most celebrated allegorical tale 'Hayy Ibn Yaqdhan' (The Living Son of the Awake) has survived. The story described in this book is though influenced by the Hidden Secrets of Ibnsena's 'Oriental Philosophy' the views presented by Ibn Tufyl about philosophers are quite opposite to those of Ibnsena's. Ibn Tufyl's work is completely original and is not an extension or amplification of Ibnsena's story.

The story in Hayy Ibn Yaqdhan is about a child named Hayy brought up in an isolated island. He grew up alone, suckled as a child by a gazelle. Despite the fact that he was cut off from human civilization he developed a system of philosophy and metaphysics by exercising reasons. This knowledge he gained through various stages, each stage taking seven years. Through fasting and meditation, Haay also gained mystical experiences. In short, Haay gained highest form of human intelligence which is only for a few by applying reasoning and rational thinking. His knowledge was still incomplete as he knew nothing about other human beings, their life style and normal human practices. Meanwhile, in a neighboring island, a wise and religious man named Asal was looking for an uninhibited place. In his search, he landed in the desolated island of Haay. Asal taught Hayy to speak and was astonished to find that Haay had developed a system of knowledge comparable to his own and in some respects even superior. Asal also taught Haay about religion and social practices of his fellow men. Hayy requested Asal to take him to the civilization where both of them could teach and propagate the secrets of wisdom to other human beings. Both men attempted to deliver their spiritual and philosophical messages to the general masses but encountered hostility. Their attempt however, failed and they concluded that ordinary people are not capable to understand the higher levels of intellect. Ultimately, both Hayy and Asal returned to the deserted island. The moral of the story is that there is a hierarchy of human intelligence. There are only few people who can attain truth by the use of reasons whereas others can achieve the same through the symbols of religious revelations. Yet there are a majority of people who neither care for the reasons nor for the laws of religion but are only interested in a materialistic world. Ibn Tufyl's work was translated into Latin in 1671 and in English in 1708. It has been suggested by some scholars that Defoe's Robinson Crusoe (1719) might have been inspired by Hayy Ibn Yaqdhan.

Like the scholars of the time, Ibn Tufyl had encyclopedic knowledge. He was a philosopher, mathematician, astronomer and poet. To him philosophy was necessary for the proper understanding of religion. He maintained that the natural philosophy and the application of reasons in the thought process could lead to the insights which parallel those of revelation and mysticism. Ibn Tufyl along with Ibn Bajjah and Ibn Rushd was the last of the great Muslim philosophers who marked the highest point of the Muslim philosophy which from onward became extinct.

Ibn Muhammad Ibn Rushd (Averroes)
(1126-1198)

Contribution: Philosopher, physician, judge, commentator and administrator. He was one of the greatest philosophers of Islam. He attempted to reconcile faith with philosophy and logic. He exerted a vast influence on the Western and the Latin thinkers mainly due to his commentaries on Aristotle.

Ibn Rushd, known as 'Averroes' to the west was a theologian, philosopher, judge and commentator. Ibn Rushd was born at Cordoba (Spain) in 1126. He belonged to a distinguished family of jurists during Almoravid dynasty. His grandfather was a chief judge of Cordoba and later Ibn Rushd himself became a chief judge of this city. In the early years of his life he got himself thoroughly versed in Quranic Sciences (Hadith and Fiqha). Ibn Rushd studied medicine under a noted physician (Abu Jafar Harun Al-Tajali) in Seville. He learned philosophy and later his philosophical works gave him a worldwide fame. At the age of 30, Ibn Rushd traveled to Marakesh (Morocco), which was then ruled by Almohads. Under Almohad caliph Abd-al Mumin, the Almohads had conquered southern and central Spain as well as North Africa. In 1163, Abd-al Mumin died and his son Abu Yaqub Yusuf became the ruler. Abu Yaqub Yusuf was himself a scholar and a patron of philosophers. Ibn Rushd was introduced to Abu Yaqub Yusuf by a well known contemporary scholar and philosopher Ibn Tufayl (1105-1184). Abu Yaqub Yusuf had asked Ibn Tufayl to translate the works of Aristotle with clarity and comprehensible commentary. Ibn Tufayl suggested the name of Ibn Rushd, since Ibn Tufayl was too old to shoulder such a responsibility. This task finally fell on the shoulders of Ibn Rushd which became his life long ambition and brought him an ever lasting fame.

Ibn Rushd's fame lies in his work of reconciliation of philosophy and religion. In medicine his major work is a book known as Al-Kulliyat (General Medicine) which was written between 1153 and 1169 and in 1255 this book was translated into Latin. Ibn Rushd is also the author of many legal and theological treatises. Between 1169 and 1195, Ibn Rushd wrote an extensive series of commentaries on Aristotle's works which earned him the title of 'Commentator'. In his commentaries on Aristotle, Ibn Rushd showed remarkable admiration for Aristotle. He considered him 'Master' or an example for the highest level of human perfection. Ibn Rushd also wrote a commentary on Plato's Republic and dedicated it to Abu Yaqub, the Almohad caliph. His commentaries were written with immense observations and analysis which helped a great deal to understand Aristotle's philosophy. His commentaries on the works of Aristotle and Plato produced significant influence on the thinking of European philosophers for centuries to come. His commentaries were translated into Latin and had significant influence on both Christians and Jews. Thus Ibn Rushd not only introduced the Aristotelian philosophy to the Islamic world but also to the Latin Christian world.

Ibn Rushd's three most significant writings can be summarized as follows:

1. Treatise on the agreement between religious law and philosophy (Fasl).

2. His book Tahafut al-Tahafut (incoherence of incoherence) is based on arguments in defense of philosophy. This book provides philosophical answers to al-Ghazali's criticism of Ibnsina, Aristotle and Al-Farabi. Ibn Rushd's in depth knowledge of history of the religious sciences as well as theology helped him a great deal to speak and interpret the principles of the Islamic laws and their application to theological and philosophical issues. Ibn Rushd questioned Al-Ghazali's authority as a critic of Ibnsina and Aristotle and Al-Ghazali's view about correct beliefs and right practices.

3. Ibn Rushd's another significant writing is on theology; Kitab al-Kashf un Manahij al-Adillah (Exposition of the Methods of Proofs). In this book he tried to demonstrate how theology should be kept under the control of philosophy and the Divine Law.

Ibn Rushd like Ibnsina, believed the concept of general intelligence. In Ibn Rushd's views, motion, time and matter are all eternal, hence the world is eternal. He maintained that to consider that world is not eternal will be tantamount to accept that God lacks power and perfection. To him God was the cause of existence since the creator of matter is the creator of existence.

His philosophical views led to the thinking that his teachings are incompatible with the traditional teachings of Islam. Therefore, questions were raised whether his teachings were of double truth? The answer is in negative. Ibn Rushd believed that the objectives of the religious law and philosophy are same (On the Harmony of Religion and Philosophy). He maintained that religion through symbolic representation reveal the same truth which can also be obtained through philosophical knowledge. In Fasl he described philosophy as integral part or the companion of Shariah (Islamic laws). Despite his adaptation of Aristotelian philosophy, Ibn Rushd remained a devout Muslim and never challenged the religious beliefs. He strongly denied that there was any contradiction between philosophical truth and the teachings of the Quran and the Sharia. His commentary on Plato's Republic carried the Islamic character and tone of the time. Unfortunately, the conservative Muslim scholars of the time tried to silence Ibn Rushd. They insisted that Ibn Rushd's commentaries on Aristotelian theory are against the teachings of Islam. These orthodox Muslim scholars believed that Aristotelian theory denies God's act of creation and questions God's omniscience. Ibn Rushd's books were publicly burned and false accusations were labeled against him. Ibn Rushd was exiled to Lucena (south of Cordoba). However, in 1195, Abu Yusuf invited Ibn Rushd to join him to his capital Marrakesh which he accepted. Ibn Rushd died in 1198 in Morocco. He was initially buried in Morocco but later his remains were brought to Cordoba.

Ibn Rushd was undoubtedly one of the greatest thinkers of the Islamic world. Surprisingly he was ignored in the east and produced little influence. Some of Ibn Rushd's works in Arabic have been lost but almost all his works have been translated into Latin. Ibn Rushd's philosophical works had immense significant impact on the medieval and the Renaissance philosophers. In Europe he was considered as a great authority on Aristotle's philosophy and was simply refered to as "Commentator". A school arose around his 'Commentaries on Aristotle" known as "Latin Averroism". According to Dante, even Ibn Rushd could not dream the extent of his influence on the philosophers and the intellectuals of medieval Europe. With his death, the period of Islamic philosophy which spanned over 500 years came to an abrupt end.

The abrupt demise of the Islamic philosophy was mainly due to the continuous efforts of the orthodox clergy of Islam who only cherished their limited views and thinking. By the twelfth century, anti-intellectualism in Islam was on the rise. The so-called Ulema (religious scholars) had mustered enough public support to suppress rationalistic free thinking. In such a hostile environment, Ibn Rushd tried to revive rational thinking but his views were neglected in the declining Muslim societies. Lack of innovations from religion to sciences froze the Islamic thinking and progress into a fixed mold just at the time when Western Europe was getting ready to embrace intellectual curiosity.

Salahuddin Ayubi (Saladin) (1138-1193)

Contribution: Sultan of Egypt, Syria, Yemen and Palestine. He was a sound administrator and one of the greatest military commanders in history. He recaptured Jerusalem from Latin Christians after 88 years of its occupation mainly due to his new and improved military techniques. Saladin was the founder of the Ayubbid dynasty in Egypt.

Known as "Saladin' to the west, Salahuddin is considered as the most formidable and admirable foe to the Christian Crusaders. His heroic efforts, military genius and generosity remained for centuries the topics of 'Ballads' in the western hemisphere.

Salahuddin was born in Takrit, Mesopotamia in 1138 AD in a prominent Kurdish family. His father, Najmaddin Ayub was governor of Takrit but due to political circumstances he was forced to leave Takrit. He then rendered his services to Imad ad-Din Zangi, the Turkish governor of Syria. Zangi appointed Najmaddin Ayub as the governor of Balbek. Salahuddin grew up in Balbek and Damascus (Syria). He studied the Quran and learned poetry and grammar. Salahuddin's career began when he joined his uncle Asad Ad-din Shirukh who was a military commander under Nur Ad-Din Zangi, son and successor of Imad ad-Din Zangi. Salahuddin's brilliance impressed Nur Ad-Din and at the age of eighteen, Salahuddin became the administrator of Damascus. From a very young age Salahuddin demonstrated a remarkable character. He was honest, kindhearted and pious.

In the twelfth century, the Islamic world was plagued by the religious differences. At that time Egypt was ruled by the Fatimid dynasty which was founded in Tunisia in 908 by the Imam Ubaidallah. The fourth Fatimid Caliph Muizz conquered Egypt and founded Cairo in 969. The Fatimid rulers of Egypt were Shiite Muslims, whereas, Nur Ad-Din Zangi was a Sunni Muslim. The

Fatimids were weak and there was a danger that Egypt might fall into the hands of the Christians. This would have threatened the stability of the Islamic world. Sensing this danger, Nur Ad-Din planned the invasion of Egypt. On the orders of Nur Ad-Din, Shirukh led three military expeditions into Egypt against Latin-Christians. Though the objective of these expeditions was to prevent fall of Egypt into the hands of Latin Christians, soon a powerful rivalry began between Shirukh and the Egyptian Fatimid Caliph. After the death of Shirukh (1168), Salahuddin was appointed the commander of the Syrian troops in Egypt (1169). In 1171, Salahuddin abolished the Fatimid dynasty and became the ruler of Egypt. He founded Ayubid dynasty which ruled Egypt and Red sea coast till 1250.

Initially, Salahuddin faced hostility from the Zengid rulers at Mosul and Aleppo but ultimately subdued them. From 1174 to 1186, Salahuddin tried to unite the Muslim territories of Egypt, Palestine, Syria and Northern Mesopotamia. With the passage of time, Salahuddin gained reputation as a generous and virtuous ruler who was also devoid of cruelty as was the custom of the time.

The crusades were basically the struggle between the Christians and the Muslims for the occupation of Holy Land (Jerusalem). In all, there were eight Crusades and were fought between 1096 and 1291.

The first crusade was waged in 1096 by the Christian armies from Western Europe against Islam in Palestine and Asia Minor. The preparation for the first Crusade began after Pope Urban II at the Council of Clermont in 1195 called for the conquest of the Holy Land. The incentives for the Crusaders were glory, material gain, expansion of their territory, remission of sins, and the most important that the Crusade was considered a service to God. Pope Urban II also anticipated gaining several political advantages from the Crusade. The Crusade would have helped to unite the divided Christian kingdoms, increase papal prestige, and also minimize the differences between the western and eastern churches. In 1099, the Crusaders took Jerusalem and established the kingdom of Jerusalem and its three fiefs (Odessa, Tripoli and Antioch). The Crusaders indiscriminately massacred the Muslims and the Jewish civilians in the city. The victory of the Crusaders was mainly due to the internal political weaknesses of the Islamic world rather than military skills of the Crusaders.

The second crusade (1147-49) was inspired by St. Barnard. The Crusaders attacked Damascus but when Nur Ad-Din Zangi moved towards Damascus with his army, the Crusaders retreated. This crusade suffered due to the internal feuds among its leaders and petered out fruitlessly.

After establishing his power in Egypt and Syria, Salahuddin was ready to turn his attention towards the Latin Kingdom of Jerusalem. On July 4, 1187, Salahuddin's military genius overpowered and destroyed the army of Crusaders at Hattin near Tiberias in northern Palestine. Other important towns such as Acre, Jaffa and Ascalon were also captured by Salahuddin. On October 2, 1187, Salahuddin took Jerusalem ending its 88 years of occupation by the Franks (Latin-Christians).

The news of fall of Jerusalem into the hands of the Muslims shocked the Christian world. Soon Pope Urban III died presumbly hearing the shocking news and the new Pope Gregory VIII issued a Crusade Bull. A third crusade followed (1189-92) but due to indominatable military and political skills of Salahuddin, the crusaders failed in their bid to get Jerusalem back. The Muslims, however, lost control of Acre, Jaffa and Arsuf. With the treaty on September 2, 1192, the long and exhaustive crusades against the Muslims temporarily came to an end. In the third crusade, Salahuddin's military skills neutralized the crusading army of three great rulers of Western Europe at the time (Richard of England, Philip Augustus of France, and Frederick Barbarossa of Germany).

The fourth crusade (1202-4) was originally designed to attack Egypt center of the Muslim power in the late twelfth century but later this crusade was directed against Byzantium rather than the Muslims. The crusading army took Constantinople on the 13th April 1204 and for three days pillaged and massacred the civilians. The Crusaders finally set up the Latin kingdom of Constantinople with the Pope's blessings.

Salahuddin died on March 3, 1193 in Damascus at the age of fifty-five. The generosity and virtues of the most powerful ruler in the Muslim world can be gauged from the fact that after his death his family and friends were surprised to find that this great ruler had not left enough money to pay for his own funeral.

After Salahuddin's death, the Islamic world was once again in disarray and lacked a leader of Salahuddin's calibre. The Crusaders then managed to take back many territories including Jerusalem (taken by Frederick II in 1228 and then recaptured by the Muslims in 1244) from the Muslims until the Mamlukes arrived on the scene. The Mamlukes brought the end of the Crusades when they captured Acre in 1291, the last stronghold of the Crusaders. This also signaled the complete expulsion of the Latin Christians from Syria.

Crusades had no impact on the Islamic world rather these remained a localized and transient period in Islamic history. On the other hand, the Crusaders learned a lot while passing through many countries. The Crusaders learned about the Muslim administrative system, the Muslim culture, and the intellectual activities of the Muslim societies. Luxurious items such silk clothes and perfumes found their way in the life style of the Europeans. New trade routes were opened and an 'Age of Discoveries' slowly began in Europe. Especially, the Italians were vastly benefited by establishing trade connections in Egypt. With time the Crusades also became of little interest as the monarchs of Europe became more tolerant of Islam after realizing that the Muslims were in fact vastly cultured and intellectual people. Furthermore, by 1240, the Crusades had become a pure political game of the Papacy.

Undoubtedly, Salahuddin was one of the greatest military commanders of all time. He earned the title of al-Malik al-Nasir (King who saved the faith). Not only was he a brilliant military commander but also a sound administrator and a diplomat. He reformed the tax structure in Egypt and established departments for public works. He encouraged education and built institutes of higher learning. His diplomatic skills and the future vision of the Islamic world led him to unite and discipline many unruly Muslim rulers who alone could not have stood against the crusaders.

Like many other Muslim conquerors, Salahuddin showed a great deal of leniency towards his enemies and unlike the customs of the time did not slaughter the fallen enemy. Unlike the Christian conquest of Jerusalem, when the Muslim and the Jewish inhabitants of the city were slaughtered, Salahuddin made sure that such a barbaric act could not be repeated. After he captured

Jerusalem, he ordered his army that no harm should fall on the Christian civilians trapped in the city. He showed his friends and foes alike that even in victory one can be gentle, graceful and generous. He was also not cruel to his subordinates or to his subjects.

Salahuddin remains a captivating figure in the west despite the fact that zealous Christian scholars and historians tried to minimize the saracenic chivalry of Salahuddin. To them he was a pagan, yet he was a man of honesty, kindness and generosity.

Khwaja Muin al-Din Chishti
(1142-1236)

Contribution: The greatest of the Indian saints. Irrespective of the religious beliefs of the people of the Subcontinent, Khwaja Muin al-Din Chishti left behind enormous spiritual impact on them. He was also the founder of the Sufi order "Chishtiya".

The theologians of Islam derived their knowledge of theology and ethics either from the teachings of the Quran or the Traditions (Hadith) of the Prophet. Besides theologians and religious scholars, there were groups of thinkers who thought that direct religious experience can open new roads to knowledge and divine truth. This line of thinking and practice is known as 'mysticism'. The Arabic word of this is 'Tasawwaf' which in English became 'Sufism'. The word Suf or Sufi was probably derived from the robes of wool (suf) which early groups of Sufis are believed to have worn. For some time it was believed that the origin of the Islamic mysticism stems either from Christianity or Buddhism or even Hinduism. As a matter of fact Islamic mysticism evolved as a reaction to the worldliness of the Muslim Society. Islamic mysticism grew in different stages such as appearance of early asceticism which then developed into mysticism of divine love and then fraternal orders of mystics. With time the foreign concepts which were compatible with mystical theology and practices were incorporated into Islamic mysticism. Especially in India, Islamic mysticism was greatly influenced by the practices of Hindu mystics or saints. One also can not ignore the influence of Christian monks on the early Islamic mysticism. The idea behind a world of virtues was that by abandoning the worldly possession and repetition of the name of God in prayer, one may purify the heart and may help to move closer to God. Khwaja Muin al-Din Chishti was one such mystic who came to India and produced an enormous spiritual impact on the people of every cultural and religious background in India.

Born as Muin al-Din at Sanjan (Iran) in 1142, he is widely known as Khwaja Muin al-Din Chishti. His father Ghiyas al-Din Hasan died when Muin al-Din was only fifteen years old. He inherited an orchard which he sold and distributed the money among the poor. He then left his hometown and spent sometime in Khurasan. He wandered to many places to obtain religious education and met many Sufis of the time notably Shahab al-Din Suhrawardi and Awhad al-Din Kirmani. He then spent almost twenty years under Khwaja Osman Harooni, a spiritual and religious teacher. He settled in Baghdad for a while then left for Mecca to perform Hajj. As legend goes, while praying in Medina, he was told by the Prophet to go to India. He first came to Delhi but within a short period of time moved to Ajmir. Khwaja Muin al-Din's arrival was not welcomed by the local Hindu ruler, Pathura Rai who tried to uproot Khwaja Muin al-Din. Incidentally Shahab al-Din Muhammad of Ghur attacked India and Pathura Rai was killed in the battle. Many miracles were later attributed to Khwaja Muin al-Din.

At that time (the twelfth century), the Indian society particularly the Hindu society was divided into several caste systems and the life of the lower caste Hindus was chaotic and miserable. When Khwaja Muin al-Din started preaching Islam in India, a lot of people from the lower Hindu caste embraced Islam. Later, a large number of Hindus irrespective of their background embraced Islam due to the simple life and attractive preaching style of Khwaja Muin al-Din. If the Hindu society was plagued by the caste system, the Muslims were divided along the lines of communalism. Khwaja Muin al-Din brought the members of different religious groups and of different cultures together. He also impressed the Muslim rulers of Delhi and was their spiritual guide. Khwaja Muin al-Din died in Ajmir in 1236. His tomb became a popular place of pilgrimage and later a mausoleum was erected. Even today, people from different religious background visit his tomb. Emperor Akbar visited his tomb bare foot.

The Chishtiyah order (should not be confused with the Chishtiyah Sufi order of Abu Ishaq or Salim Chishti) brought by

Khwaja Muin al-Din Chishti is still a popular mystical order in India. His followers still preach his religious teachings.

Khwaja Muin al-Din Chisti was not a philosopher or a theologian but his greatest impact is that due to his teachings, hundreds of thousands of people in India embraced Islam and even today he is revered by both Muslims and Hindus.

Fakhr al-Din al-Razi
(1149-1209)

Contribution: Muslim theologian and scholar. His teachings and works left an indelible mark on the intellectual thinking of the Islamic world in Arabia and Iran during the twelfth and the thirteenth century. He wrote one of the most authoritative commentaries on the Quran.

Razi was born at Raay (Iran) in 1148 AD. His father was a preacher in Raay who shaped the future of Razi by giving him the lessons in theology which later made Razi famous. Razi's family claimed to be the descendants of Abu Bakar, the first caliph. Razi took special training in Islamic law, theology and philosophy. Razi mostly traveled to eastern provinces (Iran) of the Islamic caliphate in pursuit of knowledge. In Khwarizm, he got himself engaged in debates with a group of rationalist which resulted in his expulsion from there. Razi spent the next two years (1184-86) in Transoxiana, an Iranian Turkish frontier. In Transoxiana, Razi was also engaged in debates which in later years very much shaped his philosophical and theological views. He moved to Ghur (Afghanistan), where the ruler Muizz al-Din Muhammad took him under his patronage. In his court, Razi received special privileges and material compensations. In Ghur, Razi faced a staunch opposition from the representatives of the extremist Karramiya group (a Muslim anthropomorphist sect). Razi left Ghur and went to Khurasan where the ruler Aladin Tukush appointed Razi the tutor of his son and crown prince, Muhammad. By this time Razi had already become a reputed teacher and thinker. Wherever he went he debated with famous scholars and was patronized by local rulers. His fame also brought wealth to him.

Razi's theology is not based on the strict religious traditions rather is influenced by Greek philosophy, science and rational thinking. The orthodox Islamic religious thinkers were always reluctant to bring rational thinking in religious debates. Therefore, wherever Razi went he faced the opposition and criticism of his philosophical and religious views. This made him very aggressive, vengeful, irritable and short tempered. In 1203, Razi moved to Herat, settled there and died in 1210 AD.

The twelfth and the thirteenth century were unfortunate times for the Islamic world. The center of the Islamic empire, Baghdad, had lost its central authority and power which resulted in the emergence of many independent rulers in many parts of the empire. The Mongols took full advantage of the fragmented Islamic world and finally destroyed the caliphate at Baghdad. The religious unity was also destroyed with the emergence of many sects within Islam. Sunnis and Shiias became two dominant sects with rising popularity of Sufism. By the twelfth century, a line of thought emerged which tried to explain the contents of the Quran and Hadith by rational arguments based on the principles of logic. Thus efforts to erect a logical structure to rationalize the existence of God began but crumbled under the immense pressure of orthodoxy.

Before the advent of Mutazilite doctrine, the basic tenets of religious Islamic belief and fiqha were taught in madrasas but their origin and presentation in rational form was never discussed. Mutazilites, who called themselves rationalists emerged in the eighth century AD, believed that truth could be sought by using reasons given in the Quran and man has free will and creates his own acts. The group also believed that the Quran was written and is not the words of God. The rationalists, however, faced staunch opposition from the religious groups especially by the followers of Ibn Hanbal. The decline of Mutazilites was not only caused by the growing strength of Ibn Hanbal's followers in Baghdad and Damascus but with the line of thoughts developed by al-Ashari. Al-Ashari proposed that interpretation of the Quran can be justified by reasons up to a certain point and beyond that it must be simply accepted. This line of thinking was known as Ilm al-Kalam or is simply referred as 'Kalam'. Razi was one of those who adopted a middle road and tried to reconcile theology based on the revelation of the Quran and the philosophy taken from Aristotle and other Greek philosophers. He presented his philosophical and theological views in al-Mabahith al-Mashriquah (Eastern

Discourses). He also wrote commentaries on the philosophical views of Ibnsena but his greatest work was to write a comprehensive commentary on the Quran. His book known as Mafatih al-Ghayab or Kitab al-Tafsir al-Kabir (The Keys to the Unknown or The Great Commentary) was universally acclaimed and considered as one of the most authoritative commentaries on the Quran. His other widely acclaimed book is Muhassal Afkar al-Mutaqaddimin wa-al Mutaakhirin (Compendium of the Ideas of Scholars and Theologians). Outside philosophy and theology, Razi also seemed to have interest in medicine, astrology, geometry and mineralogy and he wrote many books on these topics. His intellectual brilliance and many-sided genius can be seen in his writings. Like al-Ghazali, Razi was also a reconciler (religion and philosophy) in Islam. After the fall of Mutazilites, it was left to al-Ashari, al-Ghazali and al-Razi to reconcile orthodox religious principles with rational thinking. For centuries Razi's works inspired Muslim philosophers and theologians.

Shahab ad-Din Yahya Suhrawardi
(1153-1191)

Contribution: Mystic theologian and philosopher. His works revolved around the synthesis between philosophy and mysticism. He was the founder of the Ishraqi (Illuminationist) school of philosophy which exerted a great influence on the Sufi thoughts in Iran.

Shahab ad-Din Yahya Suhrawardi should not be confused with Shah Umar al-Suhrawardi (1144-1234). Suhrawardi is a small town in Jibal province of Persia where Shahab ad-Din Suhrawardi was born in 1153 or 1154. Little is known about his early life except that he studied jurisprudence and theology at Maragha, wandered as a dervish through Iran, Anatolia and Syria and devoted his life to mystical philosophy. He finally settled in Halab (Aleppo). His earlier works were influenced by Aristotle but he leaned more towards Plato. His most important work is 'Philosophy of Illumination'. In his theory of illumination, he combines the Neo-Platonic philosophy and the theosophy of the sages of the ancient Persia. He believed that the philosophy of illumination was taught by Empedocles, Pythagoras, Plato and Zoroastrian sages. He did not separate philosophy from spirituality. In a sense he combined the hermeticism and Neo-Platonism. He regarded the external world as real and was always in touch with it. His philosophy was considered anti-Islamic from the orthodoxy's point of view. He was condemned and executed in 1191. He was not granted the title of 'martyr', therefore, he is known as al-maqtil (slain) by his followers. He was a bold and original thinker and never hid his progressive thoughts which were considered anti-Islamic by the orthodox doctors of the law and theology.

Ibnsina in his writings refer to Ishraq, the divine light which one can achieve to contact many levels of Intelligible. Many writers in later years used the term Ishraq to refer to the ancient wisdom of the east (sharq in Arabic means east). Suhrawardi was one of the writers who used the term Ishraq for the systematic formulation of theosophy.

The Islamic philosophy after a smooth sail of more than 400 years was challenged by traditionalism whose advocates were against any innovations in Islam. For time being, Islamic philosophy went underground but re-emerged in a different form. A new kind of Islamic philosophy known as Hikma (wisdom) emerged which integrated theology, philosophy and mysticism. Suhrawardi called this new wisdom as "Wisdom of Illumination". His philosophy of existence is based on the concept of "light" and "darkness". There are different levels of "light" and "darkness", depending on the level of perfection. The existence forms a single continuum that ultimately attains the form of pure light that is God. Other stages of existence are mixture of light and darkness and inferior to the pure light. Suhrawardi's views are in direct conflict with the traditional Islamic views about God and the creation of the world. The hallmark of the new wisdom was that all religions (including Zoroastrianism), the wisdom of ancient sages and philosophy (particularly Iranian and Greek philosophy) reveal the same truth. Therefore, one should combine them into one single religion which can serve all mankind (this concept of a single harmonious religion in place of many religions did exist in the teachings of many Muslim philosophers but was not openly presented).

About 50 works are attributed to Suhrawardi. These works are both philosophical as well as mystical. He wrote commentaries on the works of Plato and Aristotle and contributed tremendously to the Illuminationist school of thought. He also described different stages of mystics' journey before the mystic could achieve the esoteric knowledge. Suhrawardi founded a mystical order known as "Ishraqi" and his followers are known as "Ishraqis". The order Ishraqi combines the elements of Sufism with Hellenistic and Orphic philosophy, hermetic and Zoroastrian. The Ishraqi school of thought is based on mystical intellectualism rather than only on mysticism.

Shams-ud-Din Altamsh (Iltutmish)
(Died 1236)

Contribution: Third and the greatest sultan of the Delhi Sultanate. Due to his pious life style he is also known as the "Dervish Sultan of Delhi'. A brilliant administrator who consolidated the Muslim rule in Northern India and using his diplomatic skills avoided the Mongol invasion of India. He also vastly extended the Sultanate which stretched from Sind to Bengal.

Islam arrived in India during the seventh and the eighth century in the form of missionaries, tradesmen and military expedition. From the eleventh century onward, northern India became the battle ground of Muslim invaders who were either of Turkish or Afghan origin. Mahmud of Ghazna invaded India at least 17 times between 1001 and 1027. He went as far as Somnath but never established a central rule in India. After the fall of Ghaznavids, the Ghurids (of Ghur, a region between Ghazna and Herat in Afghanistan) rose to power. They seized the eastern Ghaznavid empire and by 1186, destroyed the remaining Ghaznavid power in the northwest. Muhammad of Ghur conquered the Punjab (which was under the control of Ghaznavids) and in 1192, removed the last hurdle in northern India by defeating the strong and talented Rajput leader Pirthviraj.

In 1193, Delhi was conquered by Muhammad of Ghur but was left into the hands of a Hindu king who paid tribute to Ghur. Muhammad of Ghur then returned to Ghazna leaving behind his most trusted slave, Qutub ud-Din Aybak in charge. This was the beginning of the so-called slave dynasty in India. In 1193, Aybak moved his capital from Lahore to Delhi and began a campaign of expansion. He added Benaras (1194), Kannauj (1199) and Kalinjar (1202) to the Delhi Sultanate. After the death of Muhammad of Ghur (1206), Aybak assumed the authority of Ghurid territory in India. Aybak, however, faced a challenge to his authority by one

136

of another slaves of Muhammad of Ghur, Taj-ud-Din Yildiz. Aybak defeated Yildiz (1208), captured Ghazna but quickly lost and Yildiz established his own rule in Ghazna and its surroundings. Aybak died in 1210 in a polo accident in Lahore. After Aybak's death, his son-in-law Altamsh became the Sultan of Delhi.

Altamsh (also spelled Iltutmish) was a Mamlukes by origin and was sold into slavery. In the Muslim political system of the time, the slaves were considered very important in military and government. Many talented slaves rose to great heights, became capable administrators or some even became well known rulers. Very little is known about the early life of Altamsh except that he was a slave of Aybak and was married to his daughter. Altamsh assumed throne in 1211 and ruled till his death in 1236.

By the time Altamsh assumed the throne of Delhi, the territory of Muhammad of Ghur was reduced in size. Muhammad of Ghur's former slave, Yildiz was driven out of Ghazna by Aladin Khwarizm Shah and Yildiz started claiming that he was the real successor of Muhammad of Ghur. At the battle of Tarain, Altamsh defeated and captured Yildiz, who then died in prison. Another threat came from the Hindu rulers who wanted to recover their lost territory due to the conquest of Muhammad of Ghur but could not unite themselves with enough military strength to pose a serious challenge to Altamsh's authority. Then came the most serious threat of the Mongol invasion of India. Altamsh's excellent political talents can be judged by his efforts to avoid direct conflict with the Mongols. After the defeat of Aladin Khwarizm Shah by Genghis Khan, his heir to the throne, Jalal ud-Din Khwarizm Shah fled to India. He sought military aid from Altamsh which he wisely refused but also did not take any attempt to hand him over to the Mongols. This diplomacy worked and the danger of a Mongol invasion of India was avoided.

Then Bengal rebelled. Altamsh in 1226 defeated Ghiyas ud-Din Iwaz Khalji, the rebel governor of Bengal. By 1229, Altamsh gained complete control of Bengal after the last Khalji chief Balka was defeated and killed. Meanwhile, Altamsh had to defend the Sultanate against the claims of Nasir-ud-Din Qabacha, another former slave of Muhammad of Ghur, who tried to hold Lahore and Multan under his control. In 1228, Altamsh drove Qabacha out of Multan and Uch, thus securing his frontiers. He also extended the

Sultanate by capturing Ranthambhor (1226), Mandawar (1227) and Gwaliar (1231). By the time of his death (1236), the Delhi Sultanate stretched from Sind to Bengal.

Despite the presence of Muslims in India since the beginning of the eighth century, there was no central Muslim kingdom. The Muslim invaders came from the northern frontiers of India, pillaged certain parts of Indian territory and then returned to their original country. This situation however, changed with the emergence of Muhammad of Ghur on the scene. He left behind his trusted slave Aybak to look after his conquered territories. Ghur died at Lahore in 1206 and Aybak took control of his conquered lands. In reality it was Aybak who established the Delhi Sultanate and thus a Muslim Raj based in India emerged. But the man who consolidated and strengthened the Delhi Sultanate was Altamsh. Without his political and military skills it would have been very difficult to sustain power in the treacherous political environment of the time. He made the Delhi Sultanate an independent power which was no longer subordinate to either Ghazna or Ghur. The status of Delhi changed, rather than being a frontier outpost, it became the center of the Muslim power and culture in India. Altamsh transformed the city of Delhi by building mosques, waterworks and other amenities to make the city look like a seat of government. He expanded the Sultanate and set up administrative machinery.

In his personal life, Altamsh was a devout Muslim and lived a simple and pious life. Yet he was tolerant of Hindus and other religions and despite that some religious leaders and his advisors suggested to enforce Islam on the majority, Altamsh wisely refrained from doing so. He gave an excellent education to his daughter Raziyya and nominated her to be his successor. Raziyya reigned for four years (1236-40) after Altamsh death. This indicates Altamsh open mindness and progressive thinking as this was very much against the political culture of the time. His major contribution is that he strengthened the Muslim rule in India whose seat of power was in India. As far as his personal achievement is concerned, he rose from a slave to a remarkable ruler.

Muhammad Ibn al-Arabi
(1165-1240)

Contribution: Renowned Muslim mystic philosopher. He explored the esoteric mystical Islamic thoughts in full-fledged philosophical terms. In his writings, he presented a synthesis of astrological signs, alphabetical and numerical symbolism and the science of mysticism. His works produced tremendous influence on Islamic mysticism and esoteric speculation both in the east and the west.

Ibn Arabi was born in Mauracia (Spain) in 1165 AD. He was of pure Arab blood and belonged to a prominent Arab tribe of Tai. He received his early education in Seville, an outstanding center of Islamic culture and learning at that time. In Seville, Ibn Arabi studied traditional Islamic philosophy and proved to be a brilliant student of this discipline. The students of Islamic philosophy generally learned such subjects such as cosmology, metaphysical aspects of Islam, and analysis of numbers and letters for hidden meaning. While at Seville, Ibn Arabi developed interest in mysticism and learned this art from many mystical masters. He traveled to various cities of Spain and North Africa in search of knowledge and mystical enlightenment. While visiting Cordoba, Arabi met great Muslim philosopher Ibn Rushd (Averroes; 1126-98). Ibn Rushd was a close friend of Arabi's father and had asked to meet the young man who was already known for his knowledge and intelligence. The views of Ibn Rushd and Arabi were quite opposite; Ibn Rushd believed that reasoning is the foundation of knowledge and wisdom whereas Arabi believed that knowledge resulted from spiritual vision. Ibn Rushd, however, recognized the fact that Arabi's views, knowledge and understanding were far superior than most of the contemporary thinkers.

In 1198, after a vision in which he felt that he had been ordered to leave Spain and go to east, Arabi then went to Mecca for pilgrimage which proved to be very important for the development of his thoughts. He stayed in Mecca for four years and devoted his time in studying, writing and taking part in public discussions. In Mecca, after a divine vision, he started writing his most famous book, al-Futuhat al-Makkiyya (The Meccan Revelations). In this book he envisioned the universe as an endless flow of existence from the Divine Being (God). The book consists of 560 chapters and deals with sayings of earlier Sufis, principles of metaphysics and the spiritual views of Arabi. While in Mecca, impressed by the beauty and intelligence of the young daughter of a friend (Abu Shuja Ibn Rustam), Arabi wrote a collection of romantic poems known as Tarjuman al-Ashwaq (The Interpreter of Love). His expression of love was so candid that orthodox Muslims condemned his poetry and prohibited the reading of the book.

From Mecca, Ibn Arabi went to Egypt and then to Anatolia, where in Qunya he met Sadr ad-Din al-Qunawi. Qunawi became Arabi's student and later his successor in the east. From Qunya, Arabi visited Baghdad and Aleppo. His journey finally ended in 1223 in Damascus where he eventually settled and devoted rest of his life to teaching and writing. He died in Damascus on November 16, 1240.

Arabi's philosophical views as well as the ideals of Sufism brought him fame and notoriety. By the time he arrived in Damascus (1223), he was already well known in the Islamic world. He was known among the Sufis as 'the greatest Sheikh'.

Arabi's another well known and probably the most important work in mystical philosophy is 'Fusus al-Hikam (Gems of Wisdom, 1230). In this book which consists of 27 chapters, Arabi described the basic doctrines of Islamic esotericism. In this book he presented the concept of 'Perfect Man'. Such a man manifests the nature of God, is master of knowledge and has enlightened himself. According to Arabi, such a 'Perfect Man' exists in the sequence of prophets (from Adam to Muhammad), he described Prophet Muhammad being the most perfect of the prophetic manifestations. This book made him a reputable thinker of highest order though his writings are difficult to understand due to lack of coherence.

The main theme of Ibn Arabi's doctrine is the 'Unity of Being' or 'Existence'. Though controversial in its meaning, it could mean that there exist nothing except God and all else is either unreal or is a part of God. On the other hand, it could also mean that only God is Necessary Being, existing by His Own Nature whereas all other beings owe their existence to the act of creation.

His works influenced the future generations of Sufis both in eastern and western hemisphere. To Ibn Arabi, love is the apex of mysticism not the knowledge as it is love which makes the Divine Union possible. His mystical views had great influence especially on Persian mystical poetry. His works are continued to be studied in the Subcontinent, North Africa and Middle East. There are evidence which suggest that Ibn Arabi may have some influence on the thinking and writings of Dante Alighieri whose works seem to be parallel with the spiritual quest of Sufis.

Sheikh Mosleh ud-Din Sadi
(1200-1291)

Contribution: One of the towering figures in classical Persian literature. He was Iran's greatest ethical and worldly-wise poet. He wrote two famous literary classics (The Orchard and The Rose Garden). These books consist of Sadi's experiences and views on love, religion and many aspects of life.

Muslihuddin Sadi also known as Sheikh Sadi (also written as Saadi or Sa'di), was born in Shiraz on 1200 AD. His father was a court official of Sad Ibn Zangi, the ruler of Fars province. After the death of Sadi's father, Sad Zangi assumed the responsibility of the young child (due to this patronage, Sadi was grateful to Sad Zangi and probably assumed his pen name Sadi after his benefactor). After finishing his schooling in Shiraz, Sadi was sent to Nizamiya College at Baghdad, probably one of the finest educational institutes of the time. At Nizamiya College, Sadi did not seem to have much interest in academics and spent most of his time socializing and enjoying. While at Baghdad, Sadi studied under the renowned Sufi, Sheikh Shahabuddin Suhrawardi. Between 1226 and 1256, Sadi traveled widely. He wandered all over the Middle East and parts of North Africa. He visited Iraq, Syria, Turkey, Egypt, Arabia and India. He went to Mecca for pilgrimage. He also traveled in the company of Dervishes or the members of the Sufi order. This way of traveling was not only safe but also helped Sadi to understand the Sufi practices and later helped him for his didactic works.

His journeys were not without incidents. On one occasion he was captured by Christian Crusaders and he won his freedom from his captors when one of his friends paid 10 Dinars to the Crusaders. While in India he ran into trouble when he criticized Hindus for their superstition. He finally returned to Shiraz and settled there and wrote his experiences about different cultures and religions. Indeed his travel to the different parts of the world added to his knowledge and observations which he had described skillfully both in his verses and prose.

In the thirteenth century, Mongol invasions brought disaster to the Islamic world. In 1258, the Mongols sacked Baghdad and killed almost three-quarters of its population. Though Sadi was safe and sound in Shiraz (mainly due to the diplomacy of Abu Bakar Ibn Sad, the ruler of Fars), the events in Baghdad deeply moved Sadi and he composed a eulogy to mark the fall of Baghdad, the then a seat of Islamic culture and power. Sadi died in 1292 in Shiraz.

Sadi's fame lies in his two most famous books Bustan (The Orchard) and Gulistan (The Rose Garden). Both these books depict Sadi's skill as master of the Persian language. The books provide enormous information about the era and the culture in which Sadi lived. Bustan was completed in 1257 and was written entirely in verses using the Masnavi (also spelled mathnawi) style of rhymed couplets. Bustan is collection of Sadi's moral teachings and different aspects of life reflecting literary, religious and folk themes. The Gulistan or Rose Garden was composed in both verses and prose and contains Sadi's personal experiences, love as well as humorous stories, aphorisms, anecdotes, maxims and advice. The verses in the Rose Garden were written in quatrains. Sadi also wrote a collection of lyrical poems in Arabic and Persian known as 'Divan'. Divan is biographical in nature and was completed by the end of his life.

Though Sadi wrote many Quasidas (poems generally written to praise somebody), Ghazals (poems which consist of 6 to 15 couplets expressing a unity of thoughts and have monorhythmic pattern) and Rubayaat (quatrains), he is best known to the West due to Bustan and Gulistan. Both Bustan and Gulistan made Sadi a literary giant and his fame as a poet and wise man spread beyond the borders of Iran. He was well known in Arabia and India and till today his name as a gigantic literary figure survives in these parts of the world. The writings of Sadi have been part of Iranian culture and literature for more than 700 years. The West, however, could not enjoy the wisdom and thoughts behind Sadi's poetries until the beginning of the twentieth century. Due to the difficulties in translating the lyrical poems of a poet from one language to the other, Sadi's real prowess as a literary giant will be difficult to assess in the West.

Sadi's poetry, unlike Rumi, is didactic rather than mystical. His love for mankind is earthly not spiritual. His experience, knowledge and teachings come from every day life. The influence of Sadi on the Persian language can be gauged from the fact that it is said that in Iran only the Quran is quoted more than Sadi's literary work. Sadi's influence on Persian language and literature equals to the influence of Shakespeare in English language and literature.

Jalaluddin Rumi
(1207-1273)

Contribution: The greatest Sufi poet in the Persian language. He is famous for his lyrics and spiritual couplets. Rumi exerted a great and long lasting influence on Sufi doctrine and practices. He was founder of Mevlavi Sufi order.

Jalaluddin Rumi, also known as 'Maulana Rum', was born at Balkh (Afghanistan) on September 30, 1207 AD. His father, Bahaduddin Walad was a mystical theologian and a teacher. Due to the approaching Mongol threat (led by Genghis Khan), Bahaduddin Walad gathered his family and left Balkh in 1218, passed through Iran, went to Mecca for pilgrimage and for time being settled in Rum (Anatolia), hence the surname Rumi. Anatolia at that time was under the rule of Seljuks and was enjoying peace and prosperity. In 1228, the family moved to Quanya (Turkey). In Quanya Bahaduddin Walad became a teacher in a Muslim religious school (madrasah). After the death of his father, Rumi started giving lessons. Burhanuddin Muhaquiq, a student of Rumi's father taught Rumi Sufi doctrine and Sufi practices.

Throughout his life, Rumi seemed to be influenced by theologians and mystics. The influences of these people are very much apparent in his thinking and poetry. Ibn-Arabi (1165-1240), one of the leading Muslim theologists of the time was one of the mentors of Rumi. Ibn-Arabi's student Sadruddin al-Qunawi was a friend of Rumi in Quanya and probably had a great deal of influence on Rumi's religious thinking. However, the man who turned Rumi into a mystical poet was a Dervish known as Shamshuddin Tabriz. Rumi met Shamshuddin in 1244 and was immediately impressed by his personality. Shamshuddin revealed the divine majesty to Rumi and the two became very close friends. This Sufi companionship, however, led Rumi to neglect his family and disciples. Ultimately in 1246, Rumi's family and disciples forced Shamshuddin to leave Quanya. Shamshuddin's departure caused great devastation to Rumi and finally Rumi's eldest son brought Shamshuddin back to Quanya. With the passage of time, Rumi's Sufi relationship with Shamshuddin became intense. Rumi's family, however, could not tolerate the close relationship between Rumi and Shamshuddin and one night in 1247, Shamshuddin disappeared. It is widely believed that Shamshuddin was murdered and hurriedly buried by Rumi's sons. Shamshuddin's sudden disappearance bewildered Rumi and turned him into a poet. Several years after Shamshuddin's death, Rumi formed mystical companionship with Salahuddin Zakrab (an illiterate goldsmith) and after his death Husamuddin Chelebi became Rumi's mystical companion.

Shamshuddin Tabriz left an indelible mark on the life and the poetry of Rumi. Rumi's overwhelming mystical love for Shamshuddin resulted in mystical poems (verses and rubayaats (quatrains)). Rumi used to go to enjoy nature and the radiant beauty of sun reminded him of Shamshuddin which means 'Sun of Religion'. In most of his poems, Rumi expressed his mystical love for Shamshuddin by inserting Shamshuddin's name instead of his own name (Rumi) as he found Shamshuddin in himself. The Divan-e-Shams (collected poetry of Shamsh) consists of Persian verses inspired by intense Sufi relationship between Shamshuddin and Rumi. It contains 35,000 lines of verses and was written over a thirty year period. The book consists of Ghazals based on mystical love and relationship. These verses were probably written when Rumi was experiencing the ecstasy of whirling or meditation.

Rumi's fame lies in his lyrics and didactic epic Masnavi-e-Manavi (Spiritual Couplets). Masnavi (also spelled mathnawi) though disjointed (the stories do not follow any order), is a masterpiece of lyrical description. Masnavi consists of 25,700 couplets expressing Sufi love and didactic commentary with ecstatic reflections. Rumi's poetry is composed of tales, anecdotes, human expression of mystical experiences and the reflections in the beauty of nature. For forty years, Rumi tried to illustrate the Sufi doctrine, thoughts and teachings in his poems.

Divan-e-Shams and Masnavi-e-Manavi have put Rumi as a first rank Persian poet. Rumi's poetry revolves around Sufism, though it is not systematic but he has communicated his views with immense artistic dedications, love, virtue, conviction and inspiration. In his writings he tried to reveal the nobility of human spirit. His lyrics and rhythms can also place him with Hafiz and Sadi (masters of Ghazals). Rumi was also a master of quatrain but his views may be quite opposite to Omar Khayyam. Omar Khayyam questioned the existence of God as well as immortality of the soul whereas Rumi's poetry was dedicated to the passionate love of God. Rumi also wrote a prose treatise known as Fihi Ma Fihi (What is Within is Within). This book is basically the compilation of his lectures and discussions with his students.

Rumi died in 1273 before finishing Masnavi. His mausoleum in Quanya is visited by thousands of followers and Sufis. After his death, Husamuddin became the leader of Rumi's disciples. After Husamuddin's death, Rumi's eldest son, Sultan Walad became the leader and organized the Sufi order 'Mevlevi' (founded by Rumi), its members are known as whirling Dervishes.

Rumi believed in the philosophy of oneness that is the love of one human spirit for another which finally unites them as one in the love of God. His concept of 'Perfect Man' is the one who identifies his oneness with God. Rumi, in order to express love and mystical experiences, combines intellect and imagination which appeals to the heart and soul. Rumi was not a theologian or philosopher but a poet of highest order and a philanthropist.

Ruknuddin Baybars I
(1223-1277)

Contribution: Fourth and the most famous of the Mamluke Sultans of Egypt and Syria. He rose from slavery to become the most eminent ruler of Mamluke dynasty. Baybars was a brilliant military commander and administrator. He led an army which defeated the Mongols which started the decline of Mongol military might.

The Abbasid caliphs used to recruit slaves from Central Asia and the caucuses, Spain and Africa into their armies. These military slaves were of distinct category and had different status and privileges than the non-military slaves. The Mamlukes were military slaves or freedmen for generations brought from central Asia and were employed by many Muslim rulers. A group of such slaves established a dynasty that ruled Egypt and Syria between 1250 and 1517, until defeated by the Ottomans. The Mamlukes were brought to Egypt by the Ayubbids.

Baybars, originally a Kipchak Turk, was born on 1223 on the northern shores of Black sea. In 1242, the Mongols invaded the area and Baybars was sold as a slave in Anatolia. After serving many masters, he finally landed into the hands of Sultan Najmuddin Ayub of Egypt. Baybars was sent to a military academy established by the Sultan for intelligent and skilled slaves. Baybars demonstrated outstanding military skills and was appointed the commander of the Sultan's bodyguards. Later Baybars led many military campaigns as the commander of the Ayubbid army against several adversaries. One of his early victories as a commander was achieved against a Crusader army led by Louis IX of France, whom he defeated in February 1250. Louis IX was captured but was later released in exchange of a large ransom. Within a short period of time, the Mamlukes gained enough strength to murder Ayubbid Sultan Toran Shah. The

Mamlukes took control of Egypt and Sultan Aybak became the first Mamluke ruler of Egypt. Baybars, however, angered the Sultan and was forced to flee to Syria along with other Mamluke officials. He spent 10 years in Syria, then in 1260, the third Mamluke Sultan Saifuddin Qutuz welcomed Baybars and his companions back to Egypt. On September 3, 1260, the Mamlukes inflicted a severe defeat on the Mongols near Nablus in Palestine. The Mongol general was killed and the legend of Mongol invincibility and conquest was over. Following the victory at Nabulus, Baybars anticipated a suitable reward from Sultan Qutuz but was disappointed when he did not get from the Sultan what he wanted. During a quarrel, the Mamlukes killed Sultan Qutuz (1260) and Baybars became the fourth sultan of the Mamlukes.

Immediately after assuming the throne, Baybars started consolidating and strengthening his military positions in Egypt and Syria. In Syria, he rebuilt the fortresses destroyed by the Mongols, added new arsenals, built new warships and cargo vessels. His main objectives were to crush the Crusaders and secure the Egyptian and Syrian borders from Mongol attacks. He started by undertaking the task of uniting the Muslims of Syria and Egypt into a single state. Between 1265 and 1271, his campaigns against the Crusaders ended their hopes that they would ever rise against Islam again. During this period he captured Arsuf, Atlit, Haifa, Jaffa and Antioch from the Crusaders which broke the backbone of their military campaigns. Mongols, though, not as strong as before their defeat in 1260, kept attacking Syria from both north and east. Baybars not only blunted their attack on Syria but engaged the Mongols of Persia and fought nine battles with them. In Syria, Baybars also turned his attentions towards a fanatic Islamic sect known as 'Assassins'. By 1273, he wiped them out completely from Syria. The Christian Armenians and the Muslim Seljuks, who were allies of the Mongols, also faced the wrath of Baybars. He first destroyed the Armenians then defeated the Seljuks and their Mongol allies. He also sent military expeditions to Libya and Nubia to secure the Egyptian borders in the south and the west.

The Crusaders were still a threat to Islam. Baybars military expeditions against the Latin-Christians states in the Middle East reduced them to coastal posts. He took Caesarea, Haifa and Arsuf from the Christians in 1265. He also conquered Galilee in 1266 and in 1268 he captured Antioch from the Christians. His victories against Latin-Christians were so impressive that by 1291, the Mamlukes managed to expel them from the Holy Land and Syria.

Apart from his military skills, Baybars also demonstrated high levels of diplomacy, administrative and political skills. He established friendly ties with the Byzantine emperor Michael VIII Palaeologus in Constantinople. In turn, the Byzantine emperor allowed the Egyptian merchants to sail through the Bosporus and Black sea. He also established friendly ties with the Sicilian king Manfred by sending an ambassador to his court (1261). He signed commercial treaties with James I of Aragon and Alfonso X of Leon and Castile.

As an administrator, Baybars also worked for the well being of his people. He built canals, roads, mosques and schools. He established a regular and fast postal system between Cairo and Damascus. He appointed judges representing the four main Islamic Schools of Law (Hanafi, Hanbli, Maliki and Shafii), indicating his open mindness and tolerance against different Islamic sects. Personally he was a devout Muslim. During his reign he prohibited the selling and drinking of alcohol. He was a generous almsgiver and encouraged others to do so. He facilitated the pilgrimage to Mecca and sponsored Muslim schools and mosques. Baybars died on July 1, 1277 after drinking a cup of poison intended for someone else. He was buried under the dome of al-Zahiriya library, which he had established.

Due to his achievements many consider Baybars as the founder of the Mamluke dynasty. A close examination of Baybars achievements will indicate that he stopped the annihilation of the Islamic world. He emerged on the scene at a time when the Islamic world in the Middle East was in chaos. Between the crusaders and the Mongols, Egypt, Syria and Palestine would have been divided ending the Muslim rule and power in the region. Overall, Baybars personally commanded 15 military campaigns and was never defeated. For seventeen years he played the roles of a warrior, ruler and reformer.

Muhammad Ibn Taymiyya
(1263-1328)

Contribution: Muslim theologian and Jurist. He is an important figure in fundamentalist strand of Islam. His works led to a religious movement (Wahhabis) in the eighteenth century with political implications.

Ibn Taymiyya was born in Haran (Mesopotamia) in 1263 but grew up in Damascus. Due to the Mongol invasion, his father in 1268 moved the family to Damascus. Ibn Taymiyya belonged to a Syrian family of scholars who followed the Hanbali school of thought. By the age of 20, he completed his study and was well versed in the Quranic sciences, Hadith, law and theology. Based on the Quran and Hadith, he defended the traditions of earlier Muslims but his arguments were not appreciated by the scholars of other orthodox Islamic schools. In 1292, he went to Mecca for pilgrimage. From Mecca, he went to Egypt where his teachings displeased the Shafiis and they incited the public opinion against him. Ibn Taymiyya lost his job as a teacher but in the same year (1299) he was appointed to preach against the Mongols to initiate a holy war. He was present in Damascus at the victory over the Mongols at Shakhab (near Damascus).

Ibn Taymiyya was imprisoned in Egypt and Syria several times for his political and religious beliefs. In Cairo (1306-7), he was accused of being an anthropomorphist (due to his literary interpretation of the Quran) and was imprisoned for a year and a half. He was released to return to Damascus but was forced back to Cairo and was imprisoned for a second time for a year and a half. While in prison, he taught Islamic laws and the principles of Islam to other prisoners. He was released (1309) but within a few days was again imprisoned in the fortress of Alexandria for eight months. After his release he returned to Cairo. The Fatimid Sultan, al-Nasir asked him to take revenge against his enemies which he declined and simply accepted a teaching position in the school founded by al-Nasir.

Ibn Taymiyya was once again imprisoned in August 1320 for refusing the Sultan's order that he should not give his opinions on the oath of repudiation. Five months later he was released but his adversaries objected to his opinion on visiting the tombs of the saints and Sufis and offering prayers over there. They incited the Sultan who imprisoned him in July 1326 in the citadel of Damascus. While in prison, Ibn Taymiyya wrote a commentary on the Quran and prepared a response to his critics. When his adversaries came to know about his writings, he was deprived of his books and writing materials. He sought relief in prayer and the recitation of the Quran but soon fell ill and died on September 26, 1328. The people of Damascus bestowed a great honor on him. His funeral was attended by more than twenty thousand people. He was buried in the Sufi cemetery. Many considered him a saint and his grave became a place of pilgrimage which he would have disapproved.

Ibn Taymiyya left behind a considerable amount of written work, rich in narration, style and polemic. Al-Siyasat al-Sharia (Treatise on Judicial Politics), translated in French and English, and Minahaj al-Sunnah (The Way of Tradition) a work on comparative theology are his two most famous books.

Ibn Taymiyya took the Quran in its literally sense. He opposed the innovations in religious practices. He accepted the existence of the saints and the Sufis but opposed the idea of visiting their tombs and offering prayers over the tombs. He criticized the Greek philosophy and its Islamic interpretation by declaring that philosophy leads to unbelief and creates many differing opinions. He maintained that these differing opinions had also crept in the bosom of Islam therefore, he believed that a return to revelation and tradition would help in uniting the divided Muslim community. He was critical of such gigantic Muslim philosophers like al-Ghazali, Ibn Arabi and Ibnsena. He rejected the interpretation of the mystical experiences of Ibn Arabi maintaining that man was a created being and can not be absorbed into God's being. Man could only come nearer to God by being obedient and by following His revealed Will.

Ibn Taymiyya, though, recognized the legitimacy of the first four caliphs, he was somewhat critical of Caliphs Omar and Ali. He was in favor of more than one ruler rather one Caliphate but believed that a ruler should be just and be able to keep individuals within their limits. He was less concerned with a ruler's approach of obtaining power but put a lot of emphasis on how a ruler used his power. He maintained that a just ruler should apply the religious law strictly and the people under his jurisdiction should obey his authority. The revolt or disobedience to the ruler was only justified when the ruler went against the command of God or/and His prophet.

Ibn Taymiyya belonged to Hanbali school of thought but never followed its teachings blindly. In his writings he claimed to follow the Quran and Hadith but did not hesitate to employ reasons by analogy. He played an important role in an attempt to revitalize the Muslim society of his time by advocating a return to the sources of Islam (the Quran and the Sunnah). He might not have achieved a significant success towards his goal mainly due to different religious sects or schools and their opposition to his views but his writings and teachings led to a religious movement almost five hundred years after his death. He became the source of Wahhabism, a strictly traditionalist group founded by Ibn Abd al-Wahhab (1703-92) in the eighteenth century. The movement led to the creation of modern Saudi Arabia and Wahhabism has its foothold in Qatar, India, Africa and Central Asia. In Egypt, in the early twentieth century, Muhammad Abduh's Reform Party was also influenced by the views and the writings of Ibn Taymiyya.

Ibn Taymiyya's political and religious enemies considered him as an eccentric or sometimes even as an heretic, but there were many who respected him and considered him a saint. His fundamentalist brand of Islam provided the orthodoxy with the tools which halted the progressive thinking within the Islamic world and caused serious damage to the rationalist movements for centuries to come.

Mahmud Ghazan
(1271-1304)

Contribution: The greatest Mongol Il-Khans (subordinate to Khakhan or Khan) of Iran who embraced Islam which resulted in the conversion of Il-Khanate to Islamic state. He fought many wars against the Mamlukes of Egypt. He was one of the rare Mongol rulers with reform mind and intellectual taste.

After the defeat of the Mongols at the Goliath Spring near Nazareth on September 3, 1260 by the Mamlukes, the legend of Mongol invincibility and conquest came to an end. The empire of Genghis Khan suffered from the internal feud and was divided among his descendents. Kublai Khan remained in China as the last great Khan but the Russian Khanate was divided into three: the Khanate of the Golden Horde, the White Horde, and the Khanate of Persia which included much of Asia Minor, Iraq and Iran.

It was in the Khanate of Persia Mahmud Ghazan, a descendent of Genghis Khan was born on November 5, 1271. His father Arghan was a grand son of Hilagu (a grand son of Genghis Khan) and was a Buddhist by faith. Ghazan himself was brought up in the Buddhist faith and before converting to Islam was a staunch Buddhist and had ordered the construction of many Buddhist temples. Ghazan spent his early childhood with his grandfather Abagha (1265-82). In 1284, when his father assumed throne, Ghazan was appointed governor of northeastern Iran where for the next 10 years he defended the territories against the attacks of Chagtai Mongols. After the death of Arghan, his brother Gaykhatu became the Il-Khan (1291) but was murdered in 1295 and his cousin Baydu was enthroned as Il-Khan in April 1295. His accession was challenged by Ghazan and with the help of an old adversary, Nawruz, Ghazan managed to defeat and capture Baydu in the autumn of 1295, who was then executed. Nawruz was a military commander of Khurasan when Ghazan was governor there but Nawruz had revolted against him. For the reasons best known to Nawruz, he decided to side with Ghazan for his bid to the throne. Nawruz, a long time Muslim, convinced Ghazan that for political advantage he should embrace Islam. Ghazan's conversion to Islam was publicly proclaimed on June 19, 1295. He acquired the name of 'Mahmud'. Upon his entry in Tabriz, Ghazan announced that Islam was the official religion of the Khanate.

On November 3, 1295, Ghazan officially became Il-Khan. He immediately faced several revolts against his authority which he crushed ruthlessly executing many Mongol princes. Nawruz, the man responsible for his conversion to Islam and accession to the throne was also executed on the charges of treason. During the early part of his reign, Ghazan mainly focused on the internal security and reliability of his advisors and military commanders. By 1299, the focus changed towards the frontier. Although, Ghazan himself was reputed as a formidable military commander and had a strong army, he was surrounded by many foes against whom he had to defend his territories. In the northeast, he faced the frequent attacks of Chagtai Khanate, a descendents of Genghis Khan's second son Chagtai. In the northwest, he faced the Khanate of Kipchak who was descendent of Genghis Khan's grandson Batu. The Khan of Kipchak had embraced Islam earlier than any other Mongol dynasties. They also had strong friendly ties with the Mamlukes of Egypt. In the southwest, Mamlukes were a perpetual enemy of the Mongols. In fact the Mamlukes were the first to defeat a Mongol army in 1260 and were always willing to repel Mongol invasion in the Middle East. There were many battles between Mamlukes and Ghazan. In one of the first such battles, Ghazan inflicted a crushing defeat over them on December 22, 1299 and entered into Damascus triumphantly. Upon Ghazan's return to Iran, Mamlukes however, recaptured the lost territory. In the autumn of 1300, Ghazan invaded Syria for the second time but poor weather (rain, flood and cold) kept the two armies apart. In 1301, both sides half-heartedly tried to reach a friendly settlement which soon fell apart.

Before the third campaign against the Mamlukes, Ghazan sought alliance with the Christian Europe. He wrote a letter (April 12, 1302) to Pope Boniface VIII providing the details of his invasion of Syria. In the autumn of 1302, Ghazan led a third campaign (without the help of the Christians) against the Mamlukes but left the conduct of the campaign to his commanders and returned to Euphrates in April 1303. The two armies met in the vicinity of Damascus and after a bloody battle (April 19-20, 1303), the Mamlukes inflicted a heavy defeat on the Mongols. Ghazan planned a fourth campaign against the Mamlukes in the spring of 1304 but by 1303 he fell sick. His movements were badly curtailed. He left Tabriz for Baghdad in September 1303 but the winter snow hampered his advances and he remained stranded in Western Iran. He decided to return to Khurasan but died at Quazvin (northwest Iran) on May 11, 1304. He was only 33 years old. Within thirty years after Ghazan's death the Khanate of Persia crumbled.

With the death of Kublai Khan in China in 1294, the slim unity of Mongol empire was gone. Though Ghazan broke the Mongol tradition and became a Muslim, the war between the Mamlukes and the Mongols did not cease until the death of Ghazan (1304). With Ghazan's death, a fifty years dream of Mongol conquest of Near East came to an end.

Ghazan was the last of the great Il-Khans. By the standards of his predecessors he was civilized. He had great intellectual curiosity and appeared to be quite well familiar with history, medicine and chemistry. He was also versed in many languages (Arabic, Persian, Chinese and probably French). Like other Il-Khans, Ghazan was also a great patron of history. He asked his Prime Minister, Rashad Din to compile the history of Mongols which was then extended to the history of Asian and European peoples with whom Mongols came in contact.

On the administrative side, Ghazan proved himself to be far superior to his Mongol predecessors in taking responsibility towards his subjects. He reformed the agricultural system which improved the plight of peasants. He encouraged trade, built roads and bridges, standardized weights and measures and established custom posts on the frontiers of his empire. He also acted to assimilate the Mongols into the traditional Islamic culture. He built mosques, schools, madrasas, and mausoleums. He paid enormous attention in building his capital Tabriz which became a major international trade route linking China, Russia and India.

Overall, as needed he was as ruthless and brutal as his Mongol predecessors but he also had a cultural and benign side which made him different than other Mongol rulers. He was a ruler with a passion for his subjects and worked to improve their conditions and tried to establish a social justice in his empire.

Mansa Musa
(1280-1337)

Contribution: King of Mali in West Africa. He was a political and cultural force in West Africa during the fourteenth century. His empire stretched to the edges of the Sahara, the tropical rain forest, the Atlantic and the borders of modern Nigeria. He developed Saharan trade, introduced brick buildings and founded Timbuktu as a world center of learning at the time. He promoted Islamic culture and intellectualism in the region and brought peace and prosperity to Mali.

Mansa Musa belonged to Kaita clan, whose members were the rulers of the West African state of Mali since 1250 AD. Musa was the ninth ruler of Mali and a grandnephew of its founder Sanjata. Very little is known about Musa's childhood. Though it is not known whether the founder of the dynasty, Sanjata, was a Muslim but probably Musa was brought up and educated as a Muslim. Musa succeeded his father Abu Bakar II to the throne in 1312.

Musa built a strong and growing empire in West Africa. Malian armies captured the Songhai principality of Gao, east of the Niger River. Musa controlled the lands of the middle Niger, Timbuktu and Gao, imposed his rule on South Sahara and Taghaza region in the north. In the east the boundaries of his empire reached to contemporary Nigeria and in the west he conquered Takrur and Fulani.

Under the rule of Musa, Mali achieved the level of wealth and international prestige which was never seen before in West Africa. Mali's main source of income was the export of gold to Mediterranean across Sahara where the European merchants purchased them. The demand for gold was very high in the European markets which helped Mali economically. The revenue earned from gold was used by Musa for the well being of his subjects.

Mansa Musa proved to be a highly skilled administrator with a vision. Due to Musa's effort, Timbuktu grew to become an important commercial city in West Africa having commercial caravan connection with Egypt and other trade centers in North Africa. The internal commerce and prosperity flourished as the traders of Mali were active throughout West Africa. Northbound caravans carried numerous products such as ivory, nut and hide. In turn, southbound trade brought products such as perfumes, papers, books, textiles and spices from North Africa and the Mediterranean. Musa established friendly ties with Egypt, Morocco and other African countries. His ties with his African neighbors facilitated the growth of Trans-Saharan trade, which in turn enriched Mali and strengthened Musa's rule. Musa founded the University of Sankora and inspired the architectural innovation in Mali and Songhai Empire.

Musa was actively involved in spreading Islam and building Islamic institutions. He built enormous number of mosques in his empire. He brought intellectuals to Mali from different parts of the Islamic world. Abu Ishaq al-Sahili, who was a renowned architect during the fourteenth century, came to Mali. Al-Sahili was the mastermind behind the mosques built with bricks some of these mosques are still standing. Musa encouraged education and was a great patron of learning. At the Sankora mosque in Timbuktu, he gathered scientists, mathematicians, theologians, philosophers and historians. Though Sankora was considered as the best learning seat in West Africa, Muslims intellectuals congregated around other mosques creating many seats of learning and intellectualism.

In 1324, Musa set out on his pilgrimage to Mecca. It was this pilgrimage which first time showed the world the wealth and generosity of Musa. He arrived in Egypt with 500 slaves, each carrying four pounds of gold and 80 camels with 300 pounds of gold on each. Musa distributed all this wealth as alms to the poor. This sudden surge of gold created inflation in Egypt, the impact of which was visible even twelve years after Musa's visit. This demonstration of wealth and generosity put Musa and Mali on the European map. The pilgrimage to Mecca taught him a great deal about Islam and he returned to Mali with a strong desire to convert the Malian society into an exemplary Islamic society. He brought jurists of the Maliki school of thought into Mali.

Musa's determination converted Mali into an Islamic state. His attempts to Islamize the society met with resistance but eventually he succeeded in his efforts. Today Mali's 90% population is Muslim this is mainly due to the grandeur effort of Mansa Musa. Musa died in 1332 or 1337 and his son Mansa Maghan succeeded to the throne. After Musa's death, the empire slowly started to disintegrate. Gao rebelled in 1400, Turag seized Walate and Timbuktu (1431) and Takrur became independent. By 1550, Mali's economical and political importance seized to exist.

Muhammad Ibn Battutah
(1304-1377)

Contribution: Islam's greatest explorer. He was one of the world's greatest travelers (greatest Muslim traveler). He traveled from North Africa to as far as India and China. Accounts of his journey provide important cultural and traditional information of the countries he traveled.

Ibn Battutah, the greatest traveler before the invention of steam boat or speedy means of traveling, was born on February 24, 1304 AD in Tangier (modern Morocco). He belonged to a family of religious judges. He received his early education in his native town Tangier and following the footsteps of his ancestors, he studied theology and law. In 1325, at the age of 21, Ibn Battutah headed towards Mecca for pilgrimage. This was the beginning of a life long journey in which he traveled to regions as far as China and Sumatra. In his life he traveled about 75000 miles which was simply unthinkable during his time. On his way to Mecca from Tangier, Ibn Battutah stopped in Cairo, Alexandria, Damascus, Jordan and Syria. During his journey, he decided to broaden his education and knowledge by studying under famous scholars of Egypt, Syria and Hejaz. Indeed this quest of knowledge served him well in coming years of his life as he proved an able judge and administrator. He provided the detailed accounts of his experience and impressions of Mecca of that time. Having finished his pilgrimage, Ibn Battutah set out for Iraq, Iran and Azerbaijan. In 1326, he met the last Mongol Khan (Abu Said) of Iran and the Khan of Golden Horde (Mohammad Ozbeg) in 1332. He visited Constantinople and then set out for a long journey towards India. In eight years (1325-1333), Ibn Battutah had traveled to Mecca, Southern and Eastern Mediterranean, Egypt, Arabia and Russia. On his way to India, Ibn Battutah crossed through Balkh, Samarquand, Bukhara, Afghanistan and finally arrived in India (sometime after 1333). He was greeted by the Sultan of Delhi, Muhammad Bin Tughlaq. He impressed the Sultan immensely and was appointed the judge of Delhi. Though Tughlaq was occasionally generous, he was also regarded as insane and cruel ruler. Ibn Battutah always feared for his life and despite his precautions he fell from Tughlaq's favor and only his good fortunes saved his life. Ibn Battutah, however, soon gained back Tughlaq's favor. In 1342, Tughlaq appointed Ibn Battutah as head of a delegation to visit the Chinese emperor. Unfortunately, on his way to China, there was a shipwreck and Ibn Battutah not only lost his belongings but the valuable gifts he was carrying to the emperor of china. Fearing the wrath of Tughlaq, Ibn Battutah escaped to Maldives Islands and served there as a judge for two years. From Maldives, Ibn Battutah went to Ceylon (now Sri Lanka), came back to Maldives and then to Bengal and Assam. From there Ibn Battutah went to Sumatra where the Muslim ruler gave him his ship on which Ibn Battutah began his journey to China. On his way back from China he once again visited Sumatra and Malabar. He also visited Damascus and witnessed the scourge of Bubonic plague (Black Death). In his accounts, he provided the vivid descriptions of plague and the disaster and impact on the lives of people brought by this plague. In 1352, he visited Spain and later set out on a journey to the Western Sudan. His last journey was the crossing of Sahara to West Africa and then Ibn Battutah spent a year in Mali. He returned to Morocco in 1353 and remained there for the rest of his life. Ibn Battutah died in Morocco in 1368 or 1369 and was buried in Tangier. He went to Mecca four times to perform Hajj.

Ibn Battutah is the author of one of the most famous travel books known as 'Rihlah' (journey or travel). Rihlah should not be considered as a daily dairy rather it is a part autobiography and part description of Ibn Battutah's journey. Unfortunately, the book remained unknown outside Islamic world until two German scholars in the early nineteenth century separately translated and published parts of Rihlah. In 1829, after its English translation, Rihlah was translated and published in many languages.

Considering the limited means of travel in his time, Ibn Battutah is undoubtedly the greatest traveler of the world. Many Western historians compare Marco Polo with Ibn Battutah. The fact of the matter is that Marco polo not only traveled far less than Ibn Battutah but Marco Polo's accounts of journey are also far less descriptive than Ibn Battutah. At a time when the speedy means of traveling was not available, a journey of 75000 miles is an astonishing achievement. During his journey to the different parts of the world he met many rulers, scholars and dignitaries. His book 'Rihlah' can be considered as a source of political history, culture, customs and different social aspects of many countries he visited.

Shamshuddin Hafiz
(1320-1390)

Contribution: One of the greatest Persian mystical poets. His style was 'Ghazal'. He preached love and humanity in his poems. Sufism is one of the main characteristics of his poetry.

One of the finest and the greatest Persian mystical poets, Shamsuddin Hafiz was born in Shiraz (Iran) in 1320 AD. Shiraz at that time was the capital of Fars (a province). His father died when Hafiz was a young boy. As was the custom of the time he received his education in Arabic and Persian literature, the Quran and science. His pen name, Hafiz, indicates that he had memorized the Quran by heart. His poetry was greatly influenced by the Persian as well as Arabic literature. He grew at a time when Persian poetry was at its zenith. After completing his early education, Hafiz lectured on the Quranic and theological issues and wrote commentaries related to religious matters. As a court poet he enjoyed the patronage of many rulers of Shiraz. His early poems were composed in praise of Abu Ishaq who was the ruler of Fars (probably ruled between 1345 and 1353). In 1353, Shiraz was captured by Mubariz al-din Muhammad (a Mozaffarid leader), who imposed a strict Sunni religious observation on the city (Hafiz was a Shiite Muslim). It appears that Hafiz became out of favor during Mubariz reign, but in 1358, Mubariz was deposed by his son Jalaluddin Shah Shuja. He gave respect and support to Hafiz. Shah Shuja ruled from 1358 to 1384 and during this period, Hafiz's reputation as a poet grew beyond the borders of Iran. He was well respected and known in the Arab world as well as in India. In 1387, Tamerlane conquered whole of Iran and when he came to Shiraz he met with Hafiz. By the end of his life, Hafiz was very well respected and known for his lyrical and mystical poems. Hafiz died in Shiraz in 1390 AD.

In his poetry, Hafiz has depicted the historical events as well as biographical descriptions of his time. He had a superb linguistic and literary command. Over 600 poems are attributed to Hafiz which are both mystical and lyrical. His verse style is known as "Ghazals'. Ghazals are poems which consist of 6 to 15 couplets expressing a unity of thoughts. Ghazals have monorhythmic pattern. The poet's title (pen name) appears in Ghazal's final couplet. Hafiz's fame lies in his Divan (an anthology of short and medium length poems). His major work is known as 'Divan-e-Hafiz', which has been translated into many languages. The simple and musical language made his poetry widely popular. Besides Iran, his poetry gained enormous popularity in Afghanistan and the Indian Subcontinent.

One of the basic characteristics of Hafiz's poetry is the adoption of Sufi thoughts or Sufism. In Islam, Sufism started as a reaction against luxury, corruption and laxity among Muslims after the establishment of the Islamic Empire. The objective of Sufism is to purify one's soul and to have a strong bond with God. Sufism in Islam was further influenced by Zoroastrian worship, Nestorian Christianity, Neo-Platonism philosophy and Buddhism. By the 14th century, Sufism was very much apparent in Islam and lots of poets and writers were influenced by this mystical movement. Though Hafiz's style of poetry was Ghazals and the Ghazals are traditionally linked to love, beauty and wine but Hafiz used this form of poetry to express the Sufi ideas. His work can be regarded as Sufi illuminates and a literary monument which produced cultural influence both in the east and the west. His poetry is not merely based on beautiful verses but it carries philosophical thoughts. His verses are neither completely mystical nor completely materialistic rather he describes the world as he sees it. Hafiz recognizes that both worldly pleasure and the religion are instrumental in developing human action therefore; in his poetry he does not ignore either of them.

Hafiz's work was not without criticism. The orthodox Muslims and the religious scholars failed to understand his work and considered his poetry as infidel, blasphemous, dangerous and superficial. Modern day theologians recognize and admire the beauty and philosophy of his works as opposed to those who wanted to excommunicate him.

Though Hafiz was well known in Iran, Middle East and India, unfortunately the Western world never really enjoyed the true lyrics, beauty and spirit of Hafiz's poems mainly due to the difficulties in translations of his works. Hafiz's poetry brings the reader both at material and spiritual planes of experience. The basic essence of Hafiz's poetry is love of humanity and relates the everyday experiences of life to mysticism and search of God. Some may see him as the combination of Omar Khayyam, Sadi and Rumi, three great Muslim poets of the12th and the 13th century.

Abd al-Rahman Ibn Khaldun
(1332-1406)

Contribution: Historian, scholar, jurist and statesman. Ibn Khaldun is considered as one of the greatest historians of the world. He developed the philosophy and art of history writing. He exerted a great influence among historians worldwide.

Ibn Khaldun, the greatest Arab historian, a sociologist and philosopher was born in Tunis on May 27, 1332. Ibn Khaldun's family had moved from Southern Arabia to Spain after the Arab conquest of Spain and settled in Seville. During the time of Christian expansion of Spain his family moved to Tunis, where both his great- grandfather and grandfather served in the court of the ruler of Tunis. His father though served as an administrator at the court of the ruler of Tunis but later gave up his position in order to study law and theology.

Ibn Khaldun's early education was on the traditional lines of the time. He learned the Quran, the Hadith, Arabic literature and jurisprudence. He also studied the Arab mysticism and the philosophy of the Moorish Spain. Ibn Khaldun was 17 years old when his parents died when the Black Death struck Tunis. By the age of 20 (1352), Ibn Khaldun had finished his early education. His mastery of language and knowledge of Jurisprudence impressed the Hafsid ruler of Tunis and Ibn Khaldun was given a post at the court. His stay in Tunis was however, short and in 1354, he moved to Morocco and served at the court of Merinid Sultan Abu Inan in Fez. After two years of service, Ibn Khaldun fell from favor and was imprisoned on charges of aiding rebels (February 1357). He remained in Jail for two years and was only released after the death of Abu Inan. The new ruler of Morocco, Abu Selim reinstated him in office. Once again he fell from favor and decided to move to Granada. In December 1362, Ibn Khaldun arrived in Granada and received a warm welcome from

Muhammad V, the ruler of Granada. Soon Ibn Khaldun found himself on a mission to the Christian king of Castile, Pedro. Ibn Khaldun's mission was to ratify the peace treaty between Castile and Granada. Pedro gave Ibn Khaldun a warm welcome and offered Ibn Khaldun to take him into his service but Ibn Khaldun declined. Ibn Khaldun came back to Granada after finishing his assignment but soon the jealousy of others and the court intrigue forced him to leave Granada and move to Africa. For the next few years, Ibn Khaldun moved from one place to another and changed his employers, yet during this time he hold many high levels of administrative positions. The ups and downs of political life embittered Ibn Khaldun and he decided to give up politics and take scholastic works.

In 1383, Ibn Khaldun traveled to Egypt. The Mumluke ruler of Egypt (al-Malik az-Zahir Barquq) bestowed great respect on Ibn Khaldun and appointed him as chief judge in one of his principal courts. During his stay in Cairo, Ibn Khaldun also taught at Al-Azhar University. In 1400, Timur (the Tartar conqueror whose empire stretched from Northern India to Syria and Anatolia) invaded Syria. The Mamluke Sultan went to meet Timur (Tamerlane) and took Ibn Khaldun with him. Timur treated Ibn Khaldun with respect. Ibn Khaldun used all his wisdom to negotiate and please the Tartar ruler. Though he could not save Damascus from pillage but secured a safe passage for himself back to Egypt (March 1401). Ibn Khaldun died in Cairo on March 17, 1406, and was buried in the Sufi Cemetery outside Cairo.

Ibn Khaldun's greatest and most significant work of universal value is 'Muquddimah' (an introduction to history). In 1375, he sought refuge with a powerful tribe of 'Awalad Arif' who allowed Ibn Khaldun and his family to stay in a castle, Qalat Ibn Salamah in the province of Oran. There in this solitary environment, Ibn Khaldun worked on his masterpiece Muquddimah for the next four years. Ibn Khaldun intended to write the history of Arabs and Berbers which he ultimately did but before doing so he discovered that there was a systematic pattern in the political and social history of human beings. He realized that one must first find a method to describe history, distinguish and isolate true history from factious elements. This led him to formulate "Philosophy of History' one of the greatest works of its kind created by a single person in any era or place. Muquddimah is not simply a chronological history of man's political and social events but it is scientific, rational and analytical.

Ibn Khaldun wrote that man is a social animal and can not survive alone; therefore, it needs co-operation with other men. This co-operation with each other results in the formation of social organization which ultimately leads to the civilization. Social organizations, however, differ in size, quality and influence. Among some social organizations there is more desire to co-operate, form stable governments and build cities and high culture than some others. Once the social organizations are established, then there is a need for a leader who can create a solidarity or corporate spirit to obtain power. Thus a leader who has a strong support by his followers can form a dynasty hence a tribe or state. However, neither the dynasty nor the state is eternal. Gradually the dynasty collapses due to political decay and lack of innovations and with that state and the civilization. Then the new dynasty takes over and after some time suffers from the same fate as of its predecessors. Thus according to Ibn Khaldun, the dynastic history moves in a circle and with time one civilization replaces other.

Ibn Khaldun's work is based on the observation and brilliant analysis of history, economics and politics. His concept of 'Social Cohesion' is based on the causes of rise and fall of dynasties. The extreme social need or a religious ideology triggers the small tribes or kingdoms to higher objectives and power. Ibn Khaldun also then skillfully analyzes the reasons for fall of such mighty powers which then make room for new powers. Overall, he has presented his accounts of history with such mastery that one can feel that he can visualize the turning points of history. In other words he can see the rise and fall of the nations.

In the 16th and the17th century, the Ottoman scholars got interested in Ibn Khaldun's work and part of Muquddimah was translated into Turkish language in the 18th century. In the 19th century, Muquddimah was translated into French and with this translation Ibn Khaldun got worldwide recognition of his work. In another book known as "Kitab Al Ibr' Ibn Khaldun has described the history of Muslim North Africa. Besides being a master historian, Ibn Khaldun studied the nature of society and social changes and called this phenomenon as 'Science of Culture'.

Ibn Khaldun faced much turmoil in his life, wandered from one place to another and bore personal tragedies of life when his family traveling from Tunis to Cairo was drowned in the Port of Alexandria (1384). Despite this emotional and physical stress, Ibn Khaldun somehow managed to maintain his mental peace and physical strength to compose his memorable historical works. The turmoil in Ibn Khaldun's life should not be interpreted as the mercurial nature of the historian rather he lived in a time when Islamic civilization was declining. The mighty Muslim empire due to its internal feud, intrigue, and lack of progressive visions was vastly reduced in size. Ibn Khaldun's concept of 'Social Cohesion' was probably an effort to revive falling Islamic culture and civilization. To him history was a great teacher as one can learn from human past which depicts social, economical and cultural aspects. Ibn Khaldun undoubtedly revived the art of history writing in the 15th century Egypt and probably still has great influence among historians worldwide.

Timur Lang
(1336-1405)

Contribution: A legendry conqueror with legendry brutality. His empire stretched from Southern Russia to Mongolia, Northern India, Persia and Mesopotamia. He made Samarqand his capital and adorned the city with splendid buildings and mosques. He was also a great patron of art.

Timur (Tamerlane), known as Timur lame or Timur Lang for his Lame leg, was of Turkish origin. He was born in Samarqand on 1336 AD. He belonged to Turkish Barlas tribe (a Mongol subgroup) which had settled in Transoxania (now in Uzbekistan). Timur claimed to be a member of Chaghatai Khanate (Chaghatai Khan was son of Genghis Khan). After the death of Amir Kazghan, the ruler of Transoxania in 1357, Timur changed his loyalty and joined forces with the Khan of Kashghar. Soon Timur betrayed him and joined Amir Hussain, the grandson of Amir Kazghan but Timur also turned against him and after his assassination in 1370, Timur declared himself as the sovereign of Samarqand and the restorer of the Mongol empire of Chaghatai line of Khans. For the first 10 years of his rule Timur fought against the Khans of Jatah (eastern Turkistan) and Khwarizm, finally capturing Kasghar in 1380. In 1383, Timur began his military campaign against Persia. After the death (1335) of the last Il-Khan, Abu Said, the ruler of Persia, Persia was going through the civil strife and succession disputes. Thus Timur faced negligible resistance from the Persians. Timur began his military campaign with the capture of Herat, then Khurasan and all of Eastern Persia fell to him by 1385. Between 1386 and 1394, Timur captured Fars, Iraq, Azerbaijan, Armenia and Georgia. One of the greatest challenges to Timur's conquest was Khan of Golden Horde, Tokhtamysh. Tokhtamysh first invaded Azerbaijan in 1385 and then Transoxania in 1388 defeating Timur's generals. Timur first defeated Tokhtamysh in 1391 and decisively in 1395. Timur then moved to capture Moscow. In his absence, revolts broke out in Persia which Timur crushed with severe brutality. In 1398, he invaded India destroying the army of Sultan of Delhi, Muhammad Bin Tughlaq. With his usual brutality, Timur reduced the city of Delhi to ruins and massacred its inhabitants. By April 1399, he was back to Samarqand and by the end of the year started a military expedition against the Mamlukes of Egypt and Syria. In 1400, he captured Aleppo and Damascus was taken in 1401. In Damascus, Timur met the great historian, Ibn Khaldun. Timur gave lot of respect to Ibn Khaldun and provided him and some Mamluke officials with safe passage out of Damascus but in the end the city was pillaged. The same year he captured Baghdad, destroying the city and killing 20,000 of its civilians. Almost all monuments of the Islamic civilization were reduced to ruins. Timur then invaded Anatolia, defeating Sultan Bayazid's army near Ankara on July 20, 1402. He then captured Symarna from the knights of Rhodes. In December 1404, Timur set out for China but died on February 1405 at Otrar and was buried in Samarqand.

Where Timur butchered hundreds of thousands of people, he also gathered a large number of talented people (artisans, intellectuals, artists, theologians and teachers) in Samarqand, Bukhara and Herat. These people provided the Timurid Dynasty with the highest standard of literary composition, paintings and historiography in Western Persia. Some great architectural monuments were erected during this time. The grand mosques in Kesh (Timur's birth place) and Samarqand (to honor his favorite wife) are the examples of the architectural achievements of Timur's era.

Timur's rise from a leader of small band of nomads in Central Asia to a great conqueror is a story of ambition, treachery and brutality. His military campaigns caused poverty, bloodshed and desolation. His military techniques and brutality resembled Genghis Khan. His historic role except his brutality is quite insignificant. He also lacked the statesmanship of some other great conquerors. Both the Christian and the Islamic world suffered due to his military ambitions. The Asiatic Christianity in its Nestorian and Jacobite form became extinct. The Muslim civilization and culture greatly suffered. Many monuments in Baghdad and Delhi were destroyed. The artisans from Damascus were deported to Samarqand. In the end, his conquests gave nothing to the civilization rather it took decades for many countries to rebuild themselves from the ruins caused by Timur.

Timur did conquer a vast land but the consolidation of these lands was never achieved. As a matter of fact the era of his descendents was more civilized and of some achievements. They lacked Timur's brutality and showed a lot of interest in reviving the artistic and intellectual life in Iran and Central Asia. The internal feud among Timur's descendents grew with the passage of time and the last Timurid of Herat finally fell to the Uzbek leader Muhammad Shaybani in 1506. Thus one hundred years after Timur's death, the vast empire he had conquered by military expeditions and brutality finally fragmented.

Abd al-Rahman Jami
(1414-1492)

Contribution: Persian scholar, mystic and poet. He is considered by many as Iran's last great classical/mystic poet. In his poetical and prose works he expressed his ethical and philosophical views, which revolved around mysticism. His writings lacked panegyrics. In his writings he touched a wide variety of subjects such as religion, philosophy and logic. He was a member of Nakshiband Sufi order.

Jami was born on November 7, 1414 in the district of Jam (hence the surname Jami) in the province of Khurasan (Iran). Jami's grandfather was one of the scholars in the city of Isfahan, then moved to Khurasan and finally settled in Jam. Jami's father was the jurist of the district of Jam but he moved to Herat (Afghanistan) when Jami was five years old. Jami received his early education in typical Islamic traditions. He learned the Arabic alphabets and when gained enough experience in reading and writing, began studying the Quran. Very soon he memorized the whole book and then started learning logic and philosophy. He also learned advance levels of mathematics and astronomy. He mastered Islamic law and Hadith (traditions) and their interpretations. Jami attended Nizamiya College under the direction of Samarqandi. He then moved to Samarqand and continued his education under the direction of renowned teacher Tabrizi. Jami spent about nine years in Samarqand and then returned to Herat.

The time in which Jami was born was of relative peace. The invasions of Mongols and Tartars on Iran, Afghanistan and India had subsided. Iran was especially recovering from these attacks and their aftermath. The process of rebuilding Iranian culture and literature was at full speed. Shahrukh, the ruler of Iran was a great patron of arts, literature, science and Sufism. His interest transformed Herat into a center of arts and literature which drew many renowned scholars of the time to the city. When Jami returned to Herat from Samarqand, he found a flourishing society in which arts and sciences were at their peak. During Jami's lifetime, his fame as a scholar and poet grew to the extent that many Muslim rulers of the time offered him patronage. He declined these offers and preferred to be a teacher in a school built by Shahrukh rather than being a court poet. In Herat, Jami was respected both by the scientific and the literary communities. Though Jami spent most of his life in Herat he also visited Meshed and Mecca. From Mecca, Jami left for Syria, Egypt and Iraq. In these countries he received highest honor and respect. He returned to Herat and spent a relatively quiet life. Jami died on November 8, 1492 at Herat.

It is not exactly known when Jami got involved into Sufism. According to one of his students (Abdul Ghafur Lori), a Sufi master Kashgari had great influence on Jami. Jami achieved the high level of perfection in Sufi practices in a short time. In 1482, Kashghari died and Jami turned to Khawaja Ahrar for more guidance. Though some other Sufi masters might have some influence on Jami but it appears that both Kashgari and Ahrar had major influence on him. Jami became the follower of the Sufi order founded by Baha al-Din Nakshiband.

Jami's writing is considerable and variable. He wrote on a variety of subjects which indicates his wide knowledge on many subjects. His written works can be divided into two categories: prose and poetry but his fame lies in his lyrical poetry which has a mastery of diction and style. His most famous collection of poetry is Haft Aurang (The seven Thrones), a collection of seven stories in the form of Mathnawi. Of these seven stories, the most famous one is the story of Yusuf and Zulikha. The story, though, has been described both in the Bible and the Quran Jami used Zulikha's love for yusuf as a spiritual beauty whereas Yusuf despite his virtues exemplifies the human soul which can surrender to the Divine beloved. He wrote three Divans (an anthology of short and medium length poems): Beginning of Youth, Central Part of the Chain, and Close of Life.

His most famous mystical treatise is 'Lavayeh' (Flashes of Light) in which Jami had described Sufi doctrines of 'Wahadal al-Wujud' (the Existential Unity of Being). He wrote a commentary on the mystical experiences of other famous mystics. His stories may be love stories but an in depth analysis of his works indicate that these are means of Sufi ways to reach God. His writings are not merely stories written in prose or poetry but have philosophical thinking. He also wrote 'Zephyrs of Intimacy', a book which is biographies of many Sufi saints. He explained and wrote commentaries on a portion of Ibn Arabi's work Fesus el-Hekam (Jewels of Wisdom) and the Quran.

Mehmed II
(1432-1481)

Contribution: Known as 'Mehmed the conqueror', he was the seventh Sultan of the Ottoman Empire and a great military commander. He conquered Constantinople and extended Ottoman control in Balkans and Anatolia. His military expeditions both in Asia and Europe enlarged the Ottoman Empire to a great proportion.

Mehmed II, son of Sultan Murad II (sixth Sultan of the Ottomans) and probably a slave girl from a non-Muslim family in the Balkans was born on March 30, 1432. At the age of two he was sent to Amasya in central Anatolia and later to Manisa near Izmir where he was educated by distinguished teachers. In August 1444, Murad surprisingly abdicated his throne in favor of his son, Mehmed. Immediately after his accession to the throne, the twelve year old Sultan faced a grave challenge from the European powers. Christian powers in Europe were joining hands in order to push Islam out of the European continent. A coalition of Christian powers was formed under the leadership of Hungary's James Hunyadi, promoted and supported by Byzantine Empire, the Papacy and Venice. In September 1444, the Crusaders crossed the Danube and then lay seize to Varna (Belgium). Murad II was requested to come out of the retirement and lead the army. On November 10, 1444, Murad led the Turkish army which decisively defeated the European coalition ending their hopes to push Islam out of Europe.

Even after his glorious victory against Crusaders, Murad kept himself away from the throne but in May 1446, decided to take the throne back. Mehmed was sent to Manisa with his newly appointed teachers, Zaganos and Shabeddin. Mehmed's first experience of battle came when in 1448 he led a Turkish army successfully against Hungarian forces. Though Mehmed had a son with a Christian Albanian slave girl, he later married a noblewoman. In February 1451, Murad II died and for the second time Mehmed ascended the throne. His first task was to eliminate those who opposed his authority. He faced the revolt from the Janissaries (an elite military corps) whom he crushed effectively. He later reorganized this military organization under his direct authority which later played an important role in his future conquests.

From his childhood and under the influence of his tutors (Zaganos and Shabeddin), Mehmed dreamt the capture of Constantinople. After ascending the throne, his first task in this direction was to build a fortress (fortress of Bogazkesan) to control Bosporus. He also built fleets and large size cannons. Meanwhile he signed a peace treaty with Venice and Hungary. This further isolated Constantinople from its Western allies. From April 6, 1453, Mehmed laid siege of Constantinople. On May 29, 1453, when the Byzantine emperor Constantine XI Paleologus rejected his terms, Mehmed ordered his troops to storm the city which fell without any serious resistance. The last Byzantine emperor was killed and Mehmed triumphantly entered into the city and marched to the great church of St Sophia which was converted into a mosque. The city was renamed 'Istanbul' and the rebuilding of the city began. The capture of Constantinople helped the expansion of Ottoman rule into northern Anatolia and dominating the straits and southern shore of Black sea.

In 1454, Mehmed turned his attention towards Balkans and the islands in the Aegean Sea. He met little resistance in the Aegan and forced Moldavia to pay annual tribute. Mehmed however, failed to take Belgrade in 1456, thus the line of middle Danube and lower Sava defined the Ottoman boundary within Hungary. In 1458, he marched towards Greece and captured Athens in August 1458 which remained under Ottoman control for almost 300 years. In 1459, the invasion of Serbia began and by the end of the year all of Serbia was occupied. He captured Morea (the southern peninsula of the Greek mainland) and then in 1461 Trebizond (northern coast of Asia Minor on the Black sea) was subjugated. In 1462, Mehmed took Walachia and by the end of 1463, Bosnia was overrun. The last of Anatolian Emirates, Karaman was annexed in 1466. Despite his victories in the West, he faced a formidable foe in the east. A Turkman leader, Uzan Hasan, in southeastern Anatolia became a major challenge to Mehmed. In 1472, Hasan marched into western Anatolia which forced Mehmed to prepare for a military expedition against Hasan. On August 11, 1473 at the Battle of Baskhent in Erzincan, Mehmed defeated Hasan. This victory extended his authority over Anatolia and the Balkans. By 1475, Crimea became a vassal state and by 1476 he overran Albania. In 1479, though a peace treaty was signed with Venice, Venice was forced to pay tribute to Mehmed. In1480, the Ottomans captured the southern Italian port of Otranto. In southern Anatolia, the Sultan of Egypt and Syria became a major military threat to him and Mehmed began preparing for a military expedition against him. His health was declining due to gout and on May 1, 1481, a severe abdominal pain struck him and he died on May 3, 1481, 15 miles from Istanbul. His relationship with his son Bayezid was very strained and it is speculated that Mehmed was poisoned by his son. His death temporarily halted the advances of the Turkish army into Europe.

All his life, Sultan Mehmed dreamt for building a universal empire. He extended the Ottoman influence deep into Europe's heart. He reorganized the Ottoman government and unified the codes of criminal law, law relating to the affairs of the government such as tax-systems and code of Ottoman justice for the conquered provinces. These laws indeed served regulatory purposes alongside the Quranic law.

Mehmed wanted Istanbul to be the center of the world both politically and culturally. He built many public buildings, hospitals, public baths and educational institutes. He encouraged the Greeks to return to Istanbul by returning their houses. He restored the Greek Orthodox Patriarch, established Jewish grand Rabbi and an Armenian Patriarch in Istanbul. In order to populate the city, he forced the Muslims and the Christians from Anatolia and Balkans to settle in Istanbul. These measures helped the city to grow rapidly and by the first quarter of the sixteenth century, Istanbul was the largest city in Europe.

He was also a patron of art and literature. He employed many Persian poets and he composed a collection of verses. He supported the visual arts and production of medals and paintings. The two most famous portraits of Mehmed were painted by Sinam

Bey, a Turkish artists and a Venetian artist, Gentile Bellini. Mehmed would gather the Muslim religious scholars and ask them to discuss theological issues in his presence. He promoted education both in sciences and theology.

Mehmed's rule was autocratic and some consider him brutal but others may argue that by the standards of the time, he was no crueler than other rulers or military commanders. His military success and the dream of a universal empire contributed a great deal to the Ottoman rule and expansion for more than four centuries and also kept Islam alive in the heart of Europe.

Muhammad Askia
(1442-1538)

Contribution: Founder of the Askia dynasty and one of the greatest rulers of the Songhai Empire with his capital at Gao in present day Mali. He expanded and consolidated the Songhai Empire. He was an excellent administrator and introduced many advanced administrative reforms in the empire. His social and political policies resulted in the expansion of trade and spread of Islam in the region.

Between 900 and 1500 AD, new states emerged in North Africa which established trade links with the rest of Africa. Northwest Africa was in the hands of Muslim rulers since the eighth century. The great Berber Empires of Almoravids (1056-1147) and Almohads (1130-1269) ruled North Africa for almost two centuries. From 1000 AD onward, Islam also spread across the Sahara into the states of 'Sudanese belt' stretching from Nile to Senegal. The great empires also emerged in western Sudan. The Trans-Saharan trade in the Sudanese belt created two great states, Ghana and Mali.

Mali prospered under the great ruler Mansa Musa (1280-1337). In 1464, one of Africa's most renowned kings Sunni Ali established the Songhai Empire. Songhai Empire was the trading state of west Africa, centered in the great bend in the Niger River (what is now Central Mali) and extending west to the Atlantic coast and east into Niger and Nigeria. Gao, the most famous city of Songhai people was established in about 800 AD and for the next 700 years remained the most important city in west Africa. After the death of Sunni Ali in 1492, his son Sunni Bare assumed power but was replaced by 'Askia the Great', who ruled from 1493 to 1528.

Muhammad Askia was born as Muhammad Ture Ibn Ali Bakr in 1442 AD in a family of military background. He received his early education in an Islamic institution but probably his military skills came from his family background. In his early adulthood, he joined the services of Songhai emperor Sunni Ali and became one of his most trusted military commanders. After Sunni Ali's death, his son Sunni Baru assumed power but in April 1493, at the battle of Anfao, he was defeated by Askia's army and was exiled. The coup staged by Askia was probably necessary as ethnic and religious divisions were running deep into the empire and a bloody civil war might have erupted. Upon assuming the throne Muhammad assumed the title of 'Askia'.

One of the major tasks which Askia undertook immediately was to consolidate the empire conquered by his predecessors by setting up an efficient administration in the region. He divided the empire into provinces and appointed a governor to each province. He established the departments of agriculture, finance, justice, water and forest and appointed a director for each department. He also reformed the army by creating a standing army and building a navy (a fleet of war canoes).

While Askia was busy in consolidating the empire and reforming the administration, his army led successful military campaigns to expand Songhai frontiers. His army battled with the Mossi tribe, captured the salt mines and Oases in the Sahara as far as the frontiers of modern Algeria and Libya. Military campaigns were also taken against the Diara (1512) kingdom of Fouta-Toro in Senegal and to the east against the Hausa states. He also captured Agadez and established a colony in Air (Niger) so that he could control the caravan markets in the north.

In 1495, Askia went to Mecca to perform Hajj. In Egypt, he was given the title 'Caliph of Blacks' by the ruler of Egypt. Like Mansa Musa, 175 years ago, Askia donated huge amounts of gold to the poor and needy. He returned to Gao in about 1497. His journey to Mecca and the Hajj probably produced great influence on Askia's thinking. He met many scholars during his journey and some of them accompanied him to Gao. He wanted to transform west Africa into an Islamic state by establishing the practices of Islam. He allied himself with Muslim clerics and intellectuals. A religious organization was set up and a Moroccan reformer al-Mehrili became his advisor on religious issues. He established the civil code of Songhai Empire based on the Quran and Arabic was declared as an official language for writing. He focused on Timbuktu, a city already well known as a center of Islamic learning and culture. He gathered Muslim scholars and intellectuals in Timbaktu in an effort to transform the city into a world class center of Islamic learning.

Though dedicated to Islam, he was tolerant of other religions and there was no persecution of peoples of other faiths. In fact, Jewish refugees flocked into Gao when persecution against them began in early sixteenth century in the Saharan Oases.

Traditionally, Niger basin produced many warrior-kings who attempted to unify the West African region. This was important for the trade especially gold and other precious commodities. Askia can also be seen as a unifier, a brilliant administrator and a contributor to Islam in West Africa. He restored commerce, contributed largely to Islam by gathering Muslim scholars and intellectuals in Timbuktu and building the city as one of the leading centers of Islamic learning and culture in the Islamic world.

Last years of Askia's life were rather tragic. His children were quarreling among themselves to become the next ruler of Songhai. Askia with time became almost half blind and in 1528, his eldest son Musa took control of the empire and exiled his father. He remained exiled till 1537 but when his son Askia Ismail became the ruler, he recalled him to Gao. Muhammad Askia died in 1538 and was buried in Gao. His sons continued to rule for the next fifty years but when the Moroccans invaded the empire, the dynasty finally came to an end in 1591.

Mohammad Askia's significant contribution was that due to his sheer administrative skill not only he consolidated the Songhai Empire but he also expanded it. He took charge of the empire at a time when it was at the verge of civil war thus saved the empire from disintegration and blood bath. His devotion to Islam resulted in the spread of Islam in West Africa as Muslim missionaries could go into the remote places of the empire to preach Islam which was not possible without his help.

Zaheeruddin Babur
(1483-1530)

Contribution: Founder of the Moghul Empire in India. He was a brilliant military commander and skilled administrator. He was also a poet and a writer.

Babur, the emperor and the founder of the Moghul dynasty in India was born on February 15, 1483 in Farghana (Central Asia). Babur was a descendent of Mongol leader Genghis Khan and Timur (Tamerlane). Babur's father Umar Sheikh Mirza was ruler of Farghana and in order to maintain his throne, Babur's father had to fight many wars with the Timurids, the dynasty founded by Timur. During all these years of trouble, wars and uncertainties, Babur remained alongside his father which proved to be a training ground for him. Babur became the ruler of Farghana at the age of 11 when his father, Umar Sheikh Mirza, died. At the age of 14, Babur tried to conquer Samarquand and he did take the city for a short time. In 1501, Babur was decisively defeated by Uzbek ruler Shaybani Khan and lost not only Samarquand but also Farghana. For the next three years, Babur wandered in central Asia finally seizing Kabul in 1504. In 1511, he attempted to take back Samarquand but once again failed. Meanwhile he consolidated his power in Afghanistan by taking Quandhar, a strategic site to road to India.

Between 1519 and 1524, Babur attacked India for three times. On April 21, 1526, Babur met Ibrahim Lodhi (Sultan of Delhi) at Panipat (50 miles north of Delhi) in a bid to take the throne of Delhi. Despite that Babar's army was about one-eighth of Ibrahim Lodhi, the military genius of Babur and the artillery power eventually resulted in Babar's victory at Paniput. Ibrahim Lodhi was killed and Babur assumed the throne of Delhi. Babur was declared emperor of India on April 27, 1526. However, he faced enormous opposition by local chiefs and rulers. Unlike his predecessors, Babur did not intend to go back to his origin rather decided to stay in India. His chief rival was Rana Sanga (Raja of Udaipur), who had amassed an enormous army by appealing to many local rulers. Babur met Rana Sanga and his allied forces on March 16, 1527 at Khanwa (37 miles west of Agra) and within a day defeated Rana Sanga and his army. Once again his military genius and intelligent use of artillery helped him to overpower an enemy which was far superior in number and resources. Meanwhile, Mahmud Lodhi, brother of Ibrahim Lodhi was building an army to take back the throne of Delhi from Babur. After defeating Mahmud Lodhi, Babur eventually secured his rule from Quandhar to parts of Northern India. In 1530, Babar's son and the crown prince Humayun became gravely ill and it is said that Babur offered his life to God in exchange for his son's life. Humayun miraculously recovered, Babur fell ill and died on December 26, 1530 in Agra (India). Several years later, his body was taken to Kabul and buried in his favorite garden with no roof over his tomb.

Babur undoubtedly was the founder of the Moghul dynasty in India though he did not have time to consolidate his empire. Babur was a military genius and showed great courage and skill against his enemies despite being outnumbered both in man power and resources. Babur learned the art of musketry and artillery from Uzbeks and used it very effectively in India against his enemies who were not very well familiar with this kind of weapon. Babur also somewhat differed from the barbaric ways of his time. When he took Delhi he prevented his soldiers from looting and sacking of the city. Not only Babur was courageous, intelligent and a great ruler he was also a poet and a writer. He was a great lover of flowers and gardens. After taking Delhi, Babur marched towards Agra and there he laid out a garden near river Jamuna. His memoirs 'Babar Nama' is a classic autobiography. In this book he has described his experiences, the conquest of India, its customs and caste system, its wildlife and flowers. His autobiography was translated into Persian (1589) and in English (1921).

The impact of Babar's invasion on India is that he established a dynasty which considered India as their mother country and had great influence on Indian culture, religion, economy, language and arts. By the time Shah Jahan (the 5th Moghul emperor of India) became the emperor, a vast Indian territory was united under one ruler that brought prosperity and peace for the people of India.

Suleyman the Magnificient
(1494/1495-1566)

Contribution: Most famous Sultan of the Ottoman Empire. To his countrymen, he was known as the 'Lawgiver' and to the west as 'the Magnificient'. He expanded the Ottoman Empire and built a formidable navy to dominate the Mediterranean. His reign was a period of internal stability mainly due to ordered system of laws he gave to his people. Under him architecture, literature and art flourished.

Originally a small principality in Western Anatolia, the Ottomans rose to a world empire which lasted more than 600 years (1281-1922). Osman, after whom the Ottoman dynasty was named, inherited a small state around the town of Sogut from his father Ertoghrul, gradually expanded the territory. From the fourteenth to the sixteenth century, the Ottoman Empire continued to grow in size, power and wealth. When Sultan Selim I died in 1520, the Empire stretched from the Red Sea to the Crimea and from Kurdistan to Bosnia. Due to an empire of this magnitude, Ottomans became a major contender and the participant in the international power politics of the time.

Suleyman, the only son of Sultan Selim I, was born on April 1494/1495. He was appointed governor of Kaffa in Crimea during the reign of his grandfather Bayezid II and of Manisa in Western Asia Minor during the reign of his father. He ascended the throne on September 1520 and immediately began his military campaign in Central Europe and Mediterranean. Belgrade and Rhodes fell to the Ottomans in 1521 and 1522, respectively. Rhodes which was only six miles off the Turkish coast, there the knights of St.John had long protected the Christian pirates. After a six-month siege, the island was taken by the Turks. At the battle of Mohacs (August 1526), the Hungarian king, Louis II lost his life and the battle against the military might of Sultan Suleyman. In 1529,

Suleyman besieged Vienna but bad weather, lack of supplies and resolute resistance by the Christian army forced the Sultan to lift the seize. Hungary, however, remained a major problem for the Ottomans as the war in Hungary continued between 1543 and 1562. Finally a peace treaty was signed in 1562. Sultan Suleyman also took his military campaigns to North Africa when Tripoli was added to the Ottoman Empire in 1551 and Tunisia in 1574. Cyprus was taken by the Ottomans in 1571.

The Ottoman navy also gained a formidable strength during Suleyman's reign. Khayr ad-Din Barbarosa was the admiral of the Ottoman fleet and won many sea battles for them. In 1538, the Ottoman navy defeated the combined fleets of Venice and Spain off Preveza, Greece. Naval adventures also brought Yemen and Aden into the Ottoman Empire. The Ottoman navy, however, did not always conduct successful campaigns. The Ottoman navy failed to take Malta from the Knights of St.John in 1565 and in 1571 was defeated at Lepanto. Earlier in 1538, the Ottoman navy failed to take the town of Diu (India) from the Portuguese.

On the eastern frontier, Suleyman led three campaigns against Persia. In the first campaign (1534-35), the Ottomans added Erzurum in eastern Asia Minor and Iraq to Ottoman territory. The second campaign (1548-49) brought much of the area around Lake Van under Ottoman control. The third campaign (1554-55) proved much difficult for the Ottomans as the Safavids (the rulers of Persia) had gained enough military strength to defy the Turks. In 1555, a peace treaty was signed between the Persians and the Turks.

The last year of Suleyman's life were troubled by the rebellion of his sons for the succession to the throne. Two of his sons, Mustafa and Bayezid were executed on his orders. After 46 years of rule, Sultan Suleyman died on September 5, 1566 while besieging the fortress of Szigetvar in Hungary.

Sultan Suleyman ruled with undisputed strength and brilliance. He earned the title of 'Quanani' or 'Lawgiver' because under his supervision 'Book of Laws' was prepared for each major province of the empire. These laws helped in maintaining the social and economical order in the empire irrespective of religion, race and culture. Predominating among these laws were criminal justice, feudal grants and the tax-systems, court ceremonies, inheritance rights, and promotion in the government and the affairs of the ruling family. Suleyman's reign was also marked by repeated demonstration of Turkish military strength. Personally he led thirteen major military campaigns; ten against European adversaries and three against Persia. The expansion of the Turkish territory, especially in Europe had great impact on European politics. In 1536, an alliance was established between the French and the Turks. Though he had inherited a strong and stable empire, he further expanded and strengthened it politically, militarily and culturally. In order to gain firm control and undisputed loyalty, he organized the Janissary (new army) corps. Though such a military corps did exist almost a century before him, he organized the entire structure in a way that every member of this corps would be absolutely loyal to the Sultan.

Sultan Suleyman was also a just ruler. After the fall of Rhode, those who chose to stay were given the civil rights and a tax remission for 5 years. He was a religious person but Islam was never forced on the non-Muslims who lived in the Ottoman territory.

Architecture also furnished under Suleyman. He commissioned a large number of mosques with domes and minarets which are still visible in Istanbul. In major Muslim cities of the time (Mecca, Baghdad and Damascus), he built mosques, bridges and roads. He transformed Byzantine Constantinople into Istanbul a center of Muslim culture and power.

Jalaluddin Muhammad Akbar
(1542-1605)

Contribution: India's most celebrated Moghul emperor. He extended the Moghul rule from North to East. Akbar was a remarkable administrator who developed an efficient bureaucratic structure in India. He adopted the policy of religious tolerance and liberty.

Jalaluddin Muhammad Akbar, known as 'Akbar the Great' in the western world, was the greatest of all Mughal emperors. He was a grandson of Babur, the founder of the Moghul dynasty in India. His father, Humayun was battling against Afghan leader Sher shah Suri to regain his throne and was wandering from place to place in despair, when Akbar was born on October 15, 1542 in Umarkot, Sind (now in Pakistan). In 1555, with the help of the Iranian troops, Humayun regained his throne but died in 1556, leaving behind a disarray kingdom in the hands of his 14 years old son, Akbar. Immediately after Humayun's death, war broke out. A rebel known as "Hemu' took Delhi and claimed the throne for himself. However, he was decisively defeated by a Moghul army at Panipat and thus Akbar's succession was ensured. Under Bayrum Khan (a loyal and capable general of Humayun) who was Akbar's mentor and guardian, Akbar's rule was extended beyond the borders of Agra and Delhi and within a short time his rule was well consolidated in India.

Akbar reigned for almost half a century. He started conquering many neighboring states. The Moghul rule was extended from Gujrat to Bengal. By 1601, many territories like Kashmir (1586), Sind (1591), Quandhar (1595) and parts of Deccan (Ahmadnagar and Berar) were added to the Moghul rule. Akbar died in 1605 but before his death he had stabilized the regime and left behind a kingdom which lasted another 250 years.

The notable feature of Akbar's reign was inclusion of Hindus, especially Rajputs (Hindu rulers of Rajhistan) in the administrative issues and policies. He faced great resistance from the Rajputs, but eventually Akbar's military as well as diplomatic skills helped him to subdue them. In 1562, Akbar married the daughter of Raja Bihari Mal of Amber, a Rajput ruler and thus established direct relationship with many notable Rajput families. She was the mother of prince Salim (later known as Jahangir, the fourth emperor of India), heir to the throne. Akbar ruled with fairness and treated both Muslims and Hindus equally. Both Hindus and Muslims were given high posts in his administration. He abolished Jizya (a tax on non-Muslims). He allowed the assimilation of Hindu and Muslim cultures. Though the civil code was based on the Muslim law, the disputes among Hindus were decided based on Hindu law. Akbar's approach to other religions besides Islam was very open and he encouraged the discussion with many religious groups. Overall, during his reign the tolerance of other religions and cultures was at the highest point in the Indian history. Such openness was essential for a country like India where so many cultures, languages and religions thrive. Akbar realized that for an efficient rule over such a vast country it is necessary to be tolerant and open minded.

The Indian subcontinent was divided into small kingdoms and there was no central government. Akbar tried to form a centralized administration which overlooked the finance and the boundaries of the Moghul territory. Taxation system was revised and the conditions of peasants were vastly improved due to the reformed tax system.

Akbar not only consolidated his power in India, but he opened the doors for friendly ties with other nations. He established a direct relation with Atlantic Europe. The East India Company was established in the sixteenth century and arrived in Akbar's court as Company's emissary in 1603.

Akbar was also a great patron of artists, painters, musicians and scholars. He maintained a very luxurious and pompous court. Though he himself was illiterate, he collected numerous scholars in his court. There were nine most celebrated people in his court known as 'Nine Jewels'

Akbar was also involved in the construction of many notable buildings which exemplify the Moghul architecture in India. The architecture of Akbar's period is elegant and graceful mainly due to the decorative work. Persian, Arabic and Indian (Hindu) decorative traditions have been assimilated into the decoration of these monumental buildings. The buildings at Fatehpur Sikri which was Akbar's capital for 16 years (1570-1586) exemplify the Islamic architecture in India. The 'Great Mosque' and the 'Victory Gate' are masterpieces of Moghul architecture. The forts at Agra, Lahore and Ajmer are also the examples of high class architectural capabilities of the Moghuls. In 1575, at Fatehpur Sikri Akbar built a house of worship where he invited scholars of different religions to discuss the theological issues. In this discussion Hindus, Muslims, Christians (Jesuits from the Portugese colony of Goa), Parsis and Jains were invited. Akbar himself did not follow the orthodox Islam and came up with his own version of religion known as Din-e-Alahi (Divine Faith or Religion of God) which was based on Hindu and Islamic beliefs. This religion however, did not exert much influence on the masses and disappeared after Akbar's death.

Akbar's reign was an era of prosperity and peace for general masses. In Europe his contemporaries were Elizabeth I of England and Philip II of Spain but Akbar surpassed both of them in wealth, power, majesty, vision, liberal thinking and administrative skills. In short, Akbar consolidated the Mughal rule in India and showed that tolerance and openness is necessary to rule a multicultural and multireligious country like India. He lived in the sixteenth century India with a vision and thinking of a twenty-first century ruler. His policy of religious tolerance and cultural harmonization makes him a model ruler.

Shah Abbas I
(1571-1629)

Contribution: Shah of Persia also known as Shah Abbas the Great. He strengthened the Safavid dynasty. Abbas built his new capital at Isfahan which was considered one of the most beautiful cities in the world at the time. Under his rule the Persian culture, trade and arts flourished.

The Safavids, a Persian dynasty gained control of Persia in 1501 and ruled till1736 AD. They named themselves after their Sufi ancestor Safiuddin. They were the first native dynasty to govern Persia after the Sasanian Empire (224-651) who were deposed by the Arab Muslims. The first ruler of the Safavid dynasty was Ismail, who in 1501 defeated a group of warriors known as 'White Sheep Turks', conquered Tabriz and proclaimed himself as Shah. For the next twenty years he stabilized Persia and started a long rivalry with Ottomans. This rivalry was of a religious nature as the Ottomans were Sunni Muslims whereas the Safavids were Shiites.

Abbas was born on January 27, 1571 AD. He was the third son of Sultan Muhammad Shah. Abbas spent his youth in Mashed and Herat. His mild mannered father could not cope with the leaders of Turkish Shiite tribes known as Kizilbash (Redheads) who had helped Safavids to gain power in Persia. The Kizilbash had gained enormous power and were very much dictating the affairs of the state. They were also instrumental in killing Abbas's mother and his brother crown prince Hamza. Abbas assumed throne at the age of 17 (1588) at a very critical moment of the Safavid dynasty. Not only there were domestic troubles but also there were family feuds for the throne. Abbas himself was marked for assassination by his uncle Shah Ismail II. Militarily it was also a turbulent time for the Safavids. On the frontiers of Persia, the Ottomans in the west and the Uzbeks in the east were advancing in the Persian territory. Sensing he could not fight at the two frontiers at the same time,

Shah Abbas signed a peace treaty with the Ottomans (1590). This treaty, however, was not without price. Shah Abbas had to give Ottomans a large area in the west and northwest of Persia. Meanwhile Uzbek offensive resulted in the loss of some Persian territory. Shah Abbas, however, did not launch any offensive against the Uzbeks for the next 10 years. This was mainly because Shah Abbas wanted a standing army. His first task to form a standing army was to tame the old tribal loyalties which had weakened his predecessors. Though the Kizilbash (Red Head) were the backbone of the Safavid military strength, Shah Abbas distrusted them. His new army was composed of the slaves brought to Persia from Georgia, Armenia and Circasia during the reign of Shah Abbas's grandfather. Shah Abbas had great faith in this standing army of slaves and some of them gained high positions during his rule. Eventually Shah Abbas was able to attack the Uzbeks and in 1598, he decisively defeated them taking control of Khurasan. After this victory, Shah Abbas moved his capital from Kazvin to Isfahan. Between 1602 and 1612, he conducted number of attacks on the Ottoman Turks and recovered most of the lands he had lost to them due to an earlier peace treaty. He, however, did not mount further attacks on Turks after recovering the lost Persian territory. In 1622, with the help of the British he took Hormoz Islands from the Portuguese.

Besides his military ventures, Shah Abbas also passionately worked for the welfare of his people. He improved the economical plight of the common people. He opened the channels of commerce and during his reign, the Dutch, the Portuguese and the English were flocked into the Persian Gulf, each trying to win his favor. This largely contributed to the economic growth of Persia. He established textile workshops which later paved the way for famous Persian carpet-weaving industry. His love and concern to the common people was genuine. He frequently visited the Bazaars and tea shops in Isfahan. Occasionally he will mix up with the people in disguise to find their conditions. He was also a patron of Persian architecture. His new capital Isfahan became one of the beautiful cities in the world. Its beauty and luxury astounded the visitors. He built mosques, colleges, baths, boulevards and spacious squares in the city.

Despite his zeal for justice and well-being for his people, Shah Abbas had a darker side. He was very suspicious of the royal family and the tribal leaders and extremely zealous in protecting his throne. He ordered the killing of many tribal leaders especially the members of Kizilbash tribes and his own son, crown prince Safi Mirza. He blinded his one son, two grandsons and two brothers. He did not allow other princes to gain necessary training for leadership. Shah Abbas died on January 19, 1629. His paranoia to save his throne created a leadership vacuum and within the next hundred years the safavid's rule in Persia came to an end.

Despite his cruelty and paranoia, Shah Abbas holds a special place in the Iranian history of this millennium. He had a vision and purpose for his rule. He not only saved the Safavid dynasty from a collapse and internal feud but raised the empire to a new height. Under his rule the safavid dynasty was at its zenith. In the end he defeated both Uzbeks and the Ottomans and restored the honor and integrity of Persia. In 1561, Anglo-Persian trade was opened and Shah Abbas had Englishmen in his services. This was part of his diplomatic strategy to have friendly ties with the west where he anticipated finding support against Turks. Politically and militarily, Shah Abbas was very successful. He secured the Persian borders and raised a standing army to defend its borders. He centralized the government and the administrative system. He improved the communication and transportation in Persia by building roads, bridges and caravansaries. He showed religious tolerance and granted privileges to many religious groups. In the eye of a modern day historian, his achievements may be overshadowed by his treatment of his own family but undeniably he remains an outstanding ruler.

Shahjahan
(1592-1666)

Contribution: Fifth Moghul emperor of India. During his reign, the Moghul Empire reached to its zenith. He is known world wide as the builder of the 'Taj Mahal'.

Shahjahan (original name Khurram) was the fifth Moghul emperor of India and best known as the builder of Taj Mahal. Shahjahan was born in Lahore on January 5, 1592, the third son of emperor Jahangir and the Rajput princess Manmati. In 1612, Shahjahan married Arjumand Bano (known as Mumtaz Mahal) who was a niece of Noor Jahan, emperor Jahamgir's most favorite wife. Though Shahjahan rebelled against his father in 1622 but reconciled with him in 1625. In 1627, Jahangir died and a war for the throne broke out between Shahjahan and his brother Khusru. Mainly due to the support of Asif Khan (Prime Minister of Moghul kingdom and father in-law of Shahjahan), Shahjahan won the war and proclaimed himself the emperor of India on February 4, 1628 at Agra.

Shahjahan ruled for the next 30 years. His reign is notable for annexing the Deccan (Southern) kingdom. From 1630 to 1636, military expeditions to Deccan resulted in the fall of independent kingdoms of Deccan. Ahmednagar (1632), Golkanda (1635) and Baijapur (1636) were taken and annexed into Moghul Empire. The notable feature of Shahjahan's conquest was that by annexing Deccan, he added more territory to the Moghul rule. His son Auranzeb was appointed the governor of Deccan and managed to maintain the law and order in the occupied territories and frequently embarked on military expedition to crush the rebels. Where Shahjahan succeeded in winning the wars in the Deccan, military ventures in the north-west did not meet with success. Quandhar was taken from the Iranians in 1638 but in 1649 the Iranians took the city back. In 1646, Badakshan and Balkh were taken by the Moghul army but in 1647, Balkh was lost and subsequent three attempts to regain the city failed. In 1648, Shahjahan moved his capital from Agra to Delhi and a new city Shahjahanabad was erected. Unfortunately, last years of his life were marred by the revolt of his son Aurangzeb. In 1657, Shahjahan fell ill and his four sons, Dara Shikoh, Shuja, Murad and Aurangzeb started fighting for the throne. Aurangzeb being most experienced and clever among all brothers managed to defeat all of them and on June 8, 1658 captured Agra. He declared himself the emperor of India and made his father captive. For the next eight years, Shahjahan remained captive in Agra Fort, most of the time gazing upon the Taj Mahal. Shahjahan died on January 22, 1666.

Shahjahan's rule was mainly peaceful and prosperous. During his reign religious tolerance continued to prevail. Shahjahan was a great patron of art, painting and calligraphy. The Moghul architecture was at its best. Mumtaz Mahal died in 1631 and Shahjahan built the Taj Mahal in her memory. Taj Mahal undoubtedly is the most remarkable building constructed anywhere in the world. In order to build this mausoleum, the artists, sculptures and craftsmen were recruited from different parts of the world. Twenty thousand men worked for 17 years to build the Taj Mahal. Besides the Taj Mahal, Shahjahan built Moti Masjid (Pearl mosque) at Agra and Jama Masjid (Grand Mosque) in Delhi. Red Fort in Delhi is another building which was built by Shahjahan. In Red Fort, Shahjahan used to hold his court and sat on his famous Peacock Throne designed by him. The Peacock Throne was built with jewels (rubies, diamond, emeralds and pearls) and gold. His court was splendor and pompous and his era is considered the richest period of the Moghul rule.

As a patron of art and music, he patronized both Hindu and Muslim poets and musicians. Sanskrit classics were translated into Persian. Overall, Shahjahan's reign was the time of peace, prosperity, wealth and grandeur.

Muhammad Ibn Abd al-Wahhab
(1703-1792)

Contribution: Theologian, reformer, and founder of the Wahhabi movement. The objective of his movement was to return the Islamic societies to the original or true principles of Islam. With time Abd al-Wahhab's movement grew in size and today its members are in many parts of the world, Saudi Arabia being the major foothold.

The plight of the Islamic world was much different in the eighteenth century than what it had been earlier. With the rise of the European powers, the Muslim dominance in the world was shrinking. Two groups of Muslim thinkers emerged from the ashes of Islam's glorious days. One group believed that reforms were needed so that Islamic societies could be compatible with the changes taking place around them, whereas another group of thinkers wanted to return to the time of the Prophet. The orthodox Muslim thinkers believed that the fall of the Muslim Empire is mainly due to the lack of 'true' practices of Islam. The emphasis was on the strict observance of 'sharia'. Many movements which advocated returning to the orthodoxy emerged in many parts of the world but their impact was short-lived. Many of these movements disappeared with the demise of their founders but one movement which though appeared to be non significant at the time, survived and has enormous impact on the Islamic world. This movement known as 'Wahhabi movement' named after its founder Muhammad Ibn Abd al-Wahhab, originated in Central Arabia.

Abd al-Wahhab, a member of Bani Sinan was born in Uyainah (now in Saudi Arabia) in 1703. He took his early education in Medina and in his early years traveled extensively. He lived and taught in Basra (Iraq) for four years, spent another five years in Baghdad where he married a wealthy woman whose property he inherited after she died. Abd al-Wahhab then traveled to

Kurdistan, Hamadan and Isfahan. In Iran he studied the Sufi system but in 1736, he began teaching against the extreme ideas of Sufi doctrines. After a visit to Quom, Abd al-Wahhab returned to Uyainah and started preaching his doctrines. Basically, Abd al-Wahhab was an advocate of Ibn Hanbal's school of thought. In Uyainah, Abd al-Wahhab wrote 'Kitab al-Tawhid' (Book of Unity), which is the main book for Wahhabi doctrines. He met with both success and opposition. Surprisingly opposition came from his own family, his brother and cousin opposed his views.

In his teachings Abd al-Wahhab, emphasized on the strict obedience to the Quran and Hadith. He opposed all innovations in Islam and believed that the past glory of Islam could be revived if only the Muslims return to the basic teaching and the principles enunciated by the Prophet. He opposed the reverence given to the dead saints and calling them intermediary between faith and God. Like Ibn Taymiyya, Abd al-Wahhab also opposed the visit of tombs of the saints. He also preached against the special devotion to Sufism and the decoration of mosques. His teachings, however, produced controversy and Abd al-Wahhab was expelled from Uyainah in 1744. He then went to Ad-Dariyah, where Muhammad Ibn Saud, the ruler of Najd accepted his doctrines.

Alliance with Ibn Saud proved to be very beneficial to Abd al-Wahhab. In 1747, a war broke out between Ibn Saud and the ruler of Riyadh. This long war which lasted for 28 years was ultimately won by the Saud clan. Ibn Saud died in 1765 and his son abd-al Aziz continued his alliance with Abd al-Wahhab. In 1773, Abd-al Aziz finally captured Riyadh and the whole of Najd came under his control. Wahhabism, though opposed by many rulers and chieftain in Arabia, continued to grow and expand. Abd al-Wahhab died in 1792 at the age of 89 but his movement did not perish with his death rather gained momentum and strength. By the end of the eighteenth century, Wahhabis not only were the ruler of the whole Najd but they occupied Karbala (Iraq) and took control of Mecca and Medina, Islam's two most holy cities. The first set back to Wahhabism came when in 1818, the Ottomans stopped the expansion of the Wahhabis. After a while, the sect was revived under the leadership of Faisal I but by the end of the nineteenth century, once again was at the verge of capitulation by the hands of Rashidyah clans of Northern Arabia. Ibn Saud, eventually created the kingdom of Saudi Arabia in 1932 which ultimately provided Wahhabis a safe political and religious heaven.

The name 'Wahhabi' was given by the opponents of the sect but the followers of Abd-al Wahhab call themselves 'Muwahhidun' (Unitarians). The members of this sect regard themselves as Sunni Muslims, their jurisprudence is based on the teachings of Ibn Hanbal and they believe in the literal meaning of the Quran and Hadith.

Mirza Muhammad Siraj ud-Dawlah
(1729-1757)

Contribution: Nawab (ruler) of Bengal who became the symbol of resistance against British imperialism in India. As a legendry folk hero, Siraj ud-Dawlah is not only admired in Bengal but in the whole Subcontinent. He was an intelligent and well respected ruler who became victim of the treachery to the British as well as his own people.

Siraj ud-Dawlah was born as Mirza Muhammad in 1729 at Murshidabad. His grandfather nawab Ali Vardi Khan was the ruler of Bengal under the nominal suzerainty of the Mughal emperor. The British had gained access to the Mughul court during Shah Jahan's reign (1592-1666). They entered India disguised as merchants but their main objective was colonization of India. By the early eighteenth century, the Mughal rulers were losing their grip over provincial territories and many independent rulers emerged in India. The British took full advantage of this situation and tried to interfere into the internal affairs of these emerging independent states. Due to the strength, skill and vision of Ali Vardi Khan, the British could not make roads into Bengal. Nawab Ali Vardi Khan mistrusted the British and kept them away from his territories. Siraj ud-Dawlah became the nawab of Bengal in 1756 after the death of his grandfather, nawab Ali Vardi Khan. He faced opposition to his succession from his family members backed by the British but in the end; he managed to remove all opposition. The British, however, continued their treacherous and illegal acts within the young nawab's territory. The British, without the permission of Siraj ud-Dawlah started fortifying Calcutta (a major port city in Bengal). Siraj ud-Dawlah asked the British governor of Calcutta to halt the Illegal activities but the governor paid no heed to Siraj ud-Dawlah's orders. Siraj ud-Dawlah finally marched on the city taking the British post at

Quasimbazar and forcing the British governor and his staff to flee. On June 20, 1757, Siraj ud-Dawlah captured Fort Williams, the stronghold of the British in Calcutta. Some British soldiers and officers were captured and confined into a small jail cell. Some prisoners were suffocated in the cell and the British described the incident as "Black Hole" and propagated this incident as an act of cruelty by Siraj ud-Dawlah. In reality this was an unintentional act by Siraj ud-Dawlah and the casualty of the British was much less as what was described by them at that time.

Calcutta remained under Siraj ud-Dawlah's control for the next six months but on January 2, 1757, the British retook Calcutta under the command of Robert Clive and Admiral Charles Watson. Robert Clive, an uneducated, corrupt and a fortune seeker English clerk had arrived in India many years ago. Though he lacked real military skills, he had a treacherous mind and a bold attitude. Upon his arrival in Calcutta, Clive realized that he was no match against Siraj ud-Dawlah in an open arm conflict; therefore, he began his treacherous act by plotting with many officials of Siraj ud-Dawlah within the army and the administration. At Plassey, on June 23, 1757, Robert Clive with an army of 3000 defeated Siraj ud-Dawlah with an army of 50,000. Siraj ud-Dawlah fled to Murshidabad but was captured and executed. In reality, the Battle of Plassey was never fought. As soon as the battle began, Mir Jafar, the commander of Siraj ud-Dawlah's army joined the British camp taking with him more than half of the army. For his treacherous act, the British made Mir Jafar the nawab of Bengal. In return, Mir Jafar paid more than a quarter million British pounds to Robert Clive as part of a deal between the two. Clive also obtained many trade concessions from Mir Jafar.

Fall of Siraj ud-Dawlah at Plassey was significant from many aspects. A victory at Plassey assured British a strong foothold in India. It also gave them a sense that there were traitors within the Subcontinent who could be easily bought. On the other hand, a defeat at Plassey might have deprived the British of their dream of colonizing India. Even in defeat Siraj ud-Dawlah, remains a symbol of freedom and courage against the imperial powers.

Fateh Ali Khan Tipu
(1750-1799)

Contribution: Sultan of Mysore also known as 'Tiger of Mysore'. He was the most able and powerful ruler among the native Indian rulers. He posed the biggest threat to the British expansion in India but due to the treachery of other Indian rulers, he was defeated and killed by the British and their Indian allies.

Popularly known as 'Tipu Sultan', Fateh Ali Khan Tipu was born at Devanhalli in1750, the eldest son of Haider Ali, the ruler of Mysore. Tipu was given an excellent education and was involved in military and political affairs of the state from a very early age. He was at his father's side in many wars against the Marathas and the British. At the age of 17, he led an army against the Marathas in Western India and fought against them on several occasions between 1775 and 1779.

In 1780, Haider Ali attacked Karnataka and the second War of Mysore began which lasted for four years. At Polilur (near Kanchipuran), a British army of four thousand was completely annihilated. An army of five thousand men were mobilized from Calcutta to Mysore but in February 1782, Tipu defeated a British army on the banks of River Coleroon. The same year, Haider Ali died and Tipu succeeded him. The war with the British continued until the British signed a peace treaty with Tipu (Treaty of Mysore, 1784).

Both economically and militarily, Mysore, under Tipu's efficient administration was becoming a strong state. This alarmed the Marathas in the northwest and the Nizam (the Muslim ruler of Hyderabad) in the north. Tipu defeated both the enemies but also tried to gain the friendship of both Marathas and the Nizam but failed in his attempts. Tipu knew very well that sooner or later the British would break the treaty and invade Mysore. Sensing the incompetency, greed and lack of vision of the rulers of Indian states, Tipu sent his emissaries to France and to the Ottomans but could not gain any real benefit out of it.

The third War of Mysore (1790-2) was initiated by Cornwallis (the general who had surrendered to George Washington at Yorktown during the American War of Independence). In 1790, the Marathas and Nizam allied with the British attacked Mysore. For the next two years, Tipu held his enemies at bay but was then forced to sign the 'Treaty of Seringapatnam' (March 1792). The treaty cost him half of his kingdom and an eight-figure indemnity. The British also took his two sons (aged 8 and 10 years) as a guarantee for the payment of indemnity.

Despite the loss of half of his kingdom, in no time Tipu re-established his military strength, paid the indemnity and reunited with his sons and once again became a dangerous foe to the British.

Richard Wellesley, the governor-general, who was responsible for the fourth war of Mysore (1799), began preparation for battle against Tipu, immediately after his arrival in India. Sensing that militarily, it would be very difficult to defeat Tipu, the British started looking for a traitor within Tipu's court. In Mir Sadique, they found their man. Mir Sadique was one of the relatives of Tipu and held a very important post in Tipu's court. In 1799, the British along with Marathas and Nizam attacked Mysore. Mir Sadique disrupted Tipu's military structure and Tipu was pushed back to his capital Seringapatnam and died on May 4, 1799, while defending Mysore. Seringapatnam was sacked and among 9000 dead Mysore's fighters, Tipu's body was found. He was cut by bayonets, shot twice and was robbed of his precious jewelries. Like Siraj ud-Dawlah, Tipu was not defeated by the British but it was the treachery and the greed of his incompetent and visionless countrymen who brought his downfall.

Tipu was not only an excellent military commander but also a very prolific administrator. His policies made Mysore a very prosperous state. He was a just ruler who treated his subjects without partiality of caste or religion. Haider Ali had turned Mysore's army into a professional army trained on the European lines. Tipu followed his father's footsteps but also paid attention to improve the economy of the state. Trade became very important. He established a trading company and encouraged investors to buy shares. Tipu experimented with new crops using seeds and plants obtained from Asia and France. Botanical acclimatization and propagation was sought. Tipu introduced sericulture in Mysore. He established factories for silk processing and weaving. He also established factories for sugar, paper and gunpowder. There were many ammunition factories and the factory at Bednur produced 20,000 muskets and guns every year.

The British indeed considered Tipu the greatest hurdle for their imperialistic dream of capitulating India. When governor-general Wellesly saw Tipu's body he shouted with joy that "Today India is ours". Indeed after Tipu, there was no body to resist the British expansion in India.

Mirza Assadullah Khan Ghalib
(1797-1869)

Contribution: Renowned Indian poet, famous for his philosophical and romantic poetry. Most of his poems were composed in Persian but his fame comes mainly due to his Urdu poetry. Ghalib was an original and independent poet. His letters, written to his friends are regarded as his mastery over the Urdu language and a model of early prose writing.

Urdu is one of the most widely spoken languages in the Indian subcontinent. The word 'Urdu' comes from Turkish, means 'army camp'. Urdu language is almost 500 years old and consists of a large number of words borrowed from other languages (Turkish, Persian, Arabic, Sanskrit and Hindi). In the twelfth and the thirteenth century, when in India Sanskrit became obsolete as a spoken language; people in different regions of India adopted their own dialect. The origin of Urdu can be traced in Delhi region where people spoke their own dialect, known as 'Khari Boli'. The Muslim rulers of Delhi, who spoke either Persian or Turkish, found 'Khari Boli' very useful to communicate with their Indian subjects. Thus a large number of Persian, Turkish and Arabic words were introduced into 'Khari Boli'. With time, Urdu became the language of the rulers of Northern India.

By the middle of the sixteenth century, Urdu established itself as the language of elite and was written, read and spoken widely in Delhi. By early eighteenth century, Urdu started replacing Persian as the language of prose and poetry writing. Once Delhi established itself as undisputed capital of India, top Urdu poets and writers flocked in. These scholars further helped in building the reputation and grandeur of Urdu language as it spread to Lucknow, Hyderabad and Lahore. Ghalib composed his poems both in Persian and Urdu but it is his Urdu poetry which made him a household name in the subcontinent.

'Ghalib' was born in Agra on December 27, 1797, as Mirza Assadullah Beg. Ghalib's ancestors migrated from Turkey to India and from his mother's side; Ghalib came from a very wealthy family. His father died when Ghalib was only four years old. His mother, brother and sister then moved to live with his maternal uncle. Ghalib was raised as an aristocrat and was provided with the education considered appropriate for the children of aristocratic Muslim families. He learned Persian at an early age and wrote poetry when he was barely eleven years old. He also wrote in Urdu and by the age of seventeen he had already composed some of his well known poems. As was the custom among the poets of the time, he adopted a pen name, 'Ghalib', means 'victorious'.

Ghalib was married at the age of thirteen. His wife was a member of a prominent Muslim family from Delhi. They had seven children but all died in infancy. Financially, Ghalib remained unstable throughout his life due to his indulgence in wine and gambling.

The time, Ghalib was born, the power of the Mughal Empire was in decline and the British East India Company was gaining foothold in India. The last Mughal emperor Bhadur Shah Zafar was a great admirer of poets and was himself a poet. Ghalib was a well established poet in Delhi but he had a great difficulty in gaining popularity into Bahadur Shah's court. Bahadur Shah's mentor or poetic advisor, Zauq (popularly known as ustad (teacher) Zauq) had no liking of Ghalib. Zauq considered Ghalib's poetry vulgar and his life style unsuitable for the court because Ghalib was flamboyant, spontaneous and did not care about the manners of the court. Relationship between Ghalib and Zauq remained strained until Zauq's death. Bahadur Shah was a great admirer of Ghalib's poetry and after the death of Zauq, he chose Ghalib as his mentor in poetry. For time being, Ghalib's financial situation considerably improved but unfortunately, it was short lived. In 1857, the War of Independence against the British failed, Bahadur Shah was exiled to Rangoon where he died in 1862. Ghalib continued composing his poetry but he faced enormous financial hardships. Ghalib died on February 15, 1869 in Delhi at the age of 72.

In his life, Ghalib was flamboyant, spontaneous and humorous. His humors are of practical nature and have become part of Urdu literature. After the failed War of Independence against the British in 1857, the British military governor of Delhi (colonel Burns) summoned the elites of Delhi to determine if they were involved in helping the political activists against the British. Colonel Burns asked Ghalib if he (Ghalib) was a Muslim. Ghalib responded that he was a half-Muslim. Burns was amused and demanded further explanation. Ghalib told him, "I do not eat pork but drink wine". Colonel Burns then excused Ghalib from further questioning.

Ghalib was not an orthodox Muslim rather he was a liberal and free thinker. He was tolerant of other religions and had both Muslim and non-Muslim friends. He never shunned from life's sensuous enjoyments. He was fond of gambling and wine, yet he was a family man and a person of high integrity and honesty.

Ghalib's poetry is universal. He touched almost every subject making him one of the most quoted Urdu poets. People from every walk of life like to recite his verses to prove a point or to describe a situation. Ghalib, though composed his poems extensively in Persian, he is known for his Urdu poetry. His elegant style, choice of words and the presentation of thoughts made his poetry very beautiful. He was criticized for being difficult as most of his verses are not easily comprehensible but later in his life he tried to compose his poems in easier and more comprehensible form.

Ghalib wrote his poetry in three forms: Ghazals (love lyrics), Mathnavi (mystical verses) and Quasidah (panegyric). Ghalib is famous for his ghazals and is considered the greatest Urdu poet of ghazals. Ghalib has spiritual intensity but it focuses on worldliness rather than beauty of the soul. His reference to wine and taverns means wine and taverns not the state or elevation of the soul.

Unlike Rumi, Hafiz, Omar Khayyam and Saadi, Ghalib is not well known in the west. The main reason may be that it is very difficult to translate Ghalib's verses from Urdu into a foreign language. Since a Urdu verse can have many meaning or can be interpreted in many ways, it is impossible to express Ghalib's poetry with the same intensity and expression as he does in Urdu. It is difficult to fathom the magnitude of Ghalib's contribution to Urdu poetry. He remains a towering and the most influential poet among the Urdu poets even today.

Abd al-Qadir
(1808-1883)

Contribution: Political, military and religious leader of Algeria. As a leader of Algerian independence movement, he fought against the French colonization of Algeria. His initial success against French made him a household name and a symbol of resistance against colonialism and imperialism.

Abd al-Qadir was born on September 26, 1807 in the small town of Guetma near Mascara, Algeria. He belonged to a family with a religious position connected with the Qadiri order. His father, Muhi al-Din, was a religious teacher who provided him with a traditional education as well as taught him Islamic theology. In 1821, Abd al-Qadir was sent to Oran to learn more about theology. There he saw the cruelty of the Turkish rulers of Algeria as well as their luxurious and unislamic life style. Though in 1820s, several rebellion movements led by the religious leaders were initiated but these were largely unsuccessful and the Turks executed many such leaders. In 1826, Abd al-Qadir went to Mecca for pilgrimage and visited several Middle Eastern countries; the visit helped him to extend his knowledge and experience.

In 1830, the French landed on the Algerian coast and occupied Algiers, bringing 300 years of Turkish rule to an end. The French invasion forced many Algerian tribes to organize themselves based on their religious beliefs. These tribes asked Muhi al-Din, the then director of a religious school near Mascara to lead the opposition movement against French. In 1832, aging Muhi al-Din had his son Abd al-Qadir elected in his place. Abd al-Qadir was already known for his religious beliefs, intelligence and military skills. In the battle of Oran (May 3-8, 1832), Abd al-Qadir with his ten thousand men fought bravely against the French but was defeated.

On November 22, 1832 Abd al-Qadir was proclaimed Amir (leader). The symbols of his resistance against the French based on the concept of Jihad (holy war) and respect for the Sharia. He began by seeking political recognition as Amir and used his power to the fullest. He established equality among different Algerian groups by suppressing the special privileges granted to those tribes which were considered warlike tribes. He imposed new but equal taxes on his subjects and used this money to build his army. Though there were sporadic skirmishes with the French, overall, these caused very little damage to Abd al-Qadir or his organization.

The Desmichels Treaty (1834) provided Abd al-Qadir with the opportunity of taking control of Oran and then occupying Miliana and Medea. In fact General Desmichels helped Abd al-Qadir to build his army on modern lines; this army was then effectively used by Abd al-Qadir to subdue his local enemies. Abd al-Qadir then defeated General Camille Trezel at Macta and drew enormous support from the Algerians who were becoming wary over the French use of violence. Abd al-Qadir's military successes were short lived and on July 6, 1836, General Bugeaud inflicted a serious defeat on Abd al-Qadir. In 1837, the Treaty of Tafna was signed. According to this treaty, Abd al-Qadir was now the ruler of Oran and Titteri. He organized his territory and though he established a theocratic state, the organization of his government was modern. He set up administrative structure, organized regular army and established the tax system based on the Islamic laws. By 1839 two-thirds of Algeria was under his control.

Abd al-Qadir's success and achievements alarmed the French and a military expedition led by General Bugeaud was sent against Abd al-Qadir. In 1841 he was again defeated by Bugeaud who captured his capital Tagdempt and destroyed the city. Abd al-Qadir then moved to a tent city, Zamalah and continued to harass the French but in 1843, a surprise attack by the French proved disastrous for Abd al-Qadir and he fled to Morocco. The French meanwhile were destroying the Algerian lands and mounted a high degree of cruelty against the Algerians. The French declared war against Morocco on the pretext of Abd al-Qadir's presence there and defeated them at the battle of Isly in 1844. The harsh rule of the French led to uprising and when in September 1845, Abd al-Qadir returned to Algeria, people gathered around him. The resistance movement against French once again began but attempts to recapture Algiers from the French were not successful and Abd al-Qadir once again fled to Morocco. The Moroccans, however, this time did not welcome Abd al-Qadir who on December 21, 1847 finally surrendered to the French. He was promised that he could stay in Africa but he was imprisoned in France where Napolean III released him in 1852. Abd al-Qadir, then went to Damascus and spent rest of his life there as a statesman, scholar and teacher. Abd al-Qadir considered Ibn Arabi his spiritual master. In 1860 there was an uprising in Damascus and local Christians were targeted. Abd al-Qadir saved hundreds of Christians by giving them refuge in his house. He died in Damascus on May 26, 1883; in 1968 his remains were brought to Algeria.

Abd al-Qadir left behind an indelible mark on the history of France and Algeria. In 1962, when Algeria gained independence from France, Abd al-Qadir was declared a national hero. By his sheer religious conviction and military prowess he transformed a small band of people into a military unit who fought for the freedom of their culture, religion and country as long as there was a chance of victory and hope.

Sir Syed Ahmed Khan
(1817-1898)

Contribution: Educator, author, journalist, jurist, politician and social reformer. His legacy is 'Aligarh Muslim University' which has produced world class scholars, scientists and politicians. He also induced modern thinking in otherwise orthodox Indian Muslims.

Syed Ahmed Khan, popularly known as Sir Syed (knighted by the British) was a reformer, educationalist, civil servant and a politician. In order to understand Sir Syed's role and contribution to the Indian Muslims one should first assess the overall plight of the Muslims in the eighteenth and the nineteenth century India. The glorious days of the Muslim rule in India were over. The East India Company was getting more and more involved into the Indian politics and the signs and symptoms of the British imperialism were very obvious. The Mughal rulers till the time of Shahjahan ruled with open mindness and treated their non-Muslim subjects with respect and fairness. Unfortunately, Aurangzeb, despite being a brilliant administrator failed to realize the necessity of open mindness to rule over India where the majority was non-Muslims. His rigidity and religious fervor helped the Muslim orthodoxy to manipulate the general Muslim masses. These orthodox clergy were against all sorts of innovations in the Muslim society and due to their own ignorance and continuous efforts, by the early nineteenth century the Muslim intellectualism in India was at the verge of complete collapse. The education was limited to the madrasas and neither the clergy nor the madrasa educated people had any understanding of the true spirit of Islam. The Muslims were much more interested in the arts, music and romantic poetry rather than learning science and technology, economics and new methods of administration. In short, the thinking of the Muslims was obsolete and their social and political

212

structures were hopelessly decayed. There was an urgent need for a healer and at this dark moment of the history of the Indian Muslims, Sir Syed appeared as a bright light.

Syed Ahmad Khan was born on October 17, 1817 in a well to do and educated family. His maternal grandfather, Khawja Fariduddin Ahmed served as prime minister in the Mughal court and also enjoyed the trust of the British. Khawja Fariduddin was also a mathematician and astronomer.

After his father's death, Syed Ahmad initially struggled financially and took some ordinary jobs. Despite financial problems he continued his education and obtained a law degree. He then started his career as a law clerk in East India Company and after three years he was promoted as a subjudge. He served in the judicial department at various capacities.

Sir Syed began his literary career around 1840. His brother had established a printing press in Delhi and started a newspaper in Urdu. Sir Syed contributed to the newspaper by becoming a regular writer. Sir Syed's writings mainly dealt with the Muslim social customs of the time.

In 1857, during the War of Independence against the British, Sir Syed not only saved the lives of many British officers but also tried to explain the British the causes of the war and the thinking of the Muslims as a nation. His first attempt was to convince the British that the Muslims of India neither instigated the War of Independence nor went against the Christian government of British due to their Islamic religious beliefs. In his commentary entitled 'Causes of Indian Revolt', Sir Syed outlined the weaknesses and the errors of the British Administrators which led to the War of Independence. This work of Sir Syed was seriously taken by the British and had some influence on the British policy in India. The British realized his contributions and in 1869, Sir Syed became a commander in the order of the star of India and in 1888 was awarded the knighthood. He also served as a member of Viceroy's Legislative Council and sat on the Advisory body until 1883.

After the War of Independence (1857), Sir Syed devoted his life for the cause of the Muslims. He realized that the progress of the Muslims (not only in India but throughout the Muslim world) lies in learning modern day technology. Keeping this in mind he established schools in Muradabad (1858) and in Ghazipur (1863).

He founded a Scientific Society whose main task was to publish translations of educational text books. He also started a journal called 'Social Reform' especially to reform the orthodox Muslim thinking and to help the Muslims of the Indian Subcontinent to realize the need of the hour. In 1875, he established a Muslim school in Aligarh and in 1876 by his efforts he converted this school into a college. The college provided training in history, science and English. This kind of training was needed not only to find a respectable job in British India but also to prepare Muslims of India for the civil service positions in the government. For his efforts he faced enormous opposition from the conservative Muslims but his undaunting efforts resulted in the establishment of a university known as 'Aligarh Muslim University'. This university since its establishment has produced a large number of Muslim scholars, scientists, researchers and politicians. The university is Sir Syed's legacy and the Muslims of India will remain indebted to him for his vision for the future of the Muslims of the subcontinent. In 1886, Sir Syed helped in organizing the All India Muhammadan Educational Conference which met every year in different parts of India. The objective of this conference was to promote education as well as political awareness among the Muslims of the Subcontinent.

Sir Syed opposed the creation of Indian National Congress established in 1885. He feared that at the time, Muslims of India may not be able to compete with Hindus for jobs and for legislative councils. His fear was appropriate as the Indian Muslims were in the grips of the orthodox Muslim clergy who had effectively blocked all intellectual thinking and progress among the Indian Muslims. In 1888, he formed 'United Patriotic Association' which drew massive support from the Muslims of India and left Indian National Congress without significant Muslim support almost for a quarter century.

Sir Syed was also an excellent writer and in his writings he addressed the social issues and provided the solutions of these issues. He published an Urdu journal 'Tahzib ul-Akhlaq' (moral reform) in which he presented his religious views and moral issues leading to reforms. His well known writings include; Essays on the 'Life of the Prophet Muhammad', 'Monuments of the Great' and the commentaries on the Bible and the Quran. In his works he tried to balance the Islamic faith with the scientific and logical beliefs of the time. He died in 1898 but left behind a legacy in the form of a University which will always keep his name alive. He demonstrated courage, vision and compassion to his people and to his country. For his efforts he faced enormous opposition from the orthodoxy but he remained firm and achieved his objectives. The time and the tide proved that he was heading in the right direction. Based on his reforms and religious ideas, Sir Syed can be described as the pioneer of the Muslim resurgence in India in the nineteenth century.

Muhammad Ahmad al-Mahdi
(1844-1885)

Contribution: Founder of a vast Muslim state in the Sudan. He assumed the title of al-Mahdi and proclaimed a divine mission to purify Islam. He captured Khartoum in1885 from the British and established the theocratic state of the Sudan with its capital at Omdurman.

Muhammad Ahmad popularly known as al-Mahdi was born on August 12, 1844. His father was a shipbuilder. From his early years, Muhammad Ahmad developed a great interest in religious studies. In 1861, he joined a religious brotherhood called Sammania order and led a strict religious life. Due to the influence of Islamic mysticism and asceticism which he learned in his youth, his interpretation of Islam was more of a Sufi tradition. He became a religious teacher and by 1870, he had a group of disciples with whom he moved to Aba Island in the White Nile, 175 miles south of Khartoum.

Sudan at the time was under the influence of Egypt which was one of the provinces of Ottoman Empire. Both Egypt and the Sudan were governed by Turkish speaking ruling class. Despite some efforts by the Turks to assimilate with the Sudanese masses, the stark differences between the two were obvious. The Turkish officers were corrupt and cruel. Tax burden, slave trade, forced labor and the appointments of non-Muslim Europeans as provincial governors addicted to alcohol and tobacco created a widespread discontent. Under these circumstances, Muhammad Ahmad emerged as a leader who transformed the diversified discontents of the people into a unified movement. He gathered a growing band of supporters through his preaching and interpretation of Islam and turned them into a military machine. By 1881, he concluded that the Egyptian Viceroy (Khedive) was a puppet in the hands of the British and his life style was also unIslamic. Therefore, he did not have the right to rule over a Muslim population. In 1881, Muhammad Ahmad revealed to his followers that God had appointed him to purify Islam and he assumed the title of al-Mahdi (Right-Guided one). This was a bold step in part of Muhammad Ahmad as according to Muslim belief al-Mahdi would appear to restore Islam. Within the next two years, al-Mahdi launched several military attacks against the Egyptian government capturing almost entire Sudanese territory ruled by Egypt. By 1883, he had defeated three Egyptian armies; the last one of 8000 men led by General Hicks was completely destroyed. These victories against the Egyptian army led by the British made al-Mahdi a hero in the eyes of the local people despite intense propaganda by the Governor-General (Hilmi Pasha) and a group of Ulema (the learned men of religion). Al-Mahdi's greatest victory was the capture of Khartoum. On January 26, 1885, after a resolute defense of the city, the British commander General Charles Gordon surrendered. General Gordon was killed against the orders of Mahdi. Mahdi's triumphant entry into the city was probably the most glorious moment of his life and his followers. Mahdi, however, did not live long and died of typhus on June, 1885 at the age of 41. Mahdi's tomb became a site of pilgrimage. So much was the impact of Mahdi that the British feared him even when he was dead. When the British finally conquered the Sudan, on the orders of the British commander Kitchener, Mahdi's body was dug out, burned and thrown into the Nile.

Victory at Khartoum was of immense significance in the short history of the Mahdist movement. It helped al-Mahdi to consolidate his religious empire. He made Omdurman (a village on the left bank of the Nile, opposite to Khartoum) his capital.

The British regarded al-Mahdi as their enemy and wrongly accused him with the killing of General Gordon. The British and the European authors painted a distorted image of him. To them he was cruel man and a false prophet. The propaganda against al-Mahdi was so great that even the Sudanese scholars did not have a clear picture of him. After the British conquest of the Sudan in 1898, a growing interest to know about real al-Mahdi among the Europeans and the Sudanese scholars emerged.

Al-Mahdi had successfully repelled the foreign influence in the Sudan and united most of the Sudan by regiopolitical movement.

His theocratic state lasted for another 13 years. His successor Abdallah was defeated and killed by Anglo-Egyptian armies on November 24, 1899. Mahdist remained politically active in the Sudan till 1970. Mahdi was a nationalistic leader whose sole objective was to liberate the people of the Sudan from foreign occupation and to build an Islamic society in the traditions of Prophet Muhammad.

Muhammad Abduh
(1849-1905)

Contribution: Theologian, jurist, journalist, political activist and the founder of the Egyptian modernist school. He started a liberal movement in Egypt and other Muslim countries to reform Islamic institutions, government and judiciary. As Mufti of Egypt, he brought reforms in Islamic laws, administration, higher education, family and social values. His writings stimulated the Egyptian nationalism and influenced the thinking of the liberal activists in the Muslim world.

Muhammad Abduh came from a peasant background. He was born in 1849 in Lower Egypt (Nile Delta). His parents, though were without any formal education, went through a substantial effort to ensure Abduh's education. He learned the basic literary skills and by the age of ten he memorized the Quran by heart. In 1862, Abduh was sent to a theological school in Tanta but he did not show much interest in learning theology, instead he developed interest in mysticism. In 1866, he went to attend al-Azhar University at Cairo. Initially at al-Azhar, he devoted his entire time to mysticism and practiced asceticism. By 1872, he left his devotion to mysticism and became a disciple of Jamal ad-Din Afghani. Afghani was a reformer and pan-Islamic political activist of Persian origin. Before coming to Cairo, Afghani had spent many years in Turkey, Iran and India as a teacher and political activist. It was Afghani at al-Azhar, who directed Abduh towards theology, politics and philosophy. Abduh received his degree of alim (scholar) in 1877 from al-Azhar.

In 1879, Abduh was appointed a teacher at Dar al-Ulum (Dar al-Ulum was established as an institution for educational reform) by the reform-minded Egyptian prime minister Riad Pasha. In the same year (1879), Khediv Ismail, the ruler of Egypt was forced to abdicate his throne in favor of his son Tawfiq. Tawfiq dismissed

Abduh and put him under house arrest in his village and expelled Afghani from Egypt. Fortunately for Abduh, Riad Pasha came to his rescue. He recalled him and appointed him the editor of government's official gazette al-Wakai al-Misriyyah. Abduh used the gazette for social and religious reforms as well as a political mouthpiece to resist Anglo-French political exploitation of Egypt and other countries.

In 1881, Egyptian army officers, led by Arabi Pasha, revolted against the government. British troops landed in Egypt in May 1882 which forced Abduh to speak out about reforms and nationalism. In September 1882, Abduh was expelled from Egypt. He first went to Beirut and then to Paris (1884) where he was reunited with Afghani. The two founded a party and started a journal al-Urwat alwuthqa. The journal lasted only for eight months but had a tremendous effect on many countries. The views expressed in the journal were mainly of Afghani who focused on nationalism and freedom from imperial powers. Due to the differences with Afghani, Abduh left the journal. He then visited England and Tunisia but for the next three years he remained in Beirut and taught at a theological school.

In 1888, he was allowed to return to Egypt. He was appointed a judge in the National Courts of first Instance and in 1891 at the court of appeals. In 1895, Khedive, Abbas II, appointed Abduh and other reformats on an administrative committee for al-Azhar. Abduh, despite opposition from the conservative and orthodox groups of al-Azhar, embarked on the institutional reforms. He intended to make al-Azhar a model learning center in the Islamic world. He made changes in the curriculum and brought modern administrative systems. The salaries of the faculty and the stipends of the students were doubled. The living conditions of the students were improved. The efforts of the committee paid off as the student success rate on examinations substantially increased over the next two years. In 1899, Abduh was appointed the Mufti of Egypt, a position he held till his death. In his capacity as Mufti, he tried to break the rigidity of the Muslim societies. Abduh died on July 11, 1905, near Alexandria. His funeral was like a state funeral attended by politicians and religious figures of all factions. The house he was born was declared a historical monument and a scholarship for the students of al-Azhar bears his name. Due to his reforms and the environment he created, al-Azhar till today remains a prestigious learning center in the world.

Besides his numerous articles in the official gazette in Egypt and in al-Urwat al-Muthqa, he wrote 'Risalat at-Tawhid (Treatise on the Oneness of God) in which he tried to prove the superiority of Islam over Christianity by arguing that Islam was more willing to accept reasoning, science and logic than Christianity, therefore, Islam is rational and closer to reality than Christianity. He also wrote a commentary on the Quran but was completed by one of his disciples after his death. He also wrote on mysticism and dogmatics.

With the rise of the European power and culture, it became evident to Muslim intellectuals and reform-minded political activists that in order to confront Europe and become the part of modern world, the Muslim societies require reforms. Therefore, the objectives of these 'Islamic modernists' was to make Islam compatible with the modern societies by organizing Islamic societies in a way that the basic Islamic spirit is not lost and yet the Muslims can compete with the demands of the modern world. Jamal ad-Din Afghani was one of the modernists who left behind an enormous influence on the Muslim thinking of his time. It was his disciple, Muhammad Abduh who strengthened Afghanis thoughts by bringing reforms in Egypt and influencing the Muslim world.

Muhammad Abduh's main objective was to reform Islam and establish a clear distinction between the essential doctrines of Islam and social practices and laws. He believed that no political revolution could take place without gradual change in the mentality of the Muslim communities. As Mufti of Egypt, his two 'fatwas' are well known, though they drew a lot of criticism from the orthodoxy. He declared that the Muslims can eat meat of animals slaughtered by Jews and Christians. He also advocated the savings and banking system and legalized the acceptance of interest paid on loans and savings.

Abduh embarked on a course of reasoning, freedom of the will and the implementation of the faith with rational thinking over the rituals and blind acceptance of traditions and customs. He also tried to break the rigid Muslim family relationships based on traditions and ignorance by promoting equity, welfare and rationality.

Law and social ethics depend on particular circumstances and only certain general principles should be applicable to these. As time and circumstances change, they too should change. These were the general principles around which Abduh's thinking revolved. He understood that the progress of the Islamic world does not depend in the orthodoxy and practices based on rituals and customs rather there should be rational thinking which could be compatible with the need of the modern world. In his reforms, he did not compromise with the basic teachings of Islam but attempted to reconcile Islam with reasons and pragmatism. He was the chief architect of the reforms in the Islamic world and tried to create a place for the Muslims and Islam in the modern world.

Muhammad Ali Jinnah
(1876-1948)

Contribution: Politician, lawyer, founder and the first governor-general of Pakistan. Early in his career he was a nationalist who believed in Hindu-Muslim unity but the attitude of some Hindu politicians forced him to believe that for the safeguard of the Muslim interest in the Subcontinent, a separate Muslim state is inevitable. His efforts and sense of direction ultimately led the Muslims of India to create a separate homeland for themselves.

Muhammad Ali Jinnah, popularly known in Pakistan as Quaid-e-Azam, (the Great Leader) was born in Karachi on October 20 or December 25, 1876 (there is some controversy about his date of birth) in a prosperous business family. He took his early education at Madrasa Alia Sind at Karachi and then attended Mission High School. In 1892, he left for England to acquire business experience but he ended up in joining Lincoln's Inn to pursue a law degree. He completed his law degree in 1896 and was admitted to the Bar as a barrister. England proved to be a great learning ground for him. He was highly impressed by the British political system and became active in student politics. The success of DadaBhai Noroji (a Parsi leader) to become the first Indian to sit in the House of Commons was mainly due to the grandeur efforts of Jinnah and many Indian students. Jinnah returned to Karachi in 1896 where he found that his father's business was in turmoil. He decided to practice law in Bombay and after several years of hard work, honesty and dedication he established himself as a renowned lawyer. For a decade he had kept himself away from politics but in 1906 he began a long and distinguished political career by participating at the 1906 session of the Indian National Congress at Calcutta. The Congress at the time was only political party representing the Indians and was calling for independence from the

British. In 1910, Jinnah was elected to the Imperial Legislative Council.

In the early years of his politics, Jinnah was a nationalist and believed in Hindu-Muslim unity. He was neither a religious leader nor a fanatic Muslim. His main political objectives were to establish a cordial relationship between the Hindus and the Muslims, raise the status of India in the international community and build a sense of Indian nationalism among different religious and cultural groups of India. His efforts to establish Hindu-Muslim unity in India was lauded even by such hardcore Indian nationalist leader like Gopal Krishna Gokhle who described Jinnah as 'the best ambassador of Hindu-Muslim unity'. On the other hand many Muslim leaders in India were thinking in terms of preserving their identity and culture rather than amalgamation in the Indian nation dominated by the Hindus. As a result the Muslim League was founded in 1906 at Dhaka (present Bangladesh). Jinnah, however, kept himself away from the Muslim League for the next seven years, finally joining the league in 1913. Even after joining the League, Jinnah continued working towards Hindu-Muslim unity. Mainly due to Jinnah's efforts, the Congress and the Muslim League began to hold their annual meetings jointly. In the Lucknow Pact of 1916, between Congress and Muslim League, separate electorates and weighted representation for the Muslims were guaranteed. Unfortunately, the cordial relationship between congress and Muslim League was short lived. By 1920 due to the internal feud in the Muslim League and the staunch Hindu approach by some of the members of the Congress disappointed Jinnah to the extent that he decided to leave both the League and the Congress.

Between 1930 and 1935, Jinnah settled in England where he practiced before the Privy Council but all this time he remained a firm nationalist who believed in a united and strong India. Between 1930 and 1932, there were three Round Table Conferences in London. Jinnah participated in these conferences and proposed his political agenda. These conferences, however, produced negligible results. In 1935, he was persuaded by the Muslim leaders to return to India. He reorganized the Muslim League and started preparing for the elections under the Government of Indian Act of 1935. In 1937, the election took place and the Indian National Congress attained majority in six provinces but refused to include the Muslim League in the formation of the provincial government. Since then, Hindu-Muslim relations started deteriorating which resulted in riots in many parts of India.

The creation of a separate land for the Muslims of India was proposed by Dr. Muhammad Iqbal in the Muslim League conference of 1930 at Allahabad. The idea of a separate Muslim homeland was mainly due to the fact that the Muslims were a small minority in India and there was a fear (rightly so) in them that the Muslims would be excluded from India's political, economical and social progress. On March 22-23, 1940 at Lahore, the Muslim League adopted a resolution known as 'Pakistan Resolution' to form a separate Muslim state. The Congress and the Hindu majority of India as anticipated opposed the creation of a separate Muslim land. Hindu-Muslim riot broke out in several parts of India and eventually the British government and the Indian National Congress agreed for the partition of India, resulting in the creation of Pakistan on August 14, 1947. Muhammad Ali Jinnah sworn in as the first governor-general of Pakistan. The new state had enormous problems and he tackled these problems with integrity and zeal. Unfortunately, his leadership lasted for only 13 months. He was worn out by the long political struggles of independence. He died on September 11, 1948 and was buried in Karachi. Till today he is revered as the father of the nation.

In his personal life Jinnah appeared to be aloof. His first wife, a child bride died when he was a student. His second wife (Ratanbai) was a Parsi, almost half of his age. The marriage was not a happy one and ended up in divorce. Ratanbai died in 1929. His ties with his daughter Dina (from Ratanbai) was severed when she married a non-Muslim. His sister, Fatima Jinnah, stood by his side and took care of the domestic aspects.

Jinnah's greatest achievement was the creation of a separate homeland for the Muslims of India. He started his political career for the freedom of India from the British colonial rule as well as for civil freedom for the Muslims of India. He was a man with a logical mind and of high integrity and principles.

Over the years, creation of Pakistan for the Muslims of India has been questioned. Practically it was never possible for every Indian

Muslim to migrate to Pakistan. It is also true that not every Indian Muslim supported the idea of Pakistan. Furthermore, the cessation of the erstwhile East Pakistan (now Bangladesh) also questions the two religion theory (the Hindus and the Muslims). The Muslims who remained in India became the target of Hindu criticism and were excluded from India's political and economical progress. Today, there are more Muslims in India or Bangladesh than Pakistan. Only the future historians will be able to judge if indeed the creation of a separate Muslim homeland was the answer for safeguarding the interest of the Muslims of the Subcontinent. Jinnah tried his best to keep India united, worked untiringly for the Hindu-Muslim unity but the staunch and the fanatic leaders of both sides did not allow him to succeed in his nationalistic objectives.

Sir Dr. Muhammad Iqbal
(1877-1938)

Contribution: Poet, reformer, political activist and philosopher. His reputation lies in his poetry and presumably for conceiving the idea of a separate Muslim homeland. His poetry influenced millions of Muslims round the globe. He exerted a great influence on the political, social and intellectual life of the Muslims of the Subcontinent in the early twentieth century.

Iqbal was born in Sialkot (now in Pakistan) on November 9, 1877 AD. He attended Government College Lahore and obtained his Master's degree in philosophy in 1899. He went to England to pursue higher education at Cambridge University. He frequently traveled to Germany and in 1908 obtained his Ph.D. degree in philosophy from Munich University. His Ph.D. thesis was 'The Development of Metaphysics in Persia'. While in England, he also studied law and obtained a law degree. After returning to India, for a while he was involved in teaching and then began practicing law. He also started writing poetry and soon gained fame as a Persian and Urdu language poet. He was knighted by the British in 1922.

Iqbal was not a full time politician but showed active interest in politics. He was elected to the Punjab Legislature in 1926 and became the president of the Muslim League in 1930. In the Muslim League session of 1930 at Allahabad, he mentioned about a 'consolidated Northwest Indian Muslim State'. Despite the limitation of this proposal (the Muslims of rest of India were ignored) it is widely believed that this was an idea which later led to the creation of Pakistan.

Before his travel to Europe, he was a nationalist but changed his views after spending some time over there. He realized that Europe's concept of nationalism caused destruction, racism and imperialism. He was also a strong critic of the western civilization.

Iqbal died on April 21, 1938. After the creation of Pakistan, he was declared the National Poet of Pakistan and in 1951, Government of Pakistan established 'Iqbal Academy' to study and promote his works. Every year Iqbal day is celebrated in Pakistan.

Iqbal can be viewed as a poet, philosopher and political activist, though his fame lies in his poetry. His earliest poems are romantic lyrics but with passage of time he used his versatile and eloquent style to give spiritual and social messages to the Muslims.

Iqbal was initially influenced by the Spanish Sufi philosopher Ibn Arabi (1165-1240). Iqbal was highly impressed by Ibn Arabi's concept of perfect man. Later Iqbal was also influenced by Rumi, Nietzsche and Kant. In 1928-29, he delivered six lectures at Madras, Hyderabad and Aligarh. These lectures have been compiled in 'The Reconstruction of Religious Thought in Islam', and represent very much his philosophical views. Basically his philosophical views are attempts to revitalize the Muslim civilization and culture with inspiration and deeds. The concept of 'perfect or super man' as presented by Arabi, Rumi and Nietzsche was very attractive to Iqbal. Throughout the world, Muslim civilization, culture, economical and financial conditions and the education were in decline. This situation was very disturbing to Iqbal and through the concept of a perfect man he wanted to induce enthusiasm and will among the Muslims of the world to take their fate in their own hands.

Khudi or 'Self' was the most important topic in Iqbal's philosophy and poetry. He maintained that for the progress of an individual as well as the nations, the development of self-reliance, self-confidence, self-respect and self-assertion is very vital. It should not be however, misunderstood that Iqbal is promoting selfishness. His concept of 'self' revolves around one's personal achievements which can then be used to promote the progress of a nation, thus in the end a collective achievement.

To Iqbal, 'self' is the basic reality and is also a power to act freely and move from a lesser freedom to a greater freedom. In his views the most free is God. Self is immortal. Averroes described immortality as the eternity of intellect. According to Iqbal, eternity is individual and personal. He maintained that immortality is not a gift rather it is a hope or aspiration depending upon one's philosophy of life.

In his poetry, Iqbal tried to rekindle the glorious past of the Muslims. The publication of his long Persian poem Asrar-e-Khudi (The Secrets of the Self) in 1915, brought him fame and criticism. He wrote this poem in Persian mainly to draw attention from the Muslim world. The madrasa educated fundamentalist Muslims however, opposed the poem as they failed to grasp Iqbal's basic objectives. In 1918, he wrote Rumuz-e-Bekhudi (The Mysteries of Selflessness) also in Persian. This poem was in response to the views presented in the Asrar-e-Khudi. He wrote Payam-e-Mashriq (Message of the East) in 1923, which is probably a response to Goethe's 'Divan of West and East'. Zabur-e-Azam (Persian Psalms), a collection of Ghazals, was published in 1927. Javed-e-Nameh (1932, The Song of Eternity) is his masterpiece where both Rumi and Dante become alive.

In Urdu he wrote Bal-e-Jibril (1935, Gabriel's Wing), Zarb-e-Kalim (1937, The Blow of Moses) and Armaghan-e-Hejaz (1938, Gift of the Hejaz). His poems Shikwah (The Complaint) and Jawab-e-Shikwah (Answer to the Complaint) were written in Urdu and published in early 1920, were enormously popular.

Iqbal was genuinely concerned with the fall of the Muslim empire and the Muslim civilization. Through his philosophical writings, poetry and lectures he tried to revive the Muslim societies round the globe. In his writings he pressed for the awareness that there is an immediate and inevitable need for the renewal of the Muslim society through reinterpretation and proper understanding of Islam as well as social reforms. He was a conservative Muslim but not a fanatic one. He felt that pantheism and the departure from the true spirit of Islam have weakened the Muslim societies. He envisioned the same glory and majesty for the Muslims they had before the fall of Baghdad, Granada, Delhi and Constantinople, the seats of mighty Muslim empire.

Abd al-Aziz Ibn Saud
(1880-1953)

Contribution: Founder of modern Saudi Arabia. His political ambition and conquest helped in unifying small groups of desert Sheikhdoms into a unified country. He brought stability to the region and initiated the exploration of oil which made Saudi Arabia a rich and prosperous nation.

The Sauds were the rulers of central Arabia at least for a hundred years. Ibn Saud was born in Riyadh in 1880. He was the son of Abd al-Rahman, Sultan of the Najd. When Ibn Saud was eleven years of age, his family was driven out of central Arabia by the Rashidi dynasty. Ibn Saud escaped with his father to Kuwait. In 1902, Ibn Saud in a bold move regained Riyadh. He attacked Riyadh with forty men. His men penetrated into the city at night and when the governor came out at Dawn for his morning pray, Ibn Saud's men attacked, killing the governor. With the help of the supporters of his dynasty, in two years, Ibn Saud took control of almost half of the central Arabia. The Rashidis appealed to the Turks for help and Ibn Saud though defeated in 1904, still kept his grip over central Arabia. In 1915, he signed a treaty with the British not to attack the British interest in the Gulf area, especially Sharif Hussain of Mecca. Sharif Hussain was an important British ally against the Turks during World War I. In return, the British provided Ibn Saud with a financial help of 5000 British pounds a month.

By 1922, Ibn Saud ended the rule of Rashidis in Arabia and doubled his territory, controlling the whole of central Arabia except Hejaz. In 1924, Ibn Saud's forces besieged Mecca and exiled Sharif Hussain. In 1925, Ibn Saud assumed the title of king of Hejaz and in 1927 king of Nejd. In 1932, he joined both the kingdoms to form Saudi Arabia.

He revived his alliance with the Wahhabis (extremist Muslim puritans) mainly because he realized that his chances of success were high if he had the support of extremist religious groups. He himself founded a religious tribal group known as Akhwan (Brothers). This group helped him to subdue many nomadic tribes in Arabia. With time, Akhwan grew out of Ibn Saud's control. In 1927, the Akhwans attacked Iraq without Ibn Saud's permission. The British pushed them back and Akhwans were finally crushed by Ibn Saud in 1929 at the battle of Sibilla.

Ibn Saud started as a tribal chief but in due process became a king. He made bold political decisions and somehow fortune favored him. Under Ibn Saud, Saudi Arabia was without any regular civil service or civil administration. Ibn Saud ruled as an absolute monarch and all decisions were made by him. There was no source of income and Ibn Saud's kingdom was without any money. In 1933, he granted permission to an American oil company to explore the oil reserves in his kingdom. In 1938, the company did find oil but due to the World War II, work was suspended. After the war, oil production was resumed and by 1953, Ibn Saud was getting almost a quarter million dollars per week. Before Ibn Saud could determine what to do with this enormous wealth, he died at Taif on November 9, 1953. He had forty-two wounds from swords and lances he received in his youth.

Ibn Saud played an important role in the Arabian Peninsula in the early twentieth century. His efforts, boldness and vision created modern Saudi Arabia and brought stability and prosperity in the region. Ibn Saud was a devout Muslim and he tried to build his kingdom around the basic teachings of Islam but by no means was he a fanatic. When he embarked on his political career, the Arabian Peninsula consisted of small tribal Sheikhdoms but by his efforts he united them and left behind a unified and prosperous country which has become an important player in the global politics.

Mustafa Kemal Ataturk
(1881-1938)

Contribution: Political and military leader. Ataturk was the founder of modern Turkey. He led a revolutionary movement which resulted in a free Turkey. His efforts led to the modernization and secularization of Turkey.

Mustafa Kemal known as 'Ataturk' or "Father of the Turks', is an immensely significant figure in the history of modern Turkey. He was a soldier, statesman, reformer and the first president of Republic of Turkey.

Mustafa Kemal was born in 1881 at Salonika in Turkish Macedonia. His father was a lieutent in a local militia and served under the Ottoman rulers. When Mustafa Kemal was seven years of age his father died. He received his early education in Salonika. He excelled in mathematics and was nicknamed 'Kemal' (the perfect one). In 1895, Mustafa Kemal entered the military school in Monastir and in 1899 joined the War College in Istanbul. In 1905, he graduated from the General Staff College as a captain. From the very beginning of his career, Mustafa Kemal was concerned with Turkey's political, social and economical plights. When it was discovered that he and some of his revolutionary minded friends have formed a group to discuss political situations in Turkey, they were sent to remote places of the empire. Thus, this initial effort of Mustafa Kemal and his revolutionary friends to establish a democratic Turkey was not successful and their political activities were halted for time being. Mustafa Kemal was sent to Damascus. The way the Turkish officials treated the local people created annoyance in Mustafa Kemal. He formed a group called 'Society for Fatherland and Freedom' which however, did not last very long. In 1907, he was called back to Salonika. There he joined a group of young reform minded Turk revolutionaries called 'The Committee of Union and Progress'. In 1915, as a division commander he fought against an Allied attack on Turkish Straits and was instrumental of a Turkish victory at Gallipoli. In 1916-17, he fought against Russians in Eastern Anatolia. Mustafa Kemal as a young military officer believed in an independent and a democratic Turkey. In World War I, Turkey had sided with Germany and after the Allied Powers won the war, British, French and Italy divided Turkey for their imperial rule. According to the treaty of Sevres, the Ottoman Kingdom was reduced in size. Armenia became an independent state. Greece was also benefited by sharing the booty. Mustafa Kemal along with some other nationalistic army officers refused to accept this humiliation of Turkey and began to form a revolutionary army to fight against Allied powers. He drove out French and Greeks from Turkey. In 1920, the Grand National Assembly elected Mustafa Kemal as its president. In 1922, he defeated the Greek Army at Dumlupinar and drove them from Anatolia. He defeated the British at Gallipoli and in 1923 forced the Allies to sign a respectable treaty (Treaty of Lausanne). The treaty forced Turkey to give up her claims to the Arab lands and also islands of Aegean, Cyprus, Rhodes and Dodecanese. This also brought the end of mighty Ottoman Empire and Turkey became a new Republic in 1923. Mustafa Kemal was elected its first president. He married a woman from a well-to-do Turkish family in 1923 but the marriage ended in divorce in 1925. He, however, adopted many children.

In 1924, he abolished the "Caliphate' and immediately started the modernization of Turkey. Turkey before Mustafa Kemal was a conservative Islamic country. Mustafa Kemal believed that orthodox Islam is the cause of many problems of Turkey. His efforts to modernize Turkey met with great resistance by the clergy but he remained undaunted in his mission and belief. His reform efforts were met with minimum of repression. The old and outdated institutions of law, politics and culture were reformed according to the need of the time. Under Mustafa Kemal, Turkey was transformed more of a European cultured country rather than a traditional Islamic society. He replaced the Arabic alphabets by the Western alphabets which were more suited to the Turkish language. The education system was reformed. The education became modern and science oriented to meet the challenge of the time. The Turkish law became secular. Muslim calendar, religious schools and religious courts were abandoned. In 1928 the constitution was amended and Turkey became a secular state. In Republic of Turkey, women enjoyed more freedom and respect than many western countries. In 1934, Turkish women were allowed to vote and were encouraged to take part in the affairs of the state. Polygamy was abolished; marriage and divorce became a civil action.

The modernization of Turkey was not without bloodshed. The orthodox clergy tried to incite people against Mustafa Kemal's reforms but failed. The Kurds of southwestern Anatolia revolted in February 1925 in the name of Islam but the revolt was quickly put down and their leader was hanged. Mustafa Kemal allowed the creation of an opposition political party led by Ali Fethi but party's success caused Mustafa Kemal to halt its activities. This was an unfortunate act by a leader who did so much to modernize Turkey yet failed to establish a democratic institution at its best.

With time Mustafa Kemal became aloof and spent most of his time in Dolmabahce palace in Istanbul. He suffered from alcoholic cirrhosis (a disease of the liver). Mustafa Kemal died on November 10, 1938. He was buried in Ankara and a mausoleum was erected on his grave.

Mustafa Kemal is a captivating figure in modern Turkey. His greatest achievement was to demonstrate that the orthodox Islam is not the solution for the revival of the Muslim societies. His remarkable courage and vision transformed a weak, religious, autocratic feudal society to a modern democratic and industrialized nation. By his sheer courage and nationalistic approach he showed the world that freedom is an unalienable right not only for an individual but also for the nations. The forces of imperial powers could be defeated by courage and vision. Modern Turkey owes a great deal to this courageous and visionary leader.

Ahmad Sukarno
(1901-1970)

Contribution: Indonesian freedom fighter and the first president of independent Indonesia. A brilliant orator and a charismatic leader, Sukarno systematically led Indonesia to independence from the Dutch colonial rule. He remains a dominant figure in modern Indonesian history.

Sukarno was born on June 6, 1901 in East Java to a Balinese mother and a Javanese father. His father, Sukemi, moved the family to Modjokerto when Sukarno was still a very young boy. His father, a school teacher and a devout Muslim provided a good education to his son. Besides his regular school education, Sukarno was trained in religion (Islam), Indonesian culture and the Western arts and sciences. His father, despite his poverty wanted to send him to a Dutch school but Dutch regulation allowed only few native students to attend their school system. Sukarno's knowledge in Dutch and an excellent educational background helped him to enroll in the Dutch elementary school. In 1916, he enrolled himself at a high school in Surabaya. Umar Sayed Tjokroaminoto, head of the Sarakat Islam (Islamic Union) provided Sukarno with room and board. At Surabaya, due to Umar Sayed's political influence, Sukarno came across many Indonesian and Dutch intellectuals and it was here he realized about the colonial exploitation of the Indonesians by the Dutch. Sukarno remained in Surabaya for the next five years (1916-21) which proved to be very important for his future intellectual and political development.

The Independence movement in Indonesia from the Dutch colonialism had started in 1908. Sarakat Islam was the political platform which attracted a wide variety of Indonesians (workers, students, religious groups, merchants and intellectuals). Within the party, however, there were two groups, the Islamic and the Marxist

(Communist). Though the common goal was the independence of Indonesia from the Dutch, the two parties had different ways to achieve this goal. The Islamic group whose members were the descendents of the Muslim sea merchants who brought Islam in Indonesia in the fourteenth century, wanted to retain the feudal system whereas communists wanted to educate the peasants and help them to achieve the self-rule. In 1920, the left wing Marxist group left Sarakat Islam and formed the Communist Party of Indonesia (PKI).

In 1921, Sukarno entered the Institute of Technology at Bandung, from which he graduated in1926 as an engineer. At that time Bandung was the center of the political activity of young Indonesian students, particularly of those who were the graduates of the Dutch school system. Sukarno in 1925 founded a study club and in 1926 embarked on a political career. He wrote number of articles (1926) in an attempt to reconcile Islam and communism and continued his efforts in this direction for the rest of his life. He believed that both imperialism and capitalism are the enemies of Indonesian people. In 1927, he transformed his study club into a political platform by forming the Nationalist Party of Indonesia (NPI). Sukarno was elected party's chairman. The party's objective was to gain independence from the Dutch by noncooperation movement.

Sukarno started unifying various nationalist groups of Indonesia in an effort to prepare ground for the independence. He was a brilliant orator and along with the use of a language which was well understood by the general masses he became a national hero. Initially, the Dutch allowed some political activity but in 1929, they arrested Sukarno. In a public trial, Sukarno was sentenced to four years in prison but served only two years. The trial of 1930 enhanced his reputation as an Indonesian freedom fighter and a natiolist leader. During this trial, in his defense he gave one of his most important speeches known as 'Indonesia Accuses'. After his release, he resumed his political activities but the Dutch moved quickly and arrested him in 1933. This time there was no trial and he was exiled to Flores. Four years later he was moved to Bencoolen in Sumatra. He remained there until 1942, when the Japanese invasion of the island brought him freedom.

Japanese recognized him as Indonesia's most influential political leader and in turn, Sukarno agreed to cooperate with them. During this time, Sukarno formulated his political principles known as Pantjasila or Five Pillars: nationalism, internationalism, democracy, social justice and belief in God. After the Japanese defeat in the World War II, Sukarno declared Indonesia as an independent republic (August 17, 1945). The Dutch refused to grant independence to Indonesia and fighting between the Indonesian freedom fighters and the Dutch began. Two years later the Dutch allowed Indonesia to be a republic but under the Dutch Crown. This political move, however, did not work and once again fighting began. Finally, in 1949, the Dutch gave in and Indonesia became an independent republic with more than 100 million people (at the time of the independence) of many races and religions, scattered over hundreds of islands. Sukarno became the first president of the republic.

With the departure of the Dutch, Indonesia's political problems however, were not over. Indonesia faced the problems of over-population, poverty and inflation. The internal strife among the political parties brought an end to the pre-independence unity. With time Sukarno's government became unpopular and there was an armed rebellion in Sumatra and political unrest in many parts of the country. In order to strengthen his political position, Sukarno allied with the Indonesian Communist Party and a conservative Islamic party. In 1959, he reintroduced the constitution of 1945 which gave him absolute power. In 1960, he dissolved the parliament and ruled by decree. He then formulated the concept of 'Guided Democracy'. He attacked the imperialism and capitalism on his way to build a socialist society. With time Sukarno leaned more and more towards the communist party of Indonesia. In 1963, he became president for life. By mid sixties, the communists had infiltrated the Indonesian army and on October 1, 1965, they staged a coup. The coup failed and the members of the Communist Party were purged and systematically killed. Sukarno could not stop this blood bath which took more than a quarter million lives. On March 11, 1966, General Suharto with the help of army forced Sukarno to transfer power to him. Suharto assumed complete power in 1968 and Sukarno disappeared from Indonesia's political scene. He was placed under house arrest and died on June 21,

1970 due to the complications of the kidneys. He was buried near his mother at Biltar (east Java) rather than in the Hero's cemetery in Jakarta. His funeral, however, was attended by almost half a million Indonesians and a mausoleum was erected on his grave.

Sukarno's revolutionary zeal was unquestionable and he remained devoted to certain aspects of his political agenda. He was a charismatic leader but his political strategies failed both Indonesia and the Indonesians. His foreign policies not only isolated Indonesia from the west but also brought economical disaster to Indonesia. He could have converted Indonesia into a stable democratic country but due to his hunger for power and political intrigue he failed to lead the country towards democracy. Due to the lack of political reforms and democratic institutions he indirectly paved the way for the future dictator Suharto, who remained in power for more than 30 years and plunged Indonesia into further political chaos, corruption, and economical hardships. In the end, a charismatic leader of enormous promise and talents failed to deliver to his countrymen what he had promised to them in pre-independence Indonesia.

Ayatollah Ruhollah Khomeini
(1902-1989)

Contribution: Iranian Shiite religious and political leader who directed the revolution against the tyrant and corrupt regime of Reza Shah Pahlavi. Khomeini took office in 1979 and for the next ten years he remained the supreme authority of Iranian political and religious affairs. He exported his brand of Islam and inspired many Muslim countries.

Khomeini was born on September 24, 1902 in the small town of Khomein. His father, Mustafa Musavi, a local Shiite cleric was murdered by the employees of a local landlord when Khomeini was only five months old. He was then raised by his mother and aunt. His early education began on the religious traditions. He attended various Islamic schools and was also tutored by his elder brother, a cleric. In 1919, both his mother and aunt passed away. Khomeini then moved to the city of Arak where he continued to pursue his theological studies under the supervision of Ayatollah Abdal Karim Yazdi. When Yazdi moved to Quom, Khomeini followed him, eventually finishing his theological education in 1926. He got married in 1930 and his first son Mustafa was born in 1932. In all, Khomeini had two sons and three daughters. By mid 1930s, Khomeini was well established in Quom where he taught Islamic jurisprudence. As a Shiite scholar and teacher Khomeini wrote many books on Islamic jurisprudence, ethics and philosophy. In the early phase of his life he was not politically active but later in his writings he advocated active participation of clerics in the politics. At a meeting (1949) of leading clerics of Iran, Khomeini sided with those who were advocates of active participation in politics.

In the early 1920s, a low ranking military officer, known as Reza Khan emerged on Iranian politics. The unrest against the Quajar dynasty was gaining momentum and in 1925, Reza Khan deposed the last Quajar ruler Ahmad Shah. In 1926, Reza Khan declared himself the emperor and founded the Phalavi dynasty. Reza Khan was a nationalist and his reforms were mostly of western and secular nature which were however, not acceptable to the Iranian clerics. In 1941, the allied powers occupied Iran and forced Reza Khan to abdicate his throne. His son Reza Shah Phalavi succeeded him as the next monarch of Iran.

The religious groups of Iran opposed Reza Shah's reforms, especially his land redistribution proposal which could have reduced the religious estates. Reza Shah was also modernizing Iran by bringing western life style into Iranian society and by giving women more rights and freedom. These reforms were also not acceptable to the Iranian clerics.

Khomeini became a 'grand Ayatollah' in 1962 which made him one of the supreme religious leaders of the Shiites in Iran and with this title under his belt, Khomeini's real political activities began. He believed that Reza Shah's government was unIslamic, corrupt and illegitimate as the real authority should lie in the hands of religious leaders. In January, 1963, Khomeini wrote against government's land reform proposal. In March of that year he was arrested after urging Iranians not to celebrate Nouruz (Iranian New Year). On June 3, 1963, Khomeini lashed out against the government and two days later he was arrested which resulted in anti-government riots. He remained in jail for three months and then was put under house arrest. In April 1964, Khomeini was allowed to return to Quom. From Quom he continued his opposition to Reza Shah's government and in November 1964, he criticized Reza Shah for extending diplomatic immunity to American military personnel in Iran which was considered by many Iranians as insult to Iran's integrity and national pride. On November 4, 1964, he was forcibly exiled from Iran to Turkey. In Turkey, he protested against the western dress code for women and was forced to leave Turkey. Khomeini eventually settled in Najaf (Iraq).

From Najaf, Khomeini continued planning to topple the Iranian monarchy and establishment of Islamic republic in Iran. In fact, Reza Shah's so-called reforms were of little help to common Iranians and as dissatisfaction mounted, Shah's regime became more and more tyrant. From 1975 onwards, Khomeini's popularity kept growing in Iran. In October 1977, his son Mustafa died, presumably killed by Shah's secret police. Civil unrest and demonstrations continued growing against Shah with demands that Khomeini be allowed to return to Iran. The year 1978 was very troublesome for Iran as public dissatisfaction against Shah was at its peak. Shah's secret police killed hundreds of civilians. On October 6, 1978, Khomeini was forced by Saddam Hussain to leave Iraq. Khomeini then settled in the suburb of Paris. From Paris, Khomeini's taped messages were distributed throughout Iran which further incited riots and civil unrest. Finally, on January 16, 1979, Reza Shah fled from Iran and Khomeini entered Tehran triumphantly on February 1, 1979. Khomeini moved to Quom on March 1, 1979 and in December 1979, Islamic Republic of Iran was created by a referendum with Khomeini as its political and religious leader for life. With time the fundamentalist groups in Iran became very powerful and cleansing of all opposition began. Newspapers which did not support Khomeini's ideology were closed. Hundreds of officials who served under Shah and the members of the opposition were either executed or imprisoned. Khomeini and his associates had no tolerance of any opposition.

On November 4, 1979, a group of Iranians seized the American embassy in Tehran and held more than 50 people hostage till January 1981. It is widely believed that Khomeini sanctioned this seizure as at that time nothing could be done in Iran without his approval.

In September 1980, a war broke out between Iran and Iraq which lasted almost a decade. The war helped Khomeini to unite many factions of the Iranians behind nationalism and his brand of Islam. This war which ended in 1988 cost hundreds of thousands of Iranian lives and devastated the Iranian economy. Despite the loss of Iranian lives and poor economy, Khomeini maintained his charismatic grip on Iran and remained unchallenged as a religious and political figure in Iran. Khomeini and his associates also tried to export their brand of Islam to many Muslim countries but the impact was short lived.

Khomeini died on June 3, 1989. Whole Iran mourned his death and millions attended his funeral. Khomeini is still a revered figure and thousands of people visit his shrine at the Behest-e-Zahra cemetery. Kashf-e-Asrar (Discovery of Secrets) and

241

Hokumat-e-Islami (Islamic Government) are his two famous books. Islamic revolution of Iran in its magnitude and impact was no less than the 1917 Bolshevik revolution of Russia and the Communist revolution of China in 1949. Unfortunately, like the other two, the Iranian revolution failed to build its lasting impact either on Iran or on the world (both Muslim and non-Muslim countries). A revolution which was so effectively directed by Khomeini and carried out by the millions of Iranians (also supported by the progressive and liberal Iranian political parties) destroyed itself due to the fanatic religious beliefs of Khomeini and his associates. The Islamic revolution of Iran failed to deliver the real issues which had plagued Iran since the turn of the twentieth century. Under Reza Shah's tyrant regime the common human rights were nonexistent. Free speech was curbed and any opposition was ruthlessly crushed. Reza Shah's secret police was busy in torturing and killing the members of the opposition. Under these circumstances, the Islamic revolution was a ray of hope for common Iranians but unfortunately, the revolution proved to be even worse than Reza Shah's regime. Khomeini and his associates wiped out all opposition including those who actively took part in the revolution against Reza Shah. The freedom of press and speech as well as the rights of women all remained under the firm control of Khomeini and his rigid single minded associates. Torture and killing of the political prisoners were as widespread as these were during Reza Shah's regime. The leaders of the Islamic revolution were on the path of vengeance in the name of Islam and forgot the very teachings of the Prophet, his kindness and his treatment to his worst enemies after the conquest of Mecca.

Faisal Ibn Saud
(1906-1975)

Contribution: King of Saudi Arabia and the most prominent Arab leader during the early 1970s. Assumed the responsibilities of the state from an early age and played a vital role in the creation of modern Saudi Arabia. After becoming king in 1964, he built the modern infrastructure of Saudi Arabia and spent the oil revenue wisely to extend social services to the Saudis and to improve the overall administrative structure.

Faisal was born in Riyadh in 1906. He was the third son of Abd al Aziz Ibn Saud, founder of Saudi Arabia. From his early childhood, Faisal was raised under the religious influence which remained with him for the rest of his life. His mother died when he was quite young and was raised by his maternal grandparents. They taught him the Quran and basic principles of Islam. These early teachings made Faisal a devout Muslim. He avoided drinking, smoking and gambling. After joining his father's army at the age of 13, he became the commander of the Saudi army at the age of 18 and played an important role when Hejaz was conquered by his father (1926). Earlier, in 1919 he went to London. The objectives and achievements of his trip rather remain obscure.

In 1926, Faisal was appointed the Viceroy of Hejaz and in 1930 he became the foreign minister of Saudi Arabia. In 1932, he visited the Soviet Union and saw the production of oil in Baku and along the Caspian Sea. In March 1934, a dispute broke out between Ibn Saud and the ruler of Yemen. Faisal led a victorious campaign against Yemen but under the pressure of western powers, the Saudis withdrew. Faisal represented Saudi Arabia to the conference on Palestine at London in 1939 and to the United Nations Conference at San Francisco in 1945. Later he also served as the ambassador of Saudi Arabia to the United Nations General Assembly. Faisal was not a proponent of the partition of

Palestine and opposed the creation of Israel in 1948. In 1953, Ibn Saud surprisingly nominated Faisal's elder brother Saud as his heir. In November 1953, Ibn Saud died and Saud became King. Faisal was named crown prince and foreign minister. Saud was an incompetent king. He was more interested in pleasure than the affairs of the state. Saud failed to provide any kind of leadership and despite the wealth Saudi Arabia was accumulating from oil, there was a financial crisis in the country. In the April of 1958, on the initiatives of the senior members of the royal family, Saud was forced to give full executive power to Faisal. Between 1958 and 1964, Faisal worked tirelessly to modernize Saudi Arabia by keeping a balance between religion and the use of modern technology. Faisal prohibited the importation of the slaves in 1959. Among his 'ten points' reform program which he developed in 1962, he emancipated the slaves within the country. Meanwhile during this period (58-64) Saud tried to regain his power twice but he failed in his bid. Eventually, on November, 1964, Saud was forced to abdicate his throne in favor of Faisal who became king.

With the accession of Faisal on the throne, a new era in Saudi Arabia began. Faisal immediately initiated badly needed internal reforms. He started building an effective bureaucracy, mobilizing and directing the national development with the wealth Saudi Arabia was amassing from oil. Faisal introduced education for both men and women. On the administrative front, investment in the public sector was increased. Plans were made to improve the standard of living for common Saudis. Health benefits were provided to every citizen and the Saudis were encouraged to engage in business by providing them with the interest-free loan. Some of Faisal's reforms, however, were opposed by the traditionalists and the fundamentalists.

During 1960, Faisal became one of the founders of the Organization of Petroleum Exporting Countries (OPEC). Though in 1967, during Arab-Israeli conflict, OPEC halted its supplies to the USA and Britain for a short while, the real use of oil boycott as a weapon came during October 1973 Arab-Israeli war. Faisal was one of the major architects of the Arab oil embargo against the United States and the western countries which supported Israel. Faisal encouraged the increase of oil prices and despite the boycott of oil supply to many countries, Saudi oil revenues kept increasing. Faisal used the oil embargo with such diplomacy and intelligence that Saudi Arabia became a major player in world politics. In 1973, a meeting between Faisal and Kissinger failed to patch the differences between the USA and Saudi Arabia but in 1974, a trip by Fahd to Washington and then a visit by president Richard Nixon of the USA to Saudi Arabia helped in improving the relationship between the two countries.

Within the Arab world, Faisal faced a very formidable foe in Gamal Nasir. In 1962, a military coup backed by Egypt overthrew and killed the monarch in Northern Yemen and the coup leaders declared the country a republic. Saudi Arabia supported the royalist and a near-war situation erupted between Saudi Arabia and Egypt over Yemen. Finally, on August 24, 1965, Nasir and Faisal signed an agreement in Jeddah. According to the treaty, Egypt agreed to withdraw its troops from Yemen within a year. Despite this treaty, Nasir remained hostile against Faisal and tried many times to de stabilize Faisal regime. Only after Egypt's defeat in 1967 against Israel, Nasir was forced to withdraw most of the Egyptian troops from Yemen but ultimately all Egyptian troops were withdrawn after his death. Faisal established more cordial ties with Sadat who succeeded Nasir as the president of Egypt. Probably Faisal played some role in convincing Sadat to seek better ties with the USA and gradual removal of Soviet influence from Egypt.

Faisal gained much support from moderate Muslim countries like Jordan, Pakistan, Turkey and Iran (before the Islamic revolution). He established strong ties with the west especially with the USA though he never refrained from criticizing the USA policies towards Israel. Though moderate in his foreign policies, Faisal distanced himself from the Soviet Union and the communist countries.

Where he gained enormous respect by the world for being a sensible and moderate politician, his reforms in Saudi Arabia brought internal opposition by more traditionalist Saudis and the extreme Islamic groups. Plots against his regime were discovered several times. He, however, survived all these calamities but on March 25, 1975, Faisal was shot and killed by one of his nephews who was later described as hallucinated. With Faisal's death the golden era of modern Saudi Arabia was over.

If Nasir championed the Arab cause and dreamt about the unity of the Arab world, King Faisal advocated the unity of the Muslim world beyond the Arabian Peninsula. The wealth Saudi Arabia amassed from oil was spent not only on the well being of Saudis but was given to many Muslim countries as financial aid.

King Faisal emerged on the international politics in the early 1970 and showed enormous political experience and diplomacy. He was a devout Muslim yet moderate and tolerant in his views. He put the interest of Saudi Arabia and its citizens before his own political interest or the interest of any super power. He strengthened his political ties with the west but also protected Saudi Arabia from undesirable influence of the west. His independence and integrity was well respected round the globe but detested by the super powers. He was a capable and responsible diplomat even before he became king. King Faisal's influence on the Islamic world was tremendous and he stood taller than any leader of his time. His honesty, integrity and character were exemplary for any monarch, head of state or a politician anywhere in the world.

Gamal Abdel Nasir
(1918-1970)

Contribution: A shrewd politician and Egyptian revolutionary leader. Nasir was a leading member of the 'Free Officers' who overthrew king Farouk. Nasir's regime was marked by socio-economic reforms in Egypt. He tirelessly worked for the unity of one Arab world and initiated the Arab Nationalist movement in the younger generation of the Arabs.

Nasir was born on June 15, 1918 in the outskirts of Alexandria where his father was a postal employee. He started his schooling in al-Khatatibah, a small Egyptian village where his father was later transferred. From there, Nasir went to Cairo to live with his uncle. In Cairo, the movement to ouster the British from Egypt was gaining momentum and Nasir actively took part in these anti-British demonstrations. Nasir attended law school for several months but then decided to join the Royal Military Academy (1937), graduating as a second lieutenant. For the next several years Nasir served in Upper Egypt and the Sudan as a military instructor.

Nasir's life took a turn when he was posted in the Sudan where he met three officers who later played an important role in the Egyptian politics with Nasir. Nasir, with the help of these three men, Zakaria Mohieddine (later the vice president of the United Arab Republic), Abdel Hakim Amer (later field marshal) and Anwar Sadat (later succeeded Nasir as president of Egypt) formed a secret revolutionary organization known as the 'Free Officers'. The objectives of this revolutionary group were to free Egypt from the British rule as well as to overthrow the Egyptian royal family. In 1948, Nasir fought with the Arab army against the newly created State of Israel. Three Egyptian battalions were surrounded by the Israeli army for more than two months. Nasir resisted the Israeli onslaught heroically until a cease-fire was declared.

On July 23, 1952, the Free Officers led by Nasir overthrew king Farouk who was then exiled (Nasir opposed the execution of king Farouk and his family as suggested by other officers). Nasir, however, did not assume power immediately but put Major General Naguib as the head of state. A Revolutionary Command Council was formed but behind the scene, Nasir's political hand and brain were working. In 1953, Naguib and Nasir's views clashed on the future of Egypt. Nasir believed in social democracy and the elimination of class distinction, whereas Naguib was only interested in some basic reforms. In June 1953, Egypt was declared a republic but tension between Nasir and Naguib continued to heighten. Eventually, in 1954, General Naguib was deposed and Nasir assumed power as the prime minister of Egypt. With time, Nasir assumed enormous power and all political parties and opposition were banned. In 1956, Nasir presented a new constitution to the nation, declaring Egypt a Socialist Arab Republic with a one-party political system. Islam was adopted as official religion of the country. In June 1956, Nasir was elected by a vast majority of the Egyptians as the president of Egypt (Nasir was the only candidate running for the presidency).

Nasir initially appeared to be pro-western but resisted to become the part of an anti-Soviet bloc promoted by some western countries. Nasir then decided to follow the policy of neutralism. At the Bandung Conference of Asian and African nations in April 1955, he joined Marshal Tito of Yugoslavia and Prime Minister Nehru of India as advocates of non alignment movement.

Nasir brought many social reforms in Egypt. He believed in socialist economy which eventually brought enormous influence of the Soviet Union over Egypt. Measures were taken to improve the life of rural Egyptians. Social reforms such as minimum wage, limitations on the hours of work and public health services were introduced. Land reforms restricted individuals to own more than 104 acres of land. With the help of the Soviet Union, Aswan Dam was built which started operating in 1968. Women were given more rights in the Egyptian society than ever before. Industrialization of Egypt was also undertaken by Nasir. Overall, Nasir's efforts improved the economical plight of the people of Egypt and a new middle class emerged in the cities.

Nasir initiated the building of Aswan Dam which could provide Egypt with electricity and irrigation. Initially, both the United States and Britain offered financial help for Aswan High Dam project but in July 1956, both the USA and Britain declined the offer. Nasir then announced the nationalization of the Suez Canal so that the toll received from the Canal could be used to build the dam. In order to establish the control of the Suez Canal, in October 1956, Israel, Britain and France invaded Egypt. The war was short lived as the USA and the Soviet Union pressured the invaders to withdraw. Nasir not only emerged as a national hero of Egypt following this brief war but gained enormous respect and popularity in the Arab world.

In 1958, at the request of Syrian Baath party, Egypt and Syria formed the United Arab Republic. This union was, however, short lived as Syrians felt that Nasir was implementing his brand of reforms in Syria and in September 1961, the United Arab Republic was dissolved.

Nasir was a great advocate of the Palestinian cause and under his auspices in 1964; Palestine Liberation Organization (PLO) was created. Nasir also vigorously promoted his political ideas in the Arab World. He supported the Republican army in Yemen's civil war in 1962 which created a tension between Egypt and Saudi Arabia. After the defeat in the six-day war (June 1967) with Israel, Nasir eventually removed most of the Egyptian troops from Yemen. The defeat in the six-day war against Israel prompted Nasir to resign but the so-called overwhelming support of the masses forced Nasir to withdraw his resignation. Nasir continued to work towards Arab Unity and the Palestine cause until he suffered heart attack on September 11, 1969 and almost became incapacitated. Nasir died after second heart attack on September 28, 1970 at the age of fifty-two.

Nasir undoubtedly, was one of the most popular and revered political figures in the Arab world in the later half of the 20th century. His dream of one Arab world, though did not materialize, (mainly due to the internal feud of the Arab leaders) was a step to strengthen the political role of the Arab nations on the global political map. This line of political thinking, however, brought criticism from the extreme right, especially the fundamentalist Islamic group, Akhwan el-Muslamin (Muslim Brotherhood). In their opinion, Nasir was emphasizing less on Islam and focusing much more on the Arab nationalism. Their opposition, however, did not deter Nasir from continuing his work in this direction, though in the end he failed in this ambitious and very difficult task.

Where Nasir brought reforms which improved the quality of life for most of the Egyptians, he completely ignored the common rights of the people and made no effort to take the country towards democracy. He instituted one party political system which remains in effect till today. He crushed the opposition ruthlessly and political prisoners were tortured and killed. The Muslim Brotherhood which opposed Nasir throughout his regime was a special target of his ruthless political cleansing of the opposition.

The western press labeled Nasir as pro-Soviet Union but ignored the fact that initially he was a pro-western and in favor of free market but when his so-called western allies deserted him in the time of need he had no choice but to turn towards communist countries.

Nasir's achievements such as nationalization of the Suez Canal in 1956 and the subsequent political victory of the Suez crisis, building of Aswan Dam despite financial and political troubles, the social reforms in Egypt, strong support for the cause of Palestine and the dream of Arab unity, all made him a very popular and appealing figure in the Arab world. 'Nasirism' was widely accepted in the Arab world, especially it influenced and appealed to the younger generation of Arabs. Probably Nasir was the most charismatic Arab leader in the later half of the twentieth century.

Anwar Sadat
(1918-1981)

Contribution: A close associate of Gamal Nasir, Sadat was one of the three leading 'Free Officers' who planned and executed the 1952 revolution against King Farouk. He held many posts in Nasir regime and after the death of Nasir; Sadat served as the president of Egypt till his assassination in 1981 by the right wing fundamentalist Islamic group. He became the first Arab leader who visited Israel and initiated the peace negotiation with them in 1977. He shared the Nobel Peace prize in 1978 with Israeli Prime Minister Menachem Begin.

Sadat was born on December 25, 1918 in Mit Abul Kom, a village about 40 miles north of Cairo in the Nile Delta. His father was a civil service clerk with a very modest income. Sadat struggled in school but eventually in 1936, succeeded in obtaining a Secondary School Certificate. Sadat's first attempt to join the Royal Military Academy did not meet with success but once admitted he graduated as a second lieutenant in 1938. He met Nasir when Sadat was posted in Upper Egypt. Sadat was a nationalist and active with other officers to expel British from Egypt. The British imprisoned him in 1942 but in October 1944, Sadat managed to escape from jail and remained underground till the Second World War was over. He then took part in an unsuccessful assassination attempt on the life of former Egyptian Prime Minister Nahas who had signed a treaty with the British in 1936 and was considered pro-British by the nationalists. Sadat's role landed him in prison in January 1946. The outbreak of Arab-Israel war in 1948 overshadowed Sadat's trial, he was acquitted and released. He was reinstated in the army where he strengthened his ties with the 'Free Officers'. By 1951, Sadat rose to the rank of lieutenant colonel and by 1952 he became one of the closest allies of Gamal Nasir. When on July 23, 1952, King Farouk was overthrown; it was Sadat who announced the news of the coup to the public on the radio.

After Nasir took complete control of Egypt in 1954 by disposing General Naguib, Sadat held many senior administrative level posts but none of them was a key position. He was the editor of al-Gamhurriya (al-Jamhurriya), a government newspaper. He was the minister of state without portfolio (1954-55) and the secretary general of Egypt's Islamic congress. After the formation of the United Arab Republic (union of Egypt and Syria), he served as speaker of the newly formed republic's joint parliament. He also served as speaker of Egyptian National Assembly in 1966. After the defeat in the 1967 six-day war against Israel, Nasir's leadership was temporarily clouded but Sadat remained loyal to Nasir. In 1969, Nasir made him vice president and when Nasir died on September 28, 1970, Sadat was elected president of Egypt in a plebiscite on October 15, 1970.

The immediate reaction to Sadat's ascendancy to the presidency was that he was weak and could be removed from power soon. One of the main opponents of Sadat was Ali Sabri, another former vice president of Egypt who was also a staunch pro-Soviet. Sadat, however, had other ideas and by May 1971, he managed to isolate Ali Sabri and his supporters politically and consolidated his grip on power. His so called 'Corrective Revolution' made the Soviet leaders in Kremlin very nervous for a while but Sadat assured them of Egypt's continuous friendship towards them.

After assuming power Sadat did not follow into Nasir's footsteps. He decentralized the Egyptian economy and relaxed the political structure. He was especially lenient towards the extreme right wing Islamic group 'Muslim Brotherhood'. Many political prisoners were freed during Sadat regime. In the summer of 1972, he realized that the Soviet Union was reluctant in providing Egypt with much needed sophisticated weapons and he expelled thousands of Soviet technicians and military advisors from Egypt. This was probably also a hint that Egypt wanted better and improved ties with the United States. Sadat also laid careful plans to attack Israel. Then on October 6, 1973, the surprise invasion of Israel began when the joint forces of Egypt and Syria attacked Israel. In the early phase of the war, the Egyptian army gained some ground by crossing the Suez Canal but the massive military supplies from the USA to Israel, eventually turned the tide. Finally, the USA and the Soviet Union intervened and a cease-fire was announced. Though it was not a victory but Sadat emerged as a prestigious Arab leader who demonstrated that by proper military planning and preparations, Israel is not militarily invincible. After the war, Sadat started working towards peace in the Middle East. He shocked the Arab world by visiting Israel in November, 1977. He visited Jerusalem where he presented his peace plan before the Knesset (Israeli parliament). The personal diplomacy of the USA president Jimmy Carter brought the Israeli Prime Minister Begin and Sadat together at Camp David in September 1978. The bilateral peace treaty between Egypt and Israel was finally signed at the White House on March 26, 1979. The 1978 Nobel Peace Prize was jointly awarded to Sadat and Begin for their efforts towards peace.

Though the world recognized Sadat's peace efforts, the Arab world chastised Sadat as they were against signing any peace treaty with Israel. The Arab countries severed their ties with Egypt and withdrew the financial aid to Egypt. The Arab League moved its headquarters from Cairo to Tunis. Sadat also faced a very strong opposition in Egypt not only for signing peace treaty with Israel but also due to worsening economy and his use of force to suppress the public dissent. His 'open door' economy policy though helped some Egyptians to improve their economical plight but overall the majority of the Egyptians remained poor. Riots broke out in January 1977 when under the pressure of the International Monetary Fund, Sadat administration cut back food subsidies.

In September 1981, Sadat ordered the arrest of hundreds of politicians, banned all political activities and expelled the Soviet ambassador. This action plunged Egypt into a political chaos. On October 6, 1981, while reviewing a military parade commemorating the Arab-Israeli war of October 1973, Sadat was assassinated by the members of the fundamentalist Muslim organization.

Sadat will always be remembered as Nasir's most trusted friend. It was not easy to assume power after a highly popular and charismatic leader. During Nasir's life, Sadat was considered as a mouthpiece of Nasir but after assuming power Sadat proved himself as his own man. He put forward his own agenda and deviated from many policies of Nasir. He started reshaping the political structure of Egypt. He relaxed the political atmosphere by freeing political prisoners and gave much more freedom to the right wing extremist Islamic groups. He fought a war with Israel and yet worked for peace in the Middle East. By signing the peace treaty with Israel, he risked his political career and isolation in the Arab world. In the end, his legacy that peace is essential in the Middle East was proven to be right and in the nineties many Arab leaders followed his suit.

Sheikh Mujibur Rahman
(1920-1975)

Contribution: Founder of Bangladesh, its first prime minister and later president. Mujib was active in politics since his early teens and fought for more than twenty years against Pakistani regime for the rights of the Bengali people. He is popularly known in Bangladesh as 'Bangabandhu' (friend of Bengal).

Pakistan emerged as an independent predominantly Muslim nation on August 15, 1947 after the partition of India. It consisted of East and West Pakistan separated by one thousand miles with India lying in between the two provinces. East Pakistan was populated by the Bengali speaking majority whereas in West Pakistan many ethnic groups lived with their own spoken languages though Urdu was spoken and understood throughout West Pakistan. The center of power was in West Pakistan which controlled the defense, economy and foreign policy.

Mujib was born on March 17, 1920, at Tungipara (then India, now Bangladesh) to a middle-class landowner. Though Mujib was not an outstanding student in school, he developed revolutionary ideas from an early age. He studied political science and law at the University of Calcutta and Dhaka. Though, he was active as a young demonstrator against the British for the independence of India, his real political career began when he joined Awami League in 1949. Hussain Shahid Suharawardy, the renowned Bengali Muslim leader was his mentor in Awami League. In 1952, Mujib was instrumental in leading the student movement demanding that Bengali should be declared as national language of Pakistan as opposed to Urdu. In 1953, Mujib was elected Awami League's general secretary. The main objective of Awami League was to work for the rights of Bengalis in united Pakistan. In the 1954 provincial election, a coalition of East-Bengal-based political parties defeated the Muslim League (the political party which had campaigned for the creation of Pakistan). Mujib served as minister in the newly formed provincial government in East Pakistan. The central government of Pakistan, however, later declared the provincial election in East Pakistan invalid.

In 1957, Mujib became the leader of Awami League and his many years of struggle with the central government of Pakistan began. His sole objective was to preserve the rights of the Bengalis in united Pakistan. In 1958, Ayub Khan, a military general took over power and throughout Pakistan martial law was imposed. Between 1960 and 1962, Mujib was arrested many times for defying martial law and ban against political activities. In the 1965 India-Pakistan war, a vast majority of people in East Pakistan felt that the eastern part of Pakistan was left defenseless against the Indian attack. This created an impression that the leaders of Pakistan who lived in West Pakistan do not care for the people in East Pakistan. This widely accepted notion further strengthened Mujib's view that the people of East Pakistan had to fight for their rights.

In early 1966, Mujib presented his six-point program which could have substantially reduced the central government's authority. According to the plan, only defense and foreign policy were left in the hands of the central government. Mujib's proposal was rejected by all political parties in Pakistan. Mujib then mobilized the general masses in East Pakistan to press the central government to accept his six-point program. He was arrested in 1966 and in 1967, he was charged of treason. Pakistan government accused him that he was conspiring with India to secede East Pakistan from Pakistan. The conspiracy, popularly known as 'Agartallah Conspiracy' was never proven by the government of Pakistan in the court. Mujib was acquitted from all charges and released on March 2, 1969. Meanwhile, in both East and West Pakistan, dissatisfaction against Ayub's regime resulted in civilian demonstration and riots. Eventually, Ayub Khan handed over power to General Yahya Khan in 1969 and the new martial law administrator announced a general election to be held on December 5, 1970. In the general election, Mujib's Awami League won 167 seats out of 313, thus gaining majority in the parliamentary election. The election was strange in its pattern and outcome. Awami League did not win a single seat in West Pakistan and no political party from West Pakistan won any seat in East Pakistan. Pakistan People's Party led by Zulfiquar Ali Bhutto won the majority of the parliamentary seats in West Pakistan. By virtue of winning the maximum number of seats in the national election, Mujib was entitled to form the central government. Unfortunately, the Pakistani military junta denied Mujib this opportunity by indefinitely postponing (March 1, 1971) the meeting of the national assembly of Pakistan which was supposed to be convened on March 3, 1971. Thus a mass movement against the military regime began in East Pakistan. The movement was violent as burning and looting of the government as well as private property became order of the day. The Urdu speaking minority (immigrants from India) was special target of the rioters. Hundreds of thousands of Urdu speaking people were killed within the first three weeks of March 1971. The passions were running so high that Mujib was unable to stop this bloodshed. The massive civilian unrest in East Pakistan forced the military regime to resume negotiation with Awami League. These talks failed to produce any result and on March 25, 1971, Pakistan army began a military operation in order to crack down Bengali activists. Top Awami League leaders, though managed to escape to neighboring India, Mujib remained in Dhaka. He was arrested by the military and taken to west Pakistan where he was tried and sentenced to death. The remaining Awami League leaders with the help of India directed guerrilla warfare against Pakistan army. Hundreds of thousands of civilians were killed between March and December 1971. The Bengali freedom fighters were not gaining much ground as their operation largely remained confined within the villages. Occasional bomb blast and violence in the major cities, however, paralyzed the normal city life. By August 1971, it appeared that peace had finally returned to East Pakistan but from October 1971, border skirmishes between India and Pakistan became more frequent and the clouds of war between these two countries started appearing on the horizon. Eventually, on December 3, 1971, war broke out between India and Pakistan. Indian army mainly due to their air supremacy and internal troubles in Pakistan won the war and a new country ' Bangladesh' was created on December 16, 1971. Once again, thousands of innocent Urdu speaking people were massacred either by the Bengali freedom fighters or the rioters. The defeat of

Pakistan army in the war brought down the military regime of Yahya Khan. The new civilian administrator (Zulfiquar Ali Bhutto) of Pakistan released Mujib and Mujib triumphantly arrived in Bangladesh capital Dhaka on January 10, 1972.

Mujib immediately took over the charge of the new nation. Rebuilding of Bangladesh was an uphill task. The war-torn country had no financial and economical resource. The foreign aid, though, poured in was insufficient and only a fraction of it reached to the needy. Mujib through his shrewd personality inspired the nation and Bangladeshis gradually started building their country. In 1973, Mujib's Awami League won a landslide victory in Bangladesh first general election but then the corruption in Mujib administration slowly crept in. Mujib himself got preoccupied with building his party's grass roots and the priority of the nation became secondary. A new elite class with considerable wealth emerged. Sensing public unrest and corruption in his government, Mujib declared a state of emergency on December 28, 1974 and amended the constitution in January 1975. Bangladesh became a presidential rather a parliamentary system and Mujib became its first president with unlimited power. Mujib also established one party system thus eliminating any political opposition. Mujib's political moves were not appreciated by majority of Bangladeshis, military officers, intellectuals and politicians. In a pre-dawn coup, on August 15, 1975, a group of junior military officers assassinated Mujib and most of his family.

Mujib certainly played a very vital role in the politics of the modern day Muslim Bengal. Throughout his life, he fought for the Bengali language, its rich culture and the mild mannered intellectually oriented Bengali people. Ultimately he created a separate land for them. Today, Bangladesh is an independent country but it has paid an enormous price for its independence. During its struggle for independence, Bangladesh lost hundreds of thousands of people and it remains one of the poorest nations in the world. Only time will tell if Mujib's dream to create a separate land for the Muslims of Bengal really proved beneficial to them.

Bibliography

1. The Times Atlas of World History. 4th edition. Geoffrey Parker (editor). Hammond, Inc., New Jersey, 1994.
2. Ibn Khaldun. The Muqaddimah. An introduction to History. Translated by Franz Rosenthal. Abridged and edited by NJ Dawood. Princeton University Press, New Jersey, 1989.
3. RE Dunn. The Adventures of Ibn Battuta. University of California Press, Berkley, 1989.
4. A Hourani. A History of Arab Peoples. Harvard University Press. Cambridge, Massachusetts, 1991.
5. JM Roberts. History of the World. Oxford University Press, New York, 1993.
6. NF Cantor. The Civilization of the Middle Ages. HarperCollins, Inc., New York, 1993.
7. M Bayat and MA Jamnia. Tales from the Land of the Sufis. Shambhala, Boston, 1994.
8. Masterpieces of the Orient. Enlarged edition. GL Anderson (editor). WW Norton and Company, Inc., New York.
9. New Catholic Encyclopedia. McGraw-Hill Book Company, New York, 1967.
10. The Encyclopedia of Philosophy. Paul Edwards (Editor in Chief). Simon and Schuster and Prentice Hall International, London, 1996.
11. The New Encyclopedia Americana. International edition. Grolier, Connecticut, 2001.
12. The New Encyclopedia Britannica. Encyclopedia Brittanica, Inc., Chicago/London, 1997.
13. The Concise Encyclopedia of Islam. Cyril Glasse, introduction by Houston Smith. Harper and Row Publishers, Inc., SanFrancisco, 1989.
14. Shorter Encyclopedia of Islam. Gibbhar & Kramers (eds). Cornell University Press, Ithaca, New York, 1965.
15. Encyclopedia of Religion and Ethics. James Hastings (editor). Charles Scibner's Sons.
16. Great Lives From History. Ancient and Medieval Series. Frank N Magill (editor), Salem Press Inc., 1988.
17. Great Lives From History. Twentieth Century Series. Frank N Magill (editor), Salem Press Inc., 1988.

18. Great Lives From History. Renaissance to 1900 Series. Frank N Magill (editor), Salem Press Inc., 1988.
19. Encyclopedia of World Biography. Second Edition. Gale Research Inc., Detroit, 1988.
20. Twentieth-century Literary Criticism (1900-1959). Gale Research Inc., Detroit, 1995.
21. An anthology of Urdu verses in English. Selected and translated by David Mathews. Oxford University Press, 1995.
22. R Payne. The Dream and the Tomb. A History of the Crusades. Stein and Day Publishers, New York, 1984.
23. B Lewis. Islam and the West. Oxford University Press, New York, 1993.
24. WA Stanley. Jinnah of Pakistan. Oxford University Press, New York, 1993.
25. C Troll. Sayyid Ahmed Khan: A Reinterpretation of Muslim Theology. Humanities Press, New Jersey, 1978.
26. S Akbar. Living Islam from Samarkand to Stornoway. Facts on File. New York, 1994.

INDEX